Beyond North-East

Insurgency·History·Development

Attention Authors

Manas Publications is fighting a war to tell the world that India can win the battle not only by the bullet but also by pen. We are converting fighters into writers. There is no dearth of intellectuals in our country. However, their knowledge is confined to them only. No sincere effort has been made by any other publisher to channelise their knowledge. That is why the talent of every intellectual remains latent. An author always presents the raw material in the shape of a manuscript and it is the job of the publisher to convert it into a completely finished book. Manas has been motivating intellectuals continually and publishing their manuscripts for more than three decades and would like to publish your manuscript too. If you or your colleagues have a manuscript ready for publication or are working on it, contact us with a detailed synopsis and list of contents. Manas can also suggest you a suitable title for writing related to your area of expertise. Manas is known for its publishing quality. We take utmost care in production and give wide publicity to the book and its author through our national and international distribution network.

Beyond North-East

Insurgency·History·Development

HN Das, IAS
Former Chief Secretary: Assam

Manas Publications
(We Convert Fighters into Writers)
New Delhi-110002 (INDIA)

MANAS PUBLICATIONS

(Publishers, Library Suppliers, Importers & Exporters)
4402/5-A, Ansari Road (Opp. HDFC Bank)
Darya Ganj, New Delhi-110 002 (INDIA)
Off. ✆ 23260783, 23265523, Res. ✆ 23842660
Fax: 011-23272766
E-mail: manaspublications@yahoo.com,
manaspublications@gmail.com
Website: www.manaspublications.in

ISBN 978-81-7049-411-9
Rs. 695/-

Designed at
Manas Publications

Printed in India at
IYN Graphics, Delhi
and published by Mrs. Suman Lata for
Manas Publications, 4402/5-A,
Ansari Road, (Opp. HDFC Bank),
Darya Ganj, New Delhi-110 002 (INDIA)

Preface

During the past half a century I have published a large number of articles on different subjects in the local and national newspapers and magazines. I have also published books on Disaster Management, Rural Development, Grameen Bank of Bangladesh and Tourism in the North East. I have now collected my ideas and information on insurgency, terrorism and the recent incidents to write the chapters in the first part of this book. The second part contains small and revised essays on certain important events particularly in the North Eastern Region of India. It also contains a few reviews of books on insurgency, terrorism, infiltration of Bangladeshis and related matters. Two chapters–one on Bangladesh and the other on the Look East Policy–are added in the hope that readers would be interested in the countries covered where NE terrorists find shelter and training grounds and from where they obtain smuggled commodities including drugs and arms. This book is offered to the general public with the hope that it would help cultivate a better understanding of the issues and problems in the disturbed areas of India's North Eastern states.

HN Das

CHAPTER – I

Ethnicity and Insurgency in the North-Eastern Region

Insurgency is rising against established authority. This has happened innumerable times all over the world ever since the dawn of civilization. A large number of insurgencies have been caused by the identity crisis. To quote Amartya Sen, "Many of the conflicts and barbarities in the world are sustained through the illusion of a unique and choiceless identity. The art of constructing hatred takes the form of invoking the magical power of some allegedly predominant identity that drowns other affiliations, and in a conveniently bellicose form can also overpower any human sympathy or natural kindness that we may normally have. The result can be homespun elemental violence, or globally artful violence and terrorism."[1]

Terrorism has been used as an instrument of violence in order to force compliance to the wishes of its perpetrators. This particular word "terrorism" was coined during the great French Revolution of 1789-1795 to describe the actions of the Jacobins who organized a "Reign of Terror" during 1793-1795. Of course, such acts were present "as a form of non sanctioned violence in response to perceived injustice" for centuries. But the word terrorism was not used earlier. It appears that 109 definitions of terrorism have been formulated during the period between 1936 and 1981 and more were added later[2]. Among the various definitions I feel that the one offered by Jessica Stern is the most acceptable. According to Jessica, terrorism is "an act or threat of violence against noncombatants with the objective of exacting revenge, intimidating, or otherwise influencing an audience."[3]

Terrorism has taken many different shapes. Terrorists have adopted quite a few methods. They have come to use a number of sophisticated weapons. The latest among the weapons which have become susceptible to such use are the weapons of mass destruction (WMD) that may be biological, chemical, nuclear or radiological. Terrorism can be considered to have graduated into insurgency when it is organized with the support of a community of people and the organization has an ideology backed by certain popular grievances. In India, such insurgencies have been organized by the Naxalites, the Mao extremists, the feudal armies of North India and the ethnic and religious outfits of Jammu and Kashmir, Punjab and NE. There are many other smaller outfits also.

Actually ever since the Second World War insurgency has become very common all over the world and particularly in the developing countries. Malayasia, for example, was in the grip of insurgency immediately after the War. How insurgency was rooted out in that erstwhile British colony is an epic story. Similar is the case with Philippines. Earlier there were quite a few outfits which used to strike terror through violent acts in a large number of countries. Many advanced countries such as Japan and the United States have been victims of such insurgencies.

A new development has been the appearance of countries whose governments give direct or indirect support to terrorism and insurgency. The United States has dubbed them as rogue states. According to the US Government, Lybia, Cuba, South Yemen, Syria, Iraq, Iran and North Korea, among others, are such rogue states, India would like that the US include the Pakistan also in the list. The US did not agree with it In their self adopted idea of global policing the US has mounted a war against Iraq in the hope to curb terrorism.[4] All the countries, cited above, have supported and sponsored insurgent outfits to settle political scores. They do not seem to believe in using the diplomatic channels.

Moreover, easy means of travel, specially by air, is now facilitating many insurgent groups to perpetrate violent acts abroad. The exploits of Abu Nidal of al-Fatah, the Berlin Olympic bombings and the Japanese Red Army's shoot-outs have passed into history.[5] In more recent times the destruction of New York's twin towers and the bombing of London's underground railways are incidents which will be remembered for a long time. The Mumbai carnage of November 26-28, 2008 and the Guwahati bomb blasts of October 30, 2008 are dealt with in subsequent chapters. A host of similar incidents can be cited to show the worldwide spread of terrorism and insurgency and the destruction that it has wrought in many countries. In India terrorism has been used extensively in ancient and modern times. In modern times the period between 1900 and 1910 is considered to be important because of the rise of the revolutionary movement, particularly in Bengal.[6]

Nation States

The idealism of nation states first made its impact felt in the late eighteenth century Europe. Two big nation states were created through the Italian and the German unifications. Then the break up of the Holy Roman Empire (aka Austrian Empire) and the Ottoman Empire gave birth to several nation states particularly in Central and Eastern Europe. In the cases of Italy and Germany, a number of feudal states were cemented together to form the new nation states on linguistic basis. In the rest of Europe new nation states emerged out of the old universal empires. The Asian and the African nation states started coming up as the aftermath of the two world wars of the twentieth century mainly as a consequence of the fall of the British and other smaller empires which the European powers had built in the earlier centuries.

Arnold Toynbee's rather esoteric definition aptly describes "the spirit of nationality" as a "sour ferment of the new wine of democracy in the old bottles of tribalism".[7] Practically, a nation is "a group of people who believe they are related ancestrally. It is the largest grouping that shares that belief."[8] Simply stated a nation state is a nation matched with territory.

India had a chequered history before the advent of the British rule. There were times when great empires brought substantial portions of the Indian sub-continent under control of one imperial power. But at other times different parts had independent kings and feudal potentates. Their territories did not always conform to the idea of nation states. Even during British times considerable areas remained outside the day-to-day administration of the Central Government. These were the princely states. But most of these states were fully covered by the principle of suzerainty of the British Empire till the paramountcy lapsed after transfer of power in 1947. When independence came, India was divided and Pakistan was created. Later Bangladesh became independent after the Indo-Pak War of 1971. But in the Indian Union all the princely states were merged by the Instruments of Accession.

Reorganisation of States

Within independent India itself fissiparous tendencies were always discernible side by side with the centripetal forces of common culture and shared values. All Indians harked back to the same traditions. It was through a tenuous process combined with great political acumen and the vision of a strong united India that late Sardar

Vallabhbhai Patel (first Union Home Minister) brought all native states and union of states within the fold of the Indian Union immediately after independence. Except for Hyderabad, Junagadh, and Jammu & Kashmir, where Army had to be deployed, the entire process was peaceful.

Soon, however, problems started arising due to revival of agitations over local languages. These movements were inspired by the influence of the European idealism of nationhood on the local intelligentia. The death of Potti Sri Ramalu after long fasting over statehood for Andhra Pradesh also added fuel to it. This and a few other incidents elsewhere in the country necessitated the setting up of the Boundary Commission in 1952. Sardar KM Panikkar was the most active member of this Commission. On their recommendations radical changes of boundaries of states were made in 1956 on linguistic lines. Their recommendations were implemented through the States Reorganisation Act, 1956. The only exceptions were the erstwhile Bombay Presidency and Punjab. Both of these were, however, ultimately partitioned within a few years. The Bombay Presidency was partitioned on linguistic lines into Gujarat and Maharashtra. The earstwhile Punjab was partitioned on linguistic and religious lines into Punjab, Himachal Pradesh and Haryana.[9]

Soon after the above mentioned states re-organisation was carried out, discordant voices were heard in some parts of India. There were sporadic disturbances also. Some people were not satisfied with the re-organisation. The sub-nationalities wanted their own states. On the other hand, patriotic Indians were genuinely concerned about the unity and integrity of the country. One American journalist Sellig Harrison wrote a book titled "India – the Most Dangerous Decades" and predicted that the country would face chaos and would break up soon. But India remained united thanks to the vision and foresight of our leaders and the strong bond of the ancient civilization which has continued for five thousand years and which inspires every Indian wherever he or she may reside. The leaders were also clear about their mandate and did not hesitate to follow a strong arm policy whenever necessity arose. This provoked the American historian Paul R. Brass to remark that : "The one consistent principle, however, that emerges strongly in both the Nehru and the post-Nehru periods is that no secessionist movement will be allowed to prevail and that massive force will be used to suppress insurrectionary activity".[10]

In recent years, three more states were created - Uttaranchal (later renamed as Uttarakhand) out of Uttar Pradesh, Jharkhand out of Bihar and Chattisgarh out of Madhya Pradesh. In the wake of the agitation launched by a section of people, the Government of India suddenly agreed to the separation of Telengana from Andhra Pradesh in late 2009 and decided that 10 backward districts of Telengana region including the city of Hyderabad will form the new state. This was opposed by the coastal Andhras. Violent agitations and disturbances ensued and the Government decision was stalled temporarily. Meanwhile, demand for new states was raised by many people all over India and specially in the North-East (NE).

It will be relevant to mention here that while the Boundary Commission of early 1950s was grappling with its gigantic task, in Assam considerable heat was generated against the demand by the Bengali Hindus for transfer to West Bengal of the earstwhile Goalpara district which then consisted of the present districts of Goalpara, Dhubri, Kokrajhar, Bongaigaon and Chirang. Led by Sarat Chandra Sinha (later Chief Minister of Assam) along with Rupnath Brahma, Prakritish Chandra Barua, Khagen Nath, Muhammed Umaruddin and others, a big movement was mounted against this demand. Ultimately, the earstwhile Goalpara district was retained in Assam. When I joined as a young Deputy Commissioner of that huge district, with headquarters at Dhubri, in 1967 the embers of the fire stoked by the decade old movement had not fully died down.

Meanwhile, in the process of re-organization of states on the basis of language, the pent-up feelings and grievances of ethnic and tribal groups and sub-groups were unleashed. This happened all over India. But it happened in a more intense manner in Assam which was then the only state encompassing the entire NE barring Tripura and Manipur which were earlier princely native states and had become union territories after independence. Later they achieved full statehood. Prolonged insurgency in the Naga Hills district, since independence, led to its separation from Assam and formation of the union territory of Nagaland. Similarly, insurgency in the Lushai Hills district led to its separation from Assam and formation of the union territory of Mizoram. Both these territories achieved full statehood later. In the 1970s, the Khasi and Jaintia Hills district and the Garo Hill district of Assam were joined together to form the autonomous state of Meghalaya, under Article 244 A (1) of the Indian Constitution. It achieved full statehood within a short time.

The erstwhile North East Frontier Agency (NEFA) was only formally with Assam. It had a separate existence, very strangely, under the Ministry of External Affairs. (This probably strengthened China's demand for the merger of Arunachal Pradesh with that country). The Government of India converted it into a union territory and later transformed it into the full state of Arunachal Pradesh.

In order to achieve co-ordination among the sub-federating units of NE, the North East Council (NEC) was constituted in 1972 after passing the North Eastern Areas (Reorganisation) Act, 1971 which created a common platform for the NE Region's seven distinct states. Sikkim was the eighth state to join NEC.

The North East : Insurgency and New States

The North Eastern Region (NER) consisting of the state of Assam and some other areas formed a separate geographical entity linked to the Indian mainland only by a narrow corridor of 26 kms in West Bengal. Here the linguistic reorganization formula could not be applied in the same way because of the existence of a very large number of small tribes and languages and territorial intermixture of such tribes. Therefore, differences arose among the various ethnic and linguistic groups which had small populations, but strong sub-regional and racial sentiments. Popular movements all over the Region and some violence and insurgency ultimately resulted in the formation of separate states. In the process, far reaching political changes were made and seven separate states emerged : Manipur, Tripura, Nagaland, Mizoram, Meghalaya, Arunachal Pradesh and Assam.

As the "Advanced History of India" remarked at that time "the reorganization of territories in north-east India was effected to enable the diverse ethnic and linguistic groups who inhabit the area to shape their own destinies without interference and to remove the feeling that they were being exploited by others."[11] This hope was belied, however, when smaller ethnic groups and sub-groups started demanding further vivisection of some of the states. Insurgent outfits also emerged demanding full independence for this or that part of the eight states and threatening to secede from the Indian Union.

It is important to realize that before independence,the British Government's policy was to keep the hill people isolated. They did not allow the hill people to be integrated with the mainstream of Indian life. This was exemplified by the Inner Line Permit system which quite successfully prevented the hill people from being swamped by others. However, this also prevented any real relationship between the hills and the plains in economic, social and cultural fields.

After independence, Prime Minister Nehru adopted a policy framework for the tribals influenced by the well-known anthropologist Verrier Elwin. In fact, Nehru wrote the foreword to Elwin's famous book *"A Philosophy for NEFA"*. NEFA became Arunachal Pradesh later. Nehru wrote "the problem of the tribal areas is to make the people feel that they have perfect freedom to live their own lives and to develop according to their wishes and genius. India should signify to them not only a protecting force but a liberating one. Any conception that India is ruling them and that they are the ruled, or that customs and habits with which they are unfamiliar are going to be imposed upon them, will alienate them"[12] Elwin's philosophy has been criticized as romantic. Adverse comments have also been made about his 1939 book *"The Baiga"* where he had advocated for some sort of "National Park" for the tribals in a wild and largely inaccessible part of the country. Later, Elwin regretted this and said that his suggestion was "badly put" and that "I should have realized the unfortunate connotation of the expression National Park".[13] Elwin explained, "there was no idea of keeping anything static and, in actual fact, there is continual creative development in all these fields".

Elwin emphasized that he was misunderstood. He retorted back at his critics in very strong words, "The main reason why it (Elwin's NEFA philosophy) was believed to have failed was that I was supposed to have advocated a policy of isolation, to have urged the separation of NEFA from the people of Assam". He further said that "In fact, I had not supported any policy of isolation of NEFA people but had devoted several pages of this book to condemning it. As for the Assamese people, for whom I have great affection and respect, I had included in my book the suggestion that every scheme of development, progress or welfare in NEFA should be submitted to the test whether it would help integrate the tribal people with Assam and, of course, with India as a whole".[14] It would probably be wrong to accuse Elwin for any mis-statement or wrong-statement. But in practice his so-called philosophy created a schism between the Assamese and the Arunachalis and it was Elwin who was primarily responsible for the lop-sided development of the tribal people. While translating these ideas into action the then Advisor, NEFA, late Nari Rustomji, worked under the conviction that "The hillman has, essentially, a clean, direct and healthy outlook; he is free, happily, from the morbid complexes induced by the unnatural life of city folk". Rustomji, therefore, condemned the "reckless talk of uplifting and civilizing the tribes. Officials and social workers must go to the people not as masters who dictate but as elder brothers who have suffered themselves and wish through their experience to spare others the pains they have had to endure".[15]

When the Indian Constitution of 1950 was drawn during the years following independence the then Chief Minister of Assam Bharat Ratna Gopinath Bordoloi personally ensured that the Constitution contained special provisions in the sixth schedule relating to the hill areas. He also initiated actions for inter-mixing of the hills and the plains through various socio-cultural activities.

In spite of all these attempts at integration, however, fissiparous tendencies appeared as mentioned earlier. Many factors were responsible for these developments. The desire for self expression, the perception of discrimination and injustice, aspirations of small time politicians, better economic development of neighbouring small states and a host of other factors were responsible for the rise of sub-national and ethnic movements all over Assam and the NER. Some of these are discussed in the following paragraphs.

The Naga Insurgency

In the wake of India's independence in 1947 the Nagas were the first to raise the flag of revolt. They were a fiercely independent people. Even during British days many interior parts of the Naga inhabited area remained unadministered by the imperial power although the British had annexed most of what is now called Nagaland around 1832.

In 1918 the Naga Club came into existence. It became the platform for Naga unity. On January 10, 1929, the Naga Club submitted a memorandum to the Simon Commission in which it pleaded, on behalf of the Nagas, to the British Government "to leave us alone to determine for ourselves as in ancient times".[16] When India became independent the Nagas demanded their own independence. Earlier they had formed the Naga National Council in 1946, which marked the beginning of political movement by the Nagas in search of their identity. Their struggle was based on the premise that the "Nagas had no affinity with India whether racially, historically, politically, culturally, religiously or any otherwise. Therefore Nagaland is not part of Indian territory, neither are Nagas Indians".[17] Insurgency began under the leadership of AZ Phizo.

It was in the Shillong Accord of November 11, 1975, that "the representatives of underground organisations of the Nagas first conveyed their decision, of their own volition, to accept, without condition, the Constitution of India". Later events showed that this promise was not carried out, in letter and spirit, by all the Naga outfits. Violence continued till the Government of India drew an agreement with the Isaac Muivah faction of the National Socialist Council of Nagaland (NSCN) for a ceasefire.

Even after the formal ceasefire and intermittent talks, sporadic incidents of violence have been recorded.

It is true that the underground Naga got divided into various groups, some of which fought against each other. But most organizations continued to demand an independent and greater Nagaland or *Nagalim*. They were not satisfied with Nagaland as a full state of India. They were certainly not happy that some Naga inhabited areas of Assam, Manipur and Arunachal Pradesh had been left out of Nagaland. The basic fact is that these Naga outfits consider Nagas to be ethnically different from other Indians and they want their right of self-determination outside India. Several rounds of talks have taken place in recent years, but a lasting solution to this vexed problem, which has plagued NE for more than half a century, is not yet in sight.

It was the last British Deputy Commissioner of the erstwhile Naga Hills district of Assam, CR Pawsey, who established the Naga Hills District Tribal Council in April, 1946, with the objective of uniting all Naga tribes under one banner. Pawsey also reported to have played a pivotal role in the formation of the Naga National Council whose policy was to establish a sovereign independent Naga country and to develop it according to the genius of Naga democratic customs and culture. That was the beginning of insurgency in Nagaland. To quote the distinguished Anthropologist, Dr. DN Majumdar, "During the British period may be due to encouragement from British officers like Charles Pawsey ethnic identity organizations grew up among many of the major tribal communities of North-East India". In fact, the ground had already been prepared by the feeling among the hill tribes that "ruling class, be it the British or Indian, tended to adopt a policy of ethnic discrimination towards the hill people."[18]

The Mizo Rebellion

In the erstwhile Lushai Hills district of Assam a similar role was played by the then Superintendent (same as Deputy Commissioner) McDonald who convened a meeting of the tribal chiefs in January, 1946 and got a constitution called the McDonald *Roral Khawl* drafted for Lushai Hills which provided for a separate legislature and a Ministry. Later, the Mizo Union was formed as a political party. They demanded, like the Nagas, that all areas with Mizo population in the neighbouring Manipur, Tripura and Chittagong Hill tracts should be included in the Mizo district as proposed by them.[19]

It was, therefore, the British administrators who planted the ideas of separation and independence in the minds of the concerned ethnic groups and organizations. It later metamorphosed into insurgencies in both Nagaland and Mizoram. The British officials named above were obviously unhappy with the decision of their home government to leave India. They made every effort to scuttle the proposal. Failing that they prepared the tribes to cause confusion and pandemonium after India's independence. But it was ethnicity which they capitalized on. The feeling was so strong in Mizoram that some secessionist groups wanted to merge with Burma (present Myanmar) because they were ethnically closer to the tribes of Upper Burma.[20]

For almost two decades after independence, the tribes of Lushai Hills district simmered with discontent over many issues. They felt deeply hurt by the alleged discriminatory treatment by the Government of Assam particularly during the 1959 "*Mautam*" (famine) in the wake of large scale flowering of wild bamboo and the 1960 introduction of Assamese as the official language. The Mizo National Famine Front, formed in 1960 to help the famine victims, converted itself into the Mizo National

Front (MNF). The MNF raised the banner of insurgency when on February 28, 1966 it attacked several important government installations, looted the Aizawl Treasury and kidnapped the Sub-Divisional Officer, Lungleh. On March 1, 1966 the MNF, under the leadership of Laldenga, formally declared independence from India.

Insurgency continued for twenty long years till the Mizoram Accord was signed on June 30, 1986. The insurgent leader Laldenga was sworn in as Chief Minister on August 21, 1986. Mizoram, which had been made a union territory on January 21, 1972, became a full-fledged state on August 29, 1988. Laldenga's Ministry lasted only for eighteen months. But since then Mizoram has been peaceful.

Tripura's Transformation

Tripura has been the homeland of 19 different tribes. It was a peaceful princely state under the British. For a thousand years Tripura was ruled by a dynasty of tribal origin. Its ethnic problem started with the partition of India in 1947. Hundreds of thousands of Bengali Hindus from erstwhile East Pakistan (present Bangladesh) came rushing into Tripura and swamped the indigenous tribals into a hopeless minority. Later even Muslim illegal migrants from Bangladesh came and swelled the ranks of non-tribal population. This created a crisis of identity for the tribals.

The Tripura Upajati Juba Samiti (TUJS) was formed on June 10, 1967 to fight Bengalee chauvinism as well as the neglect of the tribals. The tribals resented the consequences of their economic deprivation and political eclipse. About the same time, the leader Hrarangkwal revived the *Sangram* Union which had been formed earlier. This started the insurgency in Tripura. The main demands of TUJS included the creation of an autonomous district council under the Sixth Schedule of the Indian

Constitution for the tribal people, restoration to the tribals of their land which had been illegally transferred to non-tribals, recognition of tribal *Kakbarak* as a state language and adoption of Roman scripts for *Kakbarak*. The violence that was unleashed by TUJS and some of other insurgent outfits rocked Tripura for a long time resulting in the death of large number of Bengalee people and damage of property belonging to individuals and institutions. It also gave birth to the opposing organization - *Amra Bengali* - which killed a number of tribals beside fuelling the tension among the communities.

In 1977 CPI(M) came to power in Tripura. Led by an able and considerate Chief Minister Nripen Chakravorty, the Communists initiated certain reforms in order to assuage tribal feelings. *Kakbarak* was recognized as the second official language of Tripura beside Bengalee. *Kakbarak* was also made the medium of instruction in the primary schools of the tribal areas. Restoration was ordered to the tribals of whatever land that had been earlier appropriated by the Bengalis without permission of District Magistrates. Necessary steps were taken towards fulfillment of tribal quotas in employment. Enabling legislation was passed for constitution of autonomous district councils under the Sixth Schedule of the Indian Constitution, similar to those in Assam, and various other welfare steps were initiated for the benefit of the tribals. An Accord was signed with Hrarangkhawl, the insurgent leader, at New Delhi in August, 1988. Sporadic violence, however, is still continuing. In the past few years, Tripura has achieved tremendous progress in the economic field specially during the enlightened leadership of the present Chief Minister Manik Sarkar. The tribals have been enabled to share in this prosperity.

Manipur's Woes

Ethnicity is more in evidence in the insurgencies in Manipur. Here the Meiteis in the plains and the two main tribes of *Kukis* and *Nagas* in the hills are perpetually fighting. The *Meiteis,* who converted themselves to Vaishnavite Hindus in the seventeenth century and who form the majority community, feel neglected and discriminated against by the Centre. In fact, "the average Manipuri blames New Delhi for most of his woes. This sense of grievance has fanned separatist sentiment".[21]

Based on this feeling of neglect the insurgent movement took concrete shape in Manipur. N. Bisheshwar, an educated leftist extremist who had spent years in jail because of earlier terrorist activities, organized the People's Liberation Army (PLA) in the mid seventies of the last century. The other insurgent organizations which sprung up about the same time were the People's Revolutionary Party of Kangleipak (PREPAK) and the Kangleipak Communist Party (KCP). They all believed in violence for getting a fair deal from the Centre. They wanted the outsiders (*Mayangs*) to leave Manipur. They practised and propagated pan-mongoloid sentiments. As a reaction against Hinduism they prescribed revival of the old *Meitei* religion of *Sanamah.* And all of them were basically secessionists.

In the hills the *Nagas* and the *Kukis* fought against the Centre and against each other. Each had its own insurgent organization. They also had problems with the neighbouring states because the Manipuri Nagas believed in greater *Nagalim.*

The violence is still continuing. But the scale is much less. The insurgencies in Manipur, both in the hills and the plains, are based on ethnicity as in the other states of NE.

Meghalaya's Xenophobia

In Meghalaya ethnicity has been the dominant factor beside neglect and lack of economic development. Ethnicity was the basis in the very emergence of the state. What is significant, however, is the fact that three principal ethnic groups - *Khasis, Jaintias* and *Garos* - decided to live together in Meghalaya. They have had their conflicts and problems but still continue as the same state. The dominant tribe - *Khasis* - is extremely conscious of their exclusivity. They like to be left alone. Their dislike of outsiders can be described as xenophobia. Meghalaya is normally peaceful. Some sporadic violence, particularly in Shillong, against outsiders do erupt from time to time. But it is not very serious compared to what is happening in Tripura or Manipur.

Peaceful Arunachal

In Arunachal Pradesh, different tribes have different aspirations. There are pockets of dissatisfaction and many grievances. Insurgent outfits from outside cause trouble sometimes. But there has not yet been any major insurgencies or violent incidents.

Complicated Assam

Assam is bigger than other states of NE in terms of population. The problems are also multifarious. With scores of tribes living in the plains and the hills, Assam has a long history of agitation over this or that issue. Separation of Nagaland, Mizoram, Meghalaya and Arunachal Pradesh made erstwhile Assam much smaller in area. But the problems did not diminish in rump Assam. The past Assamese majority, which is fast becoming a minority, has all along been dissatisfied with the Government of India. The other tribes harbour grievances against the Assamese as also the Government of India. These became more intense in the last three decades of the twentieth century. The influx of millions of foreigners from Bangladesh, and some from Nepal, complicated the situation so much that the crisis of identity, which spawned insurgencies in Tripura, made its ugly appearance in Assam also.[22] The rich mosaic of cultural variety turned into a nightmare of political maze which engulfed the state in a spate of insurgencies and consequent violence.

The United Liberation Front of Assam (ULFA), the first Assamese insurgent outfit, was born on April 7, 1979 in the playfield of the Ahom Kings in Sibsagar. It demanded freedom for Assam and separation from the Indian Union. The violence it unleashed in the late eighties and the early nineties has no parallel in the North East. The damages it wrought can be compared with those in Jammu and Kashmir and Sri Lanka by their own insurgent outfits.[23] ULFA has gone through several phases of transformation during the past quarter of a century. Its popular support base has been eroded mainly due to the violence against the civil population, and ironically, its aligning with Pakistan's ISI as also its tacit support to the Bangladeshis. ULFA's cadre strength has been decimated by surrenders, arrests and deaths. It has lost its bases in Assam and it has been flushed out from its hideouts in Bhutan.[24]

Meanwhile Islamist militants have gathered enormous strength and are posing great danger to Assam's remaining with the Indian Union. The state and the central governments seem to have been duly warned. But action taken so far does not appear to be enough. (see Endnotes 24, 25 and 26). ULFA's overall power, however, seem to be declining fast with its leaders and ranks getting distanced from each other. That is why ULFA had joined talks with the Government albeit indirectly through the

People's Consultative Group (PCG) which ULFA formed with some of the leading citizens who seem to support ULFA's cause. But even then sporadic violence was being perpetrated by its hardcore elements particularly against soft targets. Further developments in recent times are discussed later in this book.

The Bodos have been giving vent to their grievances for a long time. But actual insurgency started only in the late eighties mainly as a reaction to the short-sighted, narrow minded and haphazard actions of the Assam Gana Parishad Government. In fact, the AGP Government did not have any proper Bodo policy at all. The Bodo insurgent outfits did tremendous damage to life and property. But they hurt themselves more in the process. The Bodos have now achieved the Bodoland Territorial Autonomous Districts (BTAD). It is doubtful, however, whether they will remain satisfied. They will probably try ethnic cleansing in the BTAD area although ethnic Bodos are a minority in a number of Blocks. The issues are discussed in detail in a later chapter.

Reorganisation of the North East

In order to arrive at a solution of the problem a couple of experiments have been tried in the past few decades including creation of separate states to satisfy the smaller sub-nationalities. The sub-federal structure of the North East Council was devised to co-ordinate the development and common affairs of these states. Then the Ministry of DONER (Department of North Eastern Region) was set up. Both of these are pumping in more money to the Region for economic development. Within Assam, several measures for democratic decentralization have been taken after the Constitution was promulgated on January 26, 1950. These are discussed in the next chapter.

Endnotes

1. Amartya Sen: *Identity and Violence, The Illusion of Destiny.* Allen Lane. London. 2006.
2. David E: Long. *The Anatomy of Terrorism.* The Free Press. New York 1990.
3. Jessica Stern: *The Ultimate Terrorists.* Harvard University Press. Cambridge, Massachusetts. 1999.
4. About Iraq many books are available. The following books written before the second Iraq War appear to be useful:
   (i) Kenneth R. Timmerman: *The Death Lobby, How the West Armed Iraq.* Bantam Books. London. 1992.
   (ii) Judith Miller and Laurie Mylroie: *Saddam Hussain and the Crisis in the Gulf.* Times Books. New York. 1990.
   (iii) John Bulloch and Harvey Morris: *Saddam's Wars.* Faber & Faber. London. 1991.
   (iv) Samir al-Khalil: *Republic of Fear.* Pantheon Books. New York 1989.
5. Yosi Melman: *The Master Terrorist. The True Story of Abu Nidal.* Avon Books. New York. July, 1987. Another book about another terrorist may be referred to: Colin Smith. *Carlos, Portrait of a Terrorist.* Mandarin Paperback. London. 1995.
6. Peter Heehs: *The Bomb in Bengal, The Rise of Revolutionary Terrorism in India, 1900-1910.* Oxford University Press. Delhi. 1993. *Also see*: S. H. Subba Rao : *Terrorism and Crimes in India.* Gangarams Publications. Bangalore. Karl A. Seger. *The Anti-Terrorism Handbook.* Lancer International. New Delhi. 1991. *Also see* Afsir Karim: *Counter Terrorism, The Pakistan Factor.* Lancer International. New Delhi. 1991.
7. Arnold Toynbee, "A Study of History", Oxford University Press, 1972, p.34
8. Walker Connor, *From Tribe to Nation,* History of European Ideas, Vol. 13, No. 1/2, 1991.

9. Percival Spear, *The Oxford History of Modern India, 1970-1975*, The Oxford University Press, 1992.
10. Paul R. Brass, *The Politics of India since Independence*, The New Cambridge History of India Vol. IV, I, Cambridge University Press, 1990. (During a visit to Seattle the author of this book was invited by Brass to speak to the faculty of the Washington State University in 1992. Brass delivered a series of lectures in the Assam Administrative Staff College in 1994).
11. Majumdar, RC, Raychaudhury, HC and Datta, Kalikinkar, *An Advanced History of India*, McMillan India, 1978.
12. Verrier Elwin, *A Philosophy for NEFA*. Published by the NEFA Administration, Shillong, 1957.
13. Verrier Elwin, *The Tribal World of Verrier Elwin*. Oxford University Press, 1989
14. Verrier Elwin quoted by Nari Rustomji, in *Enchanted Frontiers*. Oxford University Press, Calcutta, 1971.
15. CL Imchen, *Naga Politics : Regionalism or Non-State Nation*. In "Regionalism in India," ed. B. Pakem, Har-Anand Publications, New Delhi: 1993.
16. Kaka D Iralu, *Nagaland and India, The Blood and the Tears*. September, 2000.
17. DN Majumder, *Ethnicity and Regionalism in North-East India*, ed. B. Pakem *Regionalism in India*, Har-Anand Publications, New Delhi, 1993.
18. B. Pakem, *Nationality Question in the Hill areas of North-East India*, p 12.
19. Ved Marwah, *Uncivil Wars: Pathology of Terrorism in India*, Harper Collins Publishers New Delhi India.
20. Ved Marwah, p. 14.
21. Myron Weiner, *Sons of the Soil: Migration and Ethnic Conflict in India*. Oxford University Press, Delhi, 1988.
22. Ved Marwah, ... p. 14.
23. Jaideep Saikia, *Bhutan's Tryst with ULFA*, Aakrosh, July 2004.

24. For a brilliant exposition of ULFA's shenanigans with the ISI, see Jaideep Saikia, *ISI Reaches East, Studies in Conflict & Terrorism, USA*, 25, no. 3 (May-June 2002) pp. 185-197.
25. Jaideep Saikia, *Terror Sans Frontiers: Islamist Militancy in North East India*, Vision Books, New Delhi, Mumbai. Hyderabad, 2004.
26. Lt. Gen. (Retd.) SK Sinha, in his foreword to Jaideep Saikia's paper on "Terror Sans Frontiers" included in the University of Illinois' Occasional Papers. USA July, 2003.

CHAPTER – 2

Demographic Transformation and Insurgency in Assam

Two Valleys

The geographical entity of Assam consists of two valleys. The Barak valley in the south has three overwhelmingly Bengali speaking districts with some immigrant labourers in the tea plantations and some scattered tribal populations mainly in the foothills. The Brahmaputra valley in the north never had a homogeneous population or society. From time immemorial different tribes and ethnic groups have lived in the Brahmaputra valley and the hills surrounding it. Immigrants have come from outside the area throughout the past. They brought their own cultures and languages. Some retained these, albeit in modified forms, but most got merged into a nebulous ethnic mainstream. This chapter is mainly about the Brahmaputra Valley or the Assam Valley.

Hindu-Aryan Immigration

In my own view three major events which took place in the Brahmaputra valley in the past two thousand years determined its demographic profile. The first major event was the Hindu Aryan immigration from north India. This brought a highly cultured, educationally advanced and socially active group which, in course of time, came to dominate the Brahmaputra valley. It is they who developed the Assamese language, which is derived from Sanskrit and belongs to the same sub-group as Bengali, Oriya, Maitheli, Bhojpuri and other Aryan languages of eastern India.[1] The *Kamakhya* temple is the most important visible monument of those times. Worship of the Mother Goddess characterised these people of old *Kamarupa* or *Pragjyotishpura*.[2] They also built scores of other temples. The sculptural and architectural remains all over the Brahmaputra valley indicate clear and close linkages with north India.[3] It was in this age that the Assamese literature was initiated. Beside poetry, prose was also composed in Assamese by *Bhattadeva* and others.[4] The Assamese tried to get most of other tribes and ethnic groups of the Brahmaputra Valley absorbed into their fold. They partially succeeded in this effort.

Tai Ahom Assimilation

The second major event was the conquest of upper Assam by *Tai-Ahoms*, a *Shan* ethnic community, who came from China - Myanmar border in the thirteenth century. They got themselves merged into the Assamese mainstream abandoning their own culture and language.[5] They adopted the Hindu religion. *Sukapha,* the *Ahom* conqueror and the first Ahom King, is reputed to have adopted this policy of assimilation and thus helped the formation of the Assamese sub-nationality as it exists to-day.[6]

Then, in the fifteenth - sixteenth centuries the greatest Assamese of all times, Sri Sankardeva (1449-1568), who started life as a Sanskrit scholar and writer, composed his *Kirtanghosha* in Assamese and introduced far reaching reforms in the Hindu religion.[7] It is Sankardeva who introduced the *Vaishnavite* cult in Assam. He and his principal disciple, Sri Madhabdeva, who wrote the *Naamghosha,* developed Assamese literature, music, drama, painting, dance and society into very high standards. Their *Bargeets* are some of the finest nuggets of Indian classical music. The *Sattriya* dance form they developed is recognized as one of the seven national classical dances of India by the Sangeet Natak Academy.[8] They taught the Assamese how to live hygienically and neatly in cottages built around a courtyard for each family. The Assamese lived a far better, more meaningful and spiritually richer life than most other communities in India till about the fiftees of the last century. The per capita income was also higher than the national average.[9] The Assamese *Naamghars* (prayer halls) are the centres of social life in the villages even today. The 914 *Satras* (large monasteries) and the thousands of *Naamghars* are the institutional and structural frameworks of the Assamese society. To quote Dr. SK Bhuyan, "through the network of *Sattras* and *Naamghars*, spread all over the country, knowledge permeated to the masses of Assam".[10] The liberal reforms of Sankardeva and Madhabdeva attracted many more ethnic groups to adopt the Assamese language, the Hindu religion and the socio-cultural millieu which Sankardeva had initiated. In fact, an innovative *Saraniya* system was introduced in order to make gradual absorption of tribals into the Assamese mainstream possible and easy.

Bangladeshi Muslim Infiltration

The third major event was the continuous and unrelenting immigration of Bengali Muslims from east Bengal (present Bangladesh) since the beginning of the twentieth century in the wake of the British Indian Government's "grow more food campaign".[11] Later, the speed of immigration was stepped up. Such immigration was supported and encouraged by the Bangladeshi intellectuals in search of a Labensraum.[12] This problem is discussed in detail in the next chapter.

It may be mentioned, however, that there are some "indigenous Muslims" who have got completely absorbed in the Assamese mainstream. Some of them came with the invading Mughal armies and the others got converted into Islam during the past few centuries. Some Muslims of north Indian origin who came to Assam with the Mughal invading armies during the long 600 years of Ahom rule from 1228 to 1826 and remained behind in the Brahmaputra Valley, fully adopted the Assamese language and culture, although retaining the Muslim religion. Some of them were conferred Ahom titles which they use in place of surnames even today. They got some indigenous people also converted into Islam. Their religious leader, *Azan Phakir,* taught them tolerance towards other religions. Their martial hero, *Bagh Hazarika,* fought with the Ahom warriors side by side. Their freedom fighter, *Bahadur Gaonbura,* was banished to *Kalapani* by the British rulers. One President of India (Fakhruddin Ali Ahmed) and one member of the drafting committee of the Indian Constitution (Sir Muhammed Saadullah, who was earlier Prime Minister of British Assam) belonged to the Assamese Muslim community.

Similarly a small number of Sikhs came with the Mughal invaders in the seventeenth century. More Sikhs came to help the Ahoms in their fight against the Burmese invaders in the 1820s. They also remained behind. These Sikhs fully adopted the Assamese language and culture while retaining their religion. They forgot the Punjabi language.[13]

Immigration during British Days

During the British occupation of Assam in the nineteenth and the twentieth centuries, the British brought some highly educated urban Bengali Hindus to work in their offices and in the educational institutions. When the tea industry was started in the 1830s thousands of indentured labourers were brought from Bengal, Bihar, U.P., Madhya Pradesh and Orissa by the British tea planters to work in the plantations. They now form a sizeable proportion (about 10 percent) of the state's population. They are politically very active. Small numbers of Rajasthani traders, Nepali milkmen and Bihari labourers also came in the past two centuries.[14]

Current Demographic Profile

The demographic profile of Assam today presents a mosaic which is rich in cultural diversity and in the profusion of languages, music, dance, drama and the fine arts. Out of the 130 known languages of NE India the majority are extant in Assam. This amalgam is difficult to comprehend unless the three major historical events as described above are properly stated and appreciated.

In fact, the process of demographic fusion and cohesion which was brought about by Sukapha and Sankardeva continued unabated till the British occupation of Assam in 1826. The process became slow after that. But the process has been reversed since the 1960s in the wake of Assamese being declared as the state language. This official language status for the Assamese language was opposed by the Bengali Hindus. The riots that took place in the 1960s claimed many lives. The pecularity of these riots was the fact that the Bangladeshi Muslim immigrants took up the cause of Assamese language and fought against the Bengali Hindus.

Social Changes

About the same time that the political reorganization was enacted, certain far-reaching changes became discernible in the social sphere. For example, the Assamese language, which had served as the linking language for the entire NE region for centuries, was edged out of this position. Even Nagamese and Arunachalis, which actually come from Assamese, are being neglected.

Central financial assistance to Arunachal Pradesh, Meghalaya, Nagaland and Mizoram were stepped up substantially after their separation from Assam. The tribal leaders assumed importance and started enjoying all the constitutional powers and the strappings of office. This was perhaps a historic necessity. But this aroused aspirations in the minds of other tribal and ethnic groups. The Bodos, for example, organized the Plains Tribal Council of Assam (PTCA) and started a movement for a separate state. Some of the Bodo factions became insurgents and started fighting for secession and independence. The Bodos now harbour ill feelings against the ethnic Assamese and do not learn the Assamese language any more.

The tea labourers have started abandoning the Assamese language and reviving the *Sadri* language aided mainly by the Christian missionaries and the NE TV Channels. They are also fighting for tribal status. The other tribes and ethnic groups demand separate state or area and have started agitating and even insurgencies. *Dima Hasaos* and *Karbis* demand upgradation of their autonomous districts into states. Some even demand independence. Several insurgent outfits have surfaced in recent times and hundreds of people have been killed in bomb blasts and grenade attacks in *Karbi Anglong* and Dima Hasao (formerly North Cachar Hill) districts. Smaller tribes and ethnic groups make similar demands.

The tribal and ethnic groups of Assam have achieved various levels of progress in different spheres. The ethnic Assamese, including Hindus, Muslims, Christians and Sikhs, have fair to high levels of education and general prosperity. Similar is the case with the Bodos, who look healthier probably because of their genes and their protein rich food intake. The wealthiest by far, however, are the Marwaris or the Rajasthanis who control the wholesale trade, the tea industry and a sizeable number of private industrial units. They now own most of the prime real estate in Guwahati and other urban centers. The urban Bengali Hindus are as literate and prosperous as the Assamese. But their rural counterparts are not so well off. Similar is the case with the large communities of Bangladeshi immigrant Muslims and tea garden labourers. Both these communities have low rates of literacy, low land holding and generally low prosperity. Literacy and prosperity rates vary among other tribal and ethnic groups. At the lowest rung perhaps are the tribes of *Karbi Anglong* and Dima Hasao districts. Insurgency also is most virulent and most intense in these two districts.[15]

Special Financial Allocation

Special efforts have been made by the central and the state Governments for the upliftment of the down trodden communities. Assam's Five-Year and Annual Plans, for example, have Hills, Tribal and Scheduled Caste components with separate prefixed ratios for weightage to different sections of people. This has been done because according to official estimates 12.41 percent of Assam's population belongs to the scheduled tribes, 6.85 percent to the scheduled castes and approximately 27 percent to the other backward classes. Large sums are allocated to the Autonomous District Councils and the tribal and ethnic councils, both under Plan and under Non-Plan heads.[16] Development Corporations have been established for the Minorities, Scheduled Castes, Scheduled Tribes and Other Backward Classes. However, the results have not been commensurate nor have the targets been achieved. There are clamours for more funds while allocated funds are not properly utilized.

Sub-Federal Political Reorganisation (1990-2009)

A spurt of tribal and ethnic aspirations in rump Assam after separation of Nagaland, Mizoram, Meghalaya and

Arunachal Pradesh resulted in a series of agitations, disturbances and destructions which rend asunder the cohesion and unity among different sections of society in the state. With the object of quelling such disturbances innovative but mind boggling political and administrative arrangements have been arrived at in the past two decades. This has resulted in decentralization of power in a rather peculiar and haphazard manner.[17]

These arrangements came in several doses of ad hoc political decisions without any general debate on the issues concerned or examination of the pros and cons of the solutions evolved. In the process even the recommendations of the Bhupinder Singh Committee appointed in this behalf were ignored.[18] Actually these ad hoc decisions were taken to subserve political expediency. Since their implications were not properly studied or discussed before implementation certain inscrutable problems have now surfaced. In fact, units have come up with disputed jurisdictions and varied configurations of financial, legislative and administrative endowments. This has been done through constitutional amendments in some cases and statutory enactments in others. Even executive orders have brought about such units.

The pattern that has emerged consists of the following:

(1) The first autonomous district council (ADC) consisting of the Karbi Anglong and North Cachar Hills districts was formed in November, 1951. Later, it was bifurcated into two separate ADCs, one each for Karbi Anglong and NC Hills, now called Dima Hasao district. These were formed under the provisions of the Sixth Schedule of the Indian Constitution. The ADCs have wide administrative and some legislative powers. But law and order is only with the State Government. As has been stated in the previous chapter, the process of recognition of sub-nationalism

in NE started with the drafting of the Indian Constitution. On the basis of the recommendations of the Committee, appointed by the Constituent Assembly and headed by Bharat Ratna Gopinath Bordoloi, the Sixth Schedule was incorporated in the Constitution with the object of protecting the tribal people, their rights and their particular way of life.[19]

To these two hill districts, the third addition has been the Bodoland Territorial Autonomous Districts (BTAD), formed on October 31, 2003 with powers exercised under the Sixth Schedule of the Constitution by the Bodoland Territorial Council (BTC). It has jurisdiction over the four administrative districts of Kokrajhar, Chirang, Baksa and Udalguri. The BTC has wide executive and some legislative powers but law and order is not included.

(2) Seven tribal councils were formed for the *Mishings, Rabha-Hasongs, Tiwas, Deories, Sonowal Kacharis* and *Thengal Kacharis* along with the non-statutory council for the Barrak valley tribes.

(3) Seven ethnic development councils are presently in the process of formation. These will be for the *Morans, Motoks, Ahoms, Chutias, Koch-Rajbongshis, Adibasis* (also called Tea Tribes) and *Gorkhas*. These ethnic groups have been demanding tribal status for a long time. In fact, the *Koch-Rajbongshis* were once declared as tribals by an ordinance. But the ordinance was allowed to lapse. It never became an Act of Parliament. The demand for tribal status by any of these groups has not been agreed by the Government of India as yet. Only *Sarania Kacharis* have been newly included in the list of tribes. The State Government has promised a new council for the *Saranias*. A ninth council will be for the *Amri Karbis* who live in the periphery of the city of Guwahati and who are not recognized as tribals in the plains of Assam.

Kachariland and Tribal State

On February 19, 2009 a significant event took place when a number of organizations and tribal and ethnic students unions congregated in Guwahati's ITA Auditorium and passed a resolution demanding a tribal state by carving out certain Assam territories to be named as *Kachariland.* They claimed to represent 18 tribes. This was indeed a momentous resolution in which all tribals are supposed to have united.

Another development has been the demand for a "tribal state". This concept has not been defined properly. But the Communist Party of India in their 2009 election menifesto had included this demand because, according to media report, "If Assam is declared as a tribal state, the people of the state would have reservations in the State Assembly and Parliament".[20] More autonomy for Assam has been demanded in the same line as Jammu & Kashmir under Article 370 and Nagaland under Article 371A of the Indian Constitution.

In November, 2009 the ULFA Pro-Talk Group (led by Mrinal Hazarika) had proposed a more powerful upper house of the Assam Legislature and federal structure of Government for Assam.

Consequences of Sub-Federal Re-organisation

The persistence of tribal, ethnic and linguistic differences and the coming into existence of so many tiers of governmental organizations have really complicated the political scene in Assam. In most other states of India at least the overwhelming majority of population belongs to one group. This facilitates political cohesion and economic development. The absence of such integration in Assam has been a cause of concern.

The latest estimates show that the Assamese Hindus comprise only 29.30 percent of the state's population.

This has serious implications. To quote Ishania "The threat perception for the *Asomiyas* in Assam is that from time to time some of the ethnic communities of the state exclude themselves from the unofficial term "indigenous *Asomiyas*", and if this alienation of the groups cannot be erased, the future of *Asomiyas* will be bleak in Assam".[21]

The Muslims, including both Assamese and Bangladeshi, form 30.14 percent of the population. The rest of the population consists of 13.19 percent Bengali Hindus, 5.16 percent *Bodos*, 9.58 percent *Adibasis*, 1.53 percent *Karbis*, 1.76 percent *Nepalis*, 1.70 percent *Mishings*, 2.07 percent *Koch Rajbangshis*, 0.35 percent *Dimasas* and 4.95 percent others.

The existence of so many tribes and ethnic groups and their unfulfilled political aspirations have led to unrest and insurgency. Even the grant of autonomy at sub-state level has not fully satisfied the tribal and ethnic leaders. The minor party apparatchiks and political agitationists seem to have a vested interest in keeping the tribal and ethnic groups isolated mainly for their own political ambition and monetary gains. Some of these groups, specially the Bangladeshi Muslims, are used as "vote banks" by the political party in power.

The tribal and ethnic councils demand more power and more money. Already media reports suggest rampant misuse of grants, non-maintenance of accounts and siphoning off funds by politicians, bureaucrats, contractors and their cohorts. It is also alleged that substantial funds are diverted to insurgent outfits. Meanwhile the administrative control and decision making processes have been complicated by the existence of many units of different types with varying powers and confusing jurisdictions. This has adversely affected the delivery system for economic development. Actually the system itself has become fragmented.

Issues and Problems of Sub-Federal Reorganisation

The political reorganisation of Assam with autonomous, tribal and ethnic councils cannot be considered to be final because in the present arrangement many problems have been left unresolved. These are now begging for solution. In Bodoland, for example, many villages have been included where there is no or little Bodo population. These areas have been included only in order to achieve territorial contiguity. Moreover, non–Bodos are in majority in 3 out of Bodoland's 4 districts.[22] There is considerable resentment among the non-Bodo inhabitants of Bodoland.

Again, the reservation of seats in the Bodoland Territorial Council (BTC) does not reflect the population pattern of Bodoland. The 40 elected seats in BTC, out of a total of 46, are distributed as follows: 30 for tribals, 5 for non-tribal communities and 5 open for all communities. The remaining 6 seats are filled up by nomination by the Governor. This arrangement is not democratic because it debars non-tribal communities from proportionate representation. This apparently undemocratic arrangement had to be resorted to in order to satisfy the Bodos.

There are a large number of Bodos who live outside Bodoland. They have no special rights or benefits unlike their compatriots inside Bodoland. What irks the Bodos most is the fact that Bodos living in Assam's hill districts are not recognized as tribals. This is anomalous.

There have been many cases of attempted ethnic cleansing inside Bodoland. The victims are the indigenous *Koch Rajbangshis* and the immigrant Bangladeshi Muslims who form large groups of Bodoland's population. The legitimate question that is being asked is : How can the indigenous people be uprooted from their own homeland? Where will they go? And, why will they go? These are questions which will have to be answered clearly.

In the case of Bangladeshi Muslims it is true that they illegally migrated to the areas, which now form Bodoland, in the past few decades. They are apprehensive about eviction from land which they have occupied for long. Many of them have encroached upon government land including land in the reserved forests and the national parks. Some of them have bought land in tribal belts and blocks. Such transactions are illegal, being prohibited by law. Several thousand Bangladeshi Muslims from BTAD are in relief camps. These people were uprooted following ethnic violence. Their problems need to be addressed boldly.

The Koch Rajbongshis are the most unhappy lot. They are indigenous Hindu people of lower Assam. Their language is Assamese. A Koch dynasty ruled in lower Assam and north Bengal for centuries. The Koch King, Naranarayana, gave shelter to Sankardeva and helped the great saint to spread his religion and culture. Naranarayan and his brother, General Chilarai, rebuilt the Kamakhya temple about five hundred years ago. The stone statues of the two brothers adorn the ante chamber of the temple. Chilarai married Sankardeva's niece.

The Koch Rajbangshis have two main demands: tribal status and Kamatapur state. As has been already stated they had been given tribal status by an ordinance. But curiously enough the ordinance was allowed to lapse and never became an Act of Parliament. Their demand for a Kamatapur state has equal weightage as the demand for a state of Bodoland. But if Kamatapur is conceded the present boundaries of Bodoland will probably undergo a change.

The total population of scheduled tribes in Assam, in the 2001 census, has been estimated to be 33,08,570 forming 12.41 percent of the state's population.[23] This is wrong. The actual tribal population will be much more because lakhs of Bodos in the hills and Amri Karbi and other such groups in the plains are not considered to be tribals and are left out. Moreover, the demands of Ahoms, Motoks, Adibasis, Morans, Chutias and Gorkhas, beside Koch Rajbongshis, for tribal status will also need to be seriously considered. This will increase the number of tribals.

Panchayati Raj Institutions

At the grassroots level the autonomous, tribal and ethnic councils seem to be in conflict with the Panchayati Raj Institutions (PRIs) in the plains and certain traditional tribal councils in the hills. In the hills the traditional councils used to wield considerable power. These are extra constitutional and extra statutory bodies. But some intellectuals and tribal experts have romantic ideas about them. There is also an attempt to see their continued existence to be sanctified by the provisions of Article 40 of the Constitution.[24] But it is forgotten that there is no express provision in the Constitution, neither in any of the main Articles nor in the Fifth or the Sixth Schedules, which would allow continuance or revival of these tribal councils. These councils are not democratic but feudal, hereditary and oligarchic institutions. They exclude women, tenant farmers, wage labourers and poor people, they are an anachronism in a democratic country.

Again, under normal circumstances neither the tribal councils nor the ethnic councils should be allowed to replace or substitute the PRIs which are democratic entities under Article 243 in part IX of the Indian Constitution. PRIs never existed in the hill districts of Assam. PRIs have been recently abolished from Bodoland areas. The leaders of tribal and ethnic councils do not want PRIs in their jurisdiction. In the Rava-Hasong area, for example, tribals prevented election to PRIs. This led to riots in which several people were killed. How to reconcile the aspirations of tribal and ethnic groups and the necessity of PRIs at the grassroots level is a moot question which must be addressed in the proper perspective and a solution evolved for maintaining unity of the people and integrity of the state.

Insurgency based on Sub-National Aspirations

It may be appropriate to recall here that taking advantage of the ethnic and sub-national grievances a very large number of insurgent outfits have made their appearance in Assam. The political re-organisation of the state, as described earlier, has been made with a view to curb such insurgencies. However, further administrative reforms will be necessary to take care of the problems which have been mentioned in this chapter.

Political acumen in bringing about reforms in the structures of the sub-federal and sub-state units, which have been constituted recently, and their integration with PRIs, will determine whether long term peace and tranquility can be achieved. The re-organisation has been done with a view to solving the ethnic problem. But whether these will fully satisfy the aspirations of all the ethnic groups will be seen only in the future. A considerable amount of fine tuning will be absolutely essential. Meanwhile, more problems have been created by appointment of executive councils with members who support the political party in power. Elections have not been held. There is no indication when elections would be held and who would form the government. The preparation of electoral rolls itself will be a difficult exercise.

In any further political re-organisation, the existing arrangements and political structures must not be disturbed suddenly. At the same time sustained efforts must continue to ensure that no ethnic community suffers or remains permanently dissatisfied. Any new arrangement will need to be based on a very careful study of the ethnic problem and detailed discussion with the leaders of different groups. The adhocism, resorted to by politicians in the past, must be avoided. It must also be ensured that any such settlement does not give rise to further violence or grounds for insurgency. Further peace in NE will depend upon how best the ethnic problem is addressed.

Finally, there is a proposal to have a legislative council at the apex level representing all tribal and ethnic groups in the state beside the usual special interest categories of citizens. This proposal was opposed by many experts on the subject. I feel, however, that it needs to be examined with special reference to the peculiar ethnic problems of Assam.

Endnotes

1. Kakati, Dr. Banikanta, *Assamese, Its Formation and Development.* Lawyer's Book Stall, Guwahati, 1941. As remarked by Dr. SK Bhuyan "Dr. Kakati established for the first time the individuality of Assamese, placing it in the proper perspective of its sister languages." It was a thesis on the basis of which Dr. Kakati was conferred the Ph.D. degree of the Calcutta University. It was highly praised by Dr. Suniti Kumar Chatterjee among others. Dr. Kakati has acknowledged that "the incentive to undertake this work" came from Dr. Chatterjee and that "he has all through helped me with valuable suggestions in every conceivable shape and form. My indebtedness to him is beyond measure."
2. Kakati, Dr. Banikanta. "The Mother Goddess *Kamakhya*", Guwahati, 1948.
3. *Kamrupa Anusandhana Sammittee.* "Readings in the History and Culture of Assam". It contains a large number of learned papers on the temples and monuments of the Brahmaputra Valley. Published by the *Sammittee* in collaboration with Indian Archaelogical Society and Indian History and Culture Society, 1984. Distributed by Books & Books, Janakpuri, New Delhi. *Also see* Barua, Kanak Lal.

"*Early History of Kamarupa.*" Published by the Author, Shillong, 1933.

4. Sarma, Dr. Satyendra Nath. *A Socio-Economic and Cultural History of Mediaevel Assam (1200-1800. A.D.)* Published by Pratima Devi, Guwahati, 1989. Dr. Sarma writes as follows: "*Bhattadeva* is considered to be the father of Assamese prose. His works, viz, *Katha Gita, Bhakti Ratnavali* and *Katha Bhagavata* are important steps towards the great achievements of Assamese narrative prose. *Bhattadeva* was followed by a few more prose writers who translated parts of the Ramayana and some other *Puranas* in the Assamese prose". *Also see* Bhuyan, Dr. SK *Studies in the Literature of Assam*, Omson's Publications, New Delhi, 1956.
5. Among the several historians who have written about the Ahom conquest, one of the earliest is EA Gait, *A History of Assam*, Calcutta, 1906. Latest edition. 1967. *Also see* HK Barpujari, edited. *The Comprehensive History of Assam*. Volume Two. Publication Board, Assam, 1992.
6. Gohain, Dr. BK *The origin of Tai and Chaolung Sukapha*, Omson's Publications, Delhi, 1996.
7. Neog, Dr. Maheswar, *Sankardeva*, National Book Trust of India, New Delhi, 1967. For a more detailed discussion see Neog, Maheswar, *Sankardeva and His Times*, Guwahati, 1965.
8. Neog, Dr. Maheswar, *Sattriya Dances of Assam and Their Rythms*. Publication Board, Guwahati, 1973. In his foreword to the book Dr. Suniti Kumar Chatterjee has written that "the ancient pan- Indian Sanskritic or what has also been correctly described as the Hindu classical tradition of the dance has still been preserved very well in Assam."
9. Das, HN *A New Paradigm of Development : Regional Imbalance and Assam. The Economic Times*, Issue dated October 23, 1985.
10. Bhuyan, Dr. SK *Studies in the Literature of Assam*. Omson's Publications, New Delhi, 1956.
11. Bhuyan, Arun Chandra. Edited. *Political History of Assam*. Volumes Two (1920-1939) and Three (1940-47). Government of Assam, Guwahati. 1978.
12. For an authentic description of how the Assamese Muslims and the Assamese Sikhs settled down in the Brahmaputra

Valley see : Barpujari, HK edited, *The Comprehensive History of Assam.* Volume Three. Chapter VII. Publication Board, Guwahati, 1994. "There is a strong belief among the Sikhs that Guru Nanak, the founder of Sikhism, in course of his first missionary tour came to *Kamarupa* in 1505." Later, Guru Tegh Bahadur came to Dhubri in 1666. His disciples raised a mound of earth on the bank of the Brahmaputra. Later, the Damdama Sahib Gurdwara was built on this mound at Dhubri town.

13. Hazarika, Dr. BB, *Political Life in Assam During the 19th Century.* Gian Publishing House, New Delhi. 1987.
14. I have drawn these impressions on the basis of observations as also the experience of the past 50 years of working in Assam and the North Eastern Region and on media reports.
15. Figures of fund allocations to different entities are in the main Budget document of the Government of Assam. Similar information about the development Corporations are available in the Departmental Budgets.
16. I have seen the process both inside and outside the Government. The discussions in the state and the central governments were perfunctory, to say the least. On many occasions leaders like Rajesh Pilot would suddenly land up in Guwahati airport by BSF plane and dictate terms to the state Government. It is doubtful whether Pilot had studied the ground situation or was aware of the future complications which his out of the hat solutions would bring about.
17. Bhupinder Singh was a retired IAS officer. He was asked to examine the tribal and ethnic situation and to recommend measures for solution of the problems arising out of different and opposing demands. His Report was never publicly discussed nor examined by the Government. He had recommended village-centric contiguous areas to form village councils. Beside village councils he had recommended regional and apex councils.
18. Durga Das Basu, *Shorter Constitution of India.* Wadhwa. 2004 Nagpur. See Part X. *Scheduled and Tribal Areas* [Articles 247 (1) and (2) and 244A 1)]. *Also see* the *Sixth Schedule.* [Articles 244 (2) and 275 (1)]

19. *The Assam Tribune*, Guwahati, March 19, 2009.
20. The figures in this and the following paragraph are from Ishani (*The North Eastern*). Bi-monthly journal of Mahatma Gandhi Ishani Foundation. Guwahati, dated Novermber 15, 2008. "Survey on Demography finds Asomiyas a Minority". This is the report of a survey on the demography of Assam conducted by the Intelligence Bureau in 2004 and submitted to the Government of India.
21. The population figures on which this statement is based are from a State Government paper.
22. *Statistical Handbook*, Government of Assam, Guwahati, 2006.
23. Sharma, BD, *Ethnicity and Self-Governance in the North East*. In BB Kumar edited *Problems of Ethnicity in the North East India*. Ashtha Bharati. Delhi, 2007. For the opposite view see Patricia Mukhim, *Negotiating Ethnic Identity in a Democracy*, in the same collection edited by BB Kumar.
24. Barua, TL "Do We Need a Second Chamber"? *The Assam Tribune*. Issue dated August 20, 2008.

CHAPTER – 3

Bangladeshi Infiltration : A Threat to Integrity of India

Second World War and India's Partition

Momentous events have taken place in the Indian subcontinent during the twentieth century which have drastically altered the political structures and violently rearranged the communal equation. None of these radical changes could be foreseen by the politicians and intellectuals of those times to whom all these came as surprises and shocks. The contention of this chapter is that if certain events mentioned below could take place in the twentieth century, similar events can certainly occur again in the twenty first century unless the politicians and intellectuals are careful enough to study the writing on the wall.

Probably the most important event was the decline and fall of the British Empire in the wake of the Second World War (1939-1945). This signalled the downfall of other universal empires. At the same time the freedom movement in India gathered momentum under Congress. But Muslim League advanced the two-nation theory. This led to partition and emergence of two countries - India and Pakistan. From the very beginning the two countries have been at loggerhead. The stand off started with the war over Jammu and Kashmir in 1947. Then the war of 1965 increased the bitterness. In 1971 the two countries fought again and a third country - Bangladesh - emerged. The end is not yet in sight. There is every possibility that the former Pakistani Prime Minister Zulfiquar Ali Bhutto's threat of a "thousand year war" might become a reality. Being a multi-ethnic, multi-language and multi-religion country, India is always susceptible to fissiparous tendencies. Past history shows that vivisections have been caused whenever the Central Government lost strength and the bonds of common culture and tradition were weakened. The purpose of this chapter is to show that the fear of another partition is real and imminent. The apprehension is that the presently neglected North Eastern Region (NE or NER) might get divided between China and Bangladesh or at least a "Swadhin Islamic Bangabhumi", loosely translated as Independent Muslim Bengali land, as proposed by the Bangladeshi intellectuals, might emerge in this geographically isolated area through continuous and unrelenting immigration of Bangladeshi Muslims into Assam and to other states through Assam. In that process, the historical and the geo-strategic factors will also be examined in some detail.

Dimensions of North Eastern Region

Most people of India are not aware that the eight states of NER have 3.9% of India's population (3.90 crores in 2001) and 7.98% (2,62,185 km^2) of its area. NER is linked to the rest of India by a narrow 26 kms wide corridor nicknamed the "chicken's neck". More than 98% of NE's boundary is international with Bhutan, China, Myanmar and Bangladesh. Only 2% of NE's boundary is with the state of West Bengal in India. Assam is the biggest state in terms of population (2.67 crores in 2001) and Arunachal is the largest in terms of area (83,743 km^2). The density is lowest in Arunachal Pradesh (13 per sq. km) and highest in Assam (340 per sq. km). Some of the Assam districts have very high densities such as 585 in Dhubri, 582 in Nagaon and 581 in Kamrup. These figures are comparable to Kerala and West Bengal. The densities have risen again between 2001 and 2010.[1]

Beginning of Bangladeshi Immigration

Large scale immigration of Bengali speaking Muslims from the districts now forming Bangladesh to Assam started early in the twentieth century. All those people who have come to Assam from the aforesaid districts and their progeny are described as Bangladeshis in this essay. This migration increased the Muslim population of Assam from less than 10 percent in 1901 to 16.23 percent in 1911, to 24.03 percent in 1971 and to 30.14 percent in 2001. The percentage is believed to have gone up to more than 35 by 2010. An intelligent guess will be that only about 5 percent of the Muslims are indigenous Assamese people. The rest 30 percent have come from Bangladesh. Since Bangladeshi Muslims do not practice any family planning and since they tend to proliferate in the belief that more the number of children, greater the earning their growth rate tends to be higher than those of the people from other religions. For example, during the 40 year period from 1951 to 1991, the growth rate of the Muslim population was as high as 77.33% compared to 41.61% of the Hindus. At this rate, the Muslims will outnumber the Hindus in Assam by about 2025 or earlier.[2]

The Bangladeshi Muslims first started coming to the green and verdant valley of Brahmaputra in search of land for cultivation. The high growth rate of population coupled with dearth of vacant land induced the poverty stricken Bangladeshis to migrate from their native districts. In this connection what SC Mullan, ICS, Census Superintendent, Assam, 1931, said is significant and is quoted here: "Probably the most important event in the Province during the last 25 years - an event, moreover, which seems likely to alter permanently the whole future of Assam and to destroy more surely the Burmese invaders of 1821, the whole structure of Assamese culture and civilization - has been the invasion of a vast horde of land-hungry Bengali immigrants mostly Muslims from the districts of East Bengal and in particular Mymensingh

.... The only thing I can compare is the mass movement of a large body of ants........... It is sad but by no means improbable that in another thirty years, Sibsagar district will be the only part of Assam in which an Assamese will find himself at home".[3] Mullan would have been shocked to learn that even Sibsagar has now a sizeable Bangladeshi population.

The pace of immigration increased tremendously during World War II when Sir Muhammad Saadullah ministry in Assam started *Grow more Food Campaign* to support the British Indian Government's war efforts. This prompted the then Viceroy of India, Lord Archibald Wavell to remark that the Saadullah Ministry was trying "to increase the immigration into the cultivable Government lands under the slogan of 'Grow More Food' but what they are really after, is 'Grow More Muslims' ". (*Viceroy's Journal*, London, 1973, page 41, entry for December 22, 1943). The surprising thing is that the British did not do anything to stop the migration.

After partition of the country in 1947 the Hindus of the districts now forming Bangladesh were systematically pushed out so that the proportion of Hindus and Buddhists in that country, which was 33.93 percent in 1901, declined to 11.37 percent in 1991. The percentage has further declined to less than 10 by now. The displaced Hindus migrated to India and to Assam in large numbers. According to one estimate about 2 million voters are missing from the electoral rolls of Bangladesh. These are Hindus and Buddhists. These people have migrated to India and particularly to Assam.[4]

Present Population Pattern of Assam

Due to the unabated and relentless immigration of Muslims from Bangladesh, Assam's population pattern has changed over time and the ethnic Assamese seem to have become a minority in their own homeland. In this connection no less a person than SL Sankhdher, the then

Chief Election Commissioner of India had observed in 1978 as follows: "A stage would be reached when the state may have to reckon with the foreign nationals who may, in all probability constitute a sizeable percentage, if not the majority of the population in the state". The present demographic pattern in the state can be seen from the table below[5] :

Present demographic profile of Assam

Assamese Hindus	29.30 per cent
Muslims	30.14 per cent
Bengali Hindus	13.19 per cent
Adibasis	9.58 per cent
Bodos	5.16 per cent
Koch-Rajbangshis	2.07 per cent
Nepalis	1.76 per cent
Mishings	1.70 per cent
Karbis	1.53 per cent
Dimasas	0.35 per cent
Others	4.95 per cent

Source: "Ishani", November 15, 2008, quoting a report of a survey conducted by the Intelligence Bureau.

This position was realised by some leaders of the Assamese community quite some time ago. There were some agitations and even riots. The local people, including the tribals and the other ethnic communities, started riots when they found that their land had been taken over by the Bangladeshis (both Hindu refugees and Muslim infiltrators). Actually the greedy local people had sold some of their land to the Bangladeshis at high prices. Riots began to recover the land but it did not help. In

1983, for example, the Tiwa tribals killed about 3000 Bangladeshis on one night in Nellie in the Nagaon district of central Assam. That was during the Assam Movement (1979-85). The then Prime Minister Indira Gandhi personally visited the place and asked the state government to take stringent steps so that such incidents do not recur. The Bangladeshis, however, remained and got more entrenched. It may be recalled that the long and widely publicized Assam Movement, organized and run by the All Assam Students Union (AASU), had the main objective of deportation of illegal Bangladeshis from Assam. The Movement ended with the signing of the Assam Accord. AASU's expectation from the Accord was that the Bangladeshis who had come after March 25, 1971 would be detected, their names would be deleted from the voters' lists and they would be deported. Twenty five years after the Accord hardly any Bangladeshi has been deported. In fact, more of them came and got absorbed by their ever willing brethren who were already in Assam.

Support Bases of Bangladeshis

It needs to be emphasized that Bangladeshis have their support bases both inside and outside India. The existing governments of Assam, Tripura and West Bengal actually welcome them and use them as the vote banks of the respective political parties in power in each of the three states. The usual epithets applied to these Bangladeshis are "Indian Muslims" and "minority community" who have to be protected. Moreover, Bangladeshi Muslims who come to Assam use the subterfuges of reading in Assamese medium schools and declaring their mother tongue as Assamese. At first this endeared them to the sentimental ethnic Assamese because of a special historical reason: By the Yandaboo Treaty of February 24, 1826, Assam was annexed by the

British. The British brought sizeable numbers of highly educated Hindu Bengalis to work as clerks, doctors, teachers, lawyers, engineers and other professionals in Assam. These Bengalis looked down upon the Assamese. It is they who persuaded the British to remove Assamese from the courts and schools of Assam in 1837. The Assamese leaders mounted a long agitation, actively supported by the Christian missionaries, and got the Assamese language restored in courts and schools by 1873. The Assamese people, therefore, have nurtured a long grievance against the Bengali Hindus. This syndrome has remained ingrained in their blood for over a century and a half. It is very unlikely that the Assamese will ever be able to shake off this syndrome easily.[6] In the beginning this sentiment was used by the Bangladeshi Muslims to the maximum. In the language based riots of 1960s the Bangladeshi Muslims supported Assamese. But most Assamese are no longer in doubt about the real intentions of Bangladeshis. They are now convinced about the need to evict and deport the illegal Bangladeshi immigrants. It is rather unfortunate that the six-year long Assam Movement, which culminated in the Assam Accord, did not bring any relief and the processes proposed in the Accord of "detection, deletion and deportation" of Bangladeshis who had come after March 25, 1971 remained practically uninitiated.

Attempts to Restrict Bangladeshi Immigration

To go back to history some attempts were made to restrict immigration by the "Line System" introduced by the Assam Government on November 4, 1939. The line system laid down that (1) there would be no settlement of land to immigrants inside any village or in the grazing reserves, (2) not more than 30 bighas per family would be settled with legal immigrants and landless people and

(3) all immigrants be evicted from areas reserved for tribals. However, Bardoloi's efforts did not become successful. No immigrants could be evicted or sent back.

After Sir Muhammad Saadullah became Prime Minister of Assam, a resolution was passed on August 24, 1943 by the Government to start a "Grow More Food" campaign. By this resolution it was proposed that (1) the vacant land in Nagaon district along with a portion of the grazing reserves should be settled with landless people of different communities, (2) in Kamrup and Darrang districts also grazing reserves should be opened up for settlement and (3) suitable hill side land should be identified in the Sibsagar and the Lakhimpur districts for settlement with local people. The resolution looked innocuous but its impact on the demographic profile of Assam was far reaching. It opened up the flood gates for large scale migration from East Bengal. Earlier a resolution had been passed in the Bengal Legislative Assembly requesting the Government of India to persuade Assam to settle land with landless cultivators of Bengal. In effect Saadullah complied with this resolution. He appointed SP Desai, ICS to identify the land suitable for such settlement with the immigrants from Bengal. Desai toured the districts and reported back saying that there was no more land to settle. Desai's views were not accepted and the process of settlement of land with the immigrants continued. The Congress leaders were in jail. There was no one to oppose Saadullah. He utilized the opportunity fully. Desai tried to oppose the sinister move of Saadullah. But he had his limitations. The entire history of those times have been chronicled very ably by Dr. Nirode Kumar Borooah.[7]

After independence the then Director of the Intelligence Bureau, BN Mullick, brought to the notice of the Government the gravity of the Bengali Muslim infiltration from erstwhile East Pakistan. The Pakistan

Infiltration Posts (PIP) of 1960s were built as a result of the Mullick Report. But because of the vote bank politics the PIP scheme remained ineffective. It is reported that even today funds are coming from the Centre under the PIP scheme to the State Government but these are diverted for use in other sectors. Incidentally the pro-talk ULFA (United Liberation Front of Assam) has demanded a revival and revamping of the PIP scheme.[8] I had myself seen that PIP scheme was relatively successful. At that time some old stalwarts of the Assam Pradesh Congress Committee still opposed Bangladeshi infiltration. I got this impression while working as Sub-Divisional Officer, Mongaldoi (1963-65) and Deputy Commissioner of erstwhile Goalpara district at Dhubri (1967-69).

In the 1960s the then Chief Minister Bimala Prasad Chaliha tried to take action against the illegal immigrants. But he had his limitations because he had become Chief Minister after deposing Bisnu Ram Medhi with the help of the Bangladeshi lobby of Deba Kanta Barua, Sarat Chandra Sinha and their friends. In this connection the comments made by the then Governor BK Nehru are significant. He said in his book titled '*Nice Guys Finish Second*' that "Efforts were made from time to time by the Government of Assam to evict these illegal migrants but they were always frustrated by Delhi. One such effort was made during my time with my full support. What happened was that Fakhruddin Ali Ahmed (later President of India), Moinul Haque Choudhary (later Industry Minister of India) and DK Barua (later President of the Congress Party) raised a hue and cry at Delhi saying that atrocities were being committed on the Indian Muslims. The cry was heard and acted upon".[9] The Assamese people even today consider the vainglorious and arrogant DK Barua of "India is Indira and Indira is India" fame to be a renegade. Naturally, the Assamese people have only contempt for him in spite of his great contributions to Assamese literature and particularly to poetry. It is really unfortunate that the two most intelligent ethnic Assamese of the twentieth century - Saadullah and DK Barua - both worked against the Assamese people and brought calamity upon their own race. Moinul Haque Choudhury was Muhammad Ali Jinnah's private secretary and at the time of partition Jinnah is supposed to have told Choudhury as follows: "Within a decade, I shall be able to annex Assam to East Pakistan by the dint of more infiltration of Muslims there".[10]

Attempts were also made to stop Bangladeshi infiltration by fencing the border. But as recorded by the then Governor of Assam, SK Sinha, "Compared to Punjab, where fencing was completed in 2 years, the quality of fencing in Assam was very poor. Observation towers and lighting had been provided in Punjab. In Assam, Observation Towers were confined to a small sector in Dhubri with no towers elsewhere nor lighting in any part of the border. There was no fencing on Indo-Bangladesh border in the neighbouring States of West Bengal, Meghalya, Mizoram and Tripura. Further, a large portion of Assam-Bangladesh border is riverine patrolled by speedboats and country boats with outboard motors. The deployment of BSF on the ground in Assam was much thinner than in Punjab".[11] As a result of this lackadaisical approach to the problem there has been no improvement of the situation at all.

IM(DT) Act, 1983

It has also to be noted that protection had been given to illegal Bangladeshi immigrants by the Central Government by enacting the Illegal Migrants (Determination by Tribunal) Act, 1983. This Act was drafted by Abdul Muhib Majumdar who was Assam's Law Minister at one time. In a recent lecture at Golaghat Majumdar claimed that immigrants have brought prosperity to Assam all through history. He, however, forgot to mention the heavier pressure of population on land and the lowering of per capita income resulting from such immigration beside the environmental degradations that such migrants have brought about. The IM(DT) Act required that only the police or people living within a short distance of any alleged foreigner (Bangladeshi) could complain against that foreigner (Bangladeshi). It also laid down that the burden of proof will be on the complainant. This Act made it virtually impossible to detect a foreigner. It acted like a speed breaker in respect of the Assam Accord. However, after a long legal fight the Supreme Court declared this discriminatory Act as ultra vires of the Constitution in 2005. The court decided that there cannot be one Act for Assam to protect the foreigners and another for the rest of the country to push foreigners out. But even after the IM(DT) Act, 1983 was removed there has been no progress in the situation. Actually the Assam Accord of August 15, 1985 required that there should be detection, deletion of names from the voters' lists and deportation of Bangladeshis who came to Assam after March 31, 1971. This date was put in the Assam Accord because it had been arbitrarily fixed in the Indira-Mujib Pact after Bangladesh was liberated. It is reported that Indira Gandhi agreed to this date at the insistence of Sheikh Mujibur Rahman, President of Bangladesh, who refused to take back any immigrants who had come to Assam before the date on which Bangladesh was formally proclaimed. Legal experts feel that Indira Gandhi had no authority to do this because 1951 had been fixed as the "cut off" date in section 6 of the Citizenship Act passed in pursuance of the Indian Constitution of 1950. Legal experts, therefore, say that by the Assam Accord of 1985 the status of all illegal Bangladeshi immigrants who had come to Assam during 1950-71 had been regularized. The All Assam Students Union (AASU) never expected this. They could never visualize that the Assam Accord will result in legalizing the illegal immigrants. Meanwhile, a new section 6-A has been added to the Citizenship Act by which all those who were born in India upto 2004 will become citizens of India. This will further complicate the situation.

After IM(DT) Act, 1983 was declared ultra vires of the Constitution, certain provisions were again re-introduced in the relevant law to protect the Bangladeshis. The Foreigners (Tribunals for Assam) Order, 2006, was enacted by the Government of India to virtually bring back the provisions of IM(DT) Act, 1983. Many considered that by this enactment the Government of India had committed a contempt of court. On a PIL (Public Interest Litigation) by AASU this Order was also struck down by the Supreme Court. But even after the legal hurdles had been removed nothing is being done to detect the Bangladeshis, to delete their names from the voters' lists and to deport them out of India. Neither the Central Government nor the State Government seem to have any intention to do that.

Number of Bangladeshi Immigrants

At this stage it has to be mentioned that there is considerable uncertainty about the number of illegal immigrants from Bangladesh. In a statement in Parliament on May 13, 2010 the Union Home Minister gave an estimate of about 20 lakhs as the number of people who had come from other countries and illegally remained behind in India. Most Bangladeshis in Assam do not come that way. They do not come with passports and visas! They just cross the border, take shelter in some relative's or compatriot's house for some time and then settle down with the help of *dalals* (agents) and *matabbars* (ring leaders). They obtain documents such as ration cards, school certificates, revenue receipts and others by paying illegal gratifications to the concerned officials and ultimately get their names included in the voter's lists. The existence of large communities of earlier Bangladeshi immigrants in the border districts help this process of assimilation of the new waves of Bangladeshis. They also settle down in forests, reserve forests and even National Parks. There are large communities of Bangladeshis in Kaziranga, Manas and other National Parks. Neither State nor Central Governments have the guts to evict them.

On May 6, 1997, the then Union Home Minister, Indrajit Gupta, told Parliament that there were 10 million Bangladeshi immigrants in India. Intelligence agencies estimated that some 4 millions out of these were in Assam. If that is so the number must have increased to 60 lakhs by now (2010) in Assam. The Task Force on Border Management, headed by former Union Home Secretary, Madhab Godbole, submitted its Report to the Government of India in August, 2000. It estimated the number of Bangladeshi infiltrators to be 1.5 crores (15 millions) "with about three lakh Bangladeshi immigrants entering India illegally every year". On April 10, 1992 the then Chief Minister of Assam Hiteswar Saikia announced in the State Assembly that there were 49 lakh illegal Bangladeshi immigrants in Assam. When some Bangladeshi leaders protested, Saikia retracted the statement and said in a party meeting that there was not a single Bangladeshi in Assam. But he never officially corrected or withdrew his original statement made in the august house of the Legislative Assembly.

In Assam, Bangladeshis are now becoming the majority in the next decade or so as has been explained already. The usual practice for these illegal immigrants is to enter Assam first, obtain the necessary documents of residence and then go to the other states of NE. In many areas of other states Bangladeshis have established their predominant presence during the past few decades.

Assam Politicians and Bangladeshis

It is an open secret that many Assam politicians, belonging mainly to the ruling party, welcome the immigration of Bangladeshi Muslims. This is because these Bangladeshis have a habit of voting *en bloc* to the party who would support them to remain in Assam. They vote as directed by their *matabbars*. These *matabbars* in their turn have a close nexus with the politicians who assure them of protecting the Bangladeshis from police, AASU, AGP, NDFB, etc. It is this nexus which pulls the Bangladeshis to Assam and encourages them to remain in the state. To quote the former Governor Sinha, "The ethnic Assamese population is already reduced to 47 per cent. Out of 24 districts of Assam, 16 are already affected. The Congress Governments in Assam and Tripura and CPM in West Bengal shield the illegal immigrants due to their need for vote banks. It is not far-fetched to visualize a Kashmir-like situation arising in another five to ten years, wherein Bangladesh, egged on by Pakistan, may fight a proxy war and cause a serious national security problem".[12]

Lebensraum

Beside the pull from the political leaders of Assam for vote bank purposes there is a persistent push from Bangladesh which was earlier East Pakistan. Jinnah's statement has already been quoted. The former Prime Minister of Pakistan, Zulfikar Ali Bhutto, had made the policy statement that "our controversy with India is not on the problem of Kashmir only, there is the problem of Assam. In Assam, there are some Muslim majority districts which should have been given to Pakistan at the time of partition, these districts were wrongly included in India".[13]

In Bangladesh there has been a realization for some time that they need more living space (*lebensraum*) for their growing population. They do not practice family planning in the belief that more the children more is the earning. They try to send away the excess population to India and particularly to Assam. In this connection the former Bangladesh President, Sheikh Mujib-ur-Rahman, said that "the population of East Bengal (Bangladesh) is increasing at alarming speed. Their inhabitants face acute shortage of land. The Bengalis need land, which can be given by Assam. Assam abounds in good forests and beautiful scenes of nature. If some inhabitants of Bangladesh migrate to Assam and settle there permanently, they will be very happy. Actually Assam should have been included in East-Pakistan". Mujib-ur-Rahman also said that "because Eastern Pakistan must have sufficient lands for its expansion and because Assam has abundant forests and natural resources, coal, petroleum etc., Eastern Pakistan must include Assam to be financially and economically strong".[14] What is more sinister is the fact that the Jamaat-e-Islami of Bangladesh has been talking about a "Swadhin Muslim Bangabhumi" in NE India.

The intellectuals of Bangladesh have been in the forefront in seeking a *lebensraum* in Assam. The Dhaka University don Ameena Mohsin had averred long ago that "migration is a normal and natural phenomenon and cannot be stopped". She, therefore, strongly put forward the plea that "the need today is to evolve ways to legalise it". Many other writers have supported this move for a *lebensraum*. I had a tiff once with one Professor of Dhaka University, Iftekhar Hussain, who strongly put forth the view that immigration cannot be stopped. Both of us were attending a seminar in Delhi's Jamia Millia

Islamia. A prominent authority on Bangladeshi infiltration, DN Bezbarua, has quoted a former diplomat and intellectual of Bangladesh, Sadiq Khan, who had said that "there is no reason why regional and international co-operation could not be worked out to plan and execute population movements and settlements to avoid critical demographic pressures in pockets of high concentration. There is no reason why under-populated regions in the developed world cannot make room for planned colonies to relieve build up of demographic disasters in countries like Bangladesh".[15] What is surprising is that their sight is set on Assam and not on the thinly populated areas of Myanmar or for that matter any other country.

Political Clout of Bangladeshis

Politically the situation is such that no Chief Minister can remain in power in Assam who is bold enough to oppose the Bangladeshis. In the days of Pandit Jawaharlal Nehru the then Chief Minister Bisnu Ram Medhi was forced to resign because he opposed settlement of Bangladeshis, both refugees and infiltrators, in Assam. Similarly Chief Minister Mahendra Mohan Choudhury was removed because he talked of Assamese identity in his famous letter to Indira Gandhi. In 1980 the coalition Government of the then Chief Minister Golap Barbora fell only because of the withdrawal of support *en masse* by the Muslim MLAs whose forefathers had come from the districts now forming Bangladesh. Ever since then politicians and political parties have vied with each other for support of the Bangladeshi vote bank.

Isolation of Ethnic Assamese

The ethnic Assamese are isolated. The Congress Government in the Centre does not support their cause. The Congress needs the Bangladeshi vote bank. The other secular and pseudo-secular political parties also follow the Congress line. The Bharatiya Janata Party's (BJP) support is limited. BJP would like the ethnic Assamese to give up their demand for deportation of Hindu Bengalis whom BJP considers to be refugees as against the Muslim Bangladeshis whom they consider to be illegal infiltrators. Neither Assam Gana Parishad (AGP) nor AASU is prepared to make such a discrimination. The Assamese people still harbour a feeling of hurt for what the Bengali Hindus did against the Assamese language in 1837. The Assamese also remember that BJP did absolutely nothing for the Assamese when it was in power at the Centre for several years. The tribals and the other ethnic groups are completely divided. They are busy with their own demands for autonomy and separate councils of which 13 have been created in recent times. Most tribal groups no longer support the ethnic Assamese. After the Assam Movement of 1979-85 the tribals feel that AASU and AGP have neglected the tribals. In fact, the Assamese have completely alienated the tribal and the ethnic minorities so that these minorities will never join another Assam type of movement again.

Some native Assamese put a lot of trust on the United Liberation Front of Assam (ULFA). This outfit lost its credibility when it abandoned its idealism of fighting for an Assamese identity and allied itself with Bangladeshi DGFI (Directorate General of Force's Intelligence) and Pakistani ISI (Inter Services Intelligence). ULFA has been recently emasculated by the capture of almost all its main leaders except for the commander-in-chief Paresh Baruah, by Indian police with the help of Bangladesh forces. A large stream of ULFA deserters have started their beeline for Assam, back from Bangladesh.

The upper crust of the Assamese youths are obtaining higher education outside the State and abroad. They are taking up jobs elsewhere. Most of them have migrated to foreign lands and other states seeking greener pastures.

The English medium educated youths do not even know Assamese. Most of them do not seem to have much attachment to the Assamese mainstream nor do they commit themselves to the Assamese cause. There is therefore an intelligence deficit and even an intellectual vacuum in the Assamese leadership.

Barpeta Events

A new dimension has now been added to the strength of Bangladeshis in Assam by the events of July 21 and 22, 2010. On July 21 a violent crowd of thousands of Bangladeshis attacked the district town of Barpeta in Lower Assam under the leadership of All Assam Minority Students Union (AAMSU). They demanded that the work on the pilot project for updating the National Register of Citizens (NRC) should be stopped forthwith and the proforma circulated for collection of data in this behalf should be revised to favour the Bangladeshis. Police had to resort to firing in which four Bangladeshis were killed. Next day AAMSU declared an Assam Bandh in which several sporadic incidents of violence took place including one of gun firing by Bangladeshis in Tezpur. The State Government succumbed to the Bangladeshi demands, suspended the pilot project and formed a ten-member ministerial group to revise the proforma. The work of drafting a new proforma has been entrusted by the ministerial group to the Principal Secretary, Home Department and the Advocate General jointly.

Certain dangerous portents have now become obvious in the aftermath of the Barpeta incident. Barpeta is one of the holiest places for the ethnic Assamese. This is the first public show of muscle power by the Bangladeshis. The police had to use force to prevent the Bangladeshis from further damage to cars, buildings and other public and private properties. To please the agitators the Government has paid large sums as compensation to the families of the victims and transferred the Superintendent of Police who had taken action to defend public life and property. This will have demoralizing effect on the district administration. By stopping work on preparation of NRC the whole process of detection of Bangladeshis has been postponed probably for a long time. The Bangladeshis are now upbeat and are going about holding meetings and rallies in support of their demand for regularization of illegal immigrants. The present State Government will probably help the Bangladeshis, directly or indirectly, to achieve their objectives.

AGP's Betrayal

The majority of Assamese people are now frustrated and resigned to their fate. This feeling has been accentuated in the past 25 years because the AGP leaderships have betrayed the trust reposed on them. Most of the AGP leaders are accused of enriching themselves personally through corrupt practices and by betraying the ideals of the Assam movement, during the two terms that AGP, with Prafulla Mahanta as Chief Minister were in power at Dispur. Mahanta has proved to be the worst Chief Minister that Assam ever had. The images of AGP and Mahanta have also been sullied by allegations of *Gupt Hatya* (secret killing) and ignoring the claims of the family members of the victims of the Assam Movement. In any case, the Assamese people have been engulfed by a fatigue syndrome and there is no way in which they can be enthused again to join another movement in the future.

The situation is becoming really difficult. Assam's population is rising at an alarming rate due to the continuous immigration from Bangladesh. As has been mentioned already according to the 2001 census, the average density in Assam was 340 people per sq. kms against 324 for India and up from 286 in 1991. In the districts of Dhubri, Nagaon and Kamrup the district densities were 585, 582 and 581 respectively. These densities are rising. The other districts are also catching up. The average size of operational holdings has fallen to 1.15 hectares by 2001. In case of the Bongaigaon district it has fallen to 0.98 hectares, in Kamrup to 1.00 hectares and in Goalpara to 1.01 hectares. These figures have fallen further in the past 10 years.[16] The Brahmaputra and the Bank valleys of Assam are now over populated.

Many suggestions have been made to control the influx. These include early completion of border fencing, strengthening of riverine police, more deployment of Border Security Forces personnel, photo identity cards in border districts for Indian nationals, updating of the National Register of Citizens which had been prepared in 1951, and deportation of illegal migrants under the Foreigners' Act.

But who will do all these ? Neither the State nor the Central Governments appear to be genuinely interested. They are more interested in opening up the Bangladesh border for trade, commerce and direct connectivity. The 14 agreements signed recently, along with the huge aid package of US $1 billion (Rs. 5,000 crores) to Bangladesh, are aimed at achieving this objective. But the question of Bangladeshi infiltration was never discussed in the talks leading to these agreements. The Government, therefore, is unlikely to take any steps against the Bangladeshis. On the other hand, the Assamese people can no longer mount united political pressure as they did during the Assam Movement of 1979-85. Only the local media, an aging and outdated AASU leadership which has lost its clout with the youth and a few sincere but ineffective intellectuals are adhering to the cause of the Assamese identity. These people do not seem to have any chance in the present millieu.

Future Chief Minister of Assam

It is unfortunate that many top Indian leaders do not understand the gravity of the complicated and piquant situation that has been created in Assam and the NE states. They also do not realize the ultimate danger to the country's security and integrity from such illegal Bangladeshi infiltration. The ignorance seems to be much more among the top bureaucrats. They need to be properly apprised and motivated. Among those who realize the dangers is Gen. (Retd.) Shankar Roy Chowdhury, former Chief of Army Staff, who told the Rajya Sabha in April, 2000 that "on account of illegal migration, Bangladesh's demographic border intruded upon India's political border over a 10-20 km. deep area". A former civil servant Madhab Godbole, who was Union Home Secretary, had candidly stated that "it would not be surprising if the future Chief Minister of Assam is one of the illegal migrants". In fact, the past history of emergence of Pakistan and then of Bangladesh should teach us that "there is a distinct danger of another Muslim country, speaking Bengali predominantly, emerging in the eastern part of India in future". This is the view considered by TV Rajeswar, former Director of the Intelligence Bureau.[17]

Severence of NE from India

This possibility of severance of NE from the rest of India was clearly and forcefully brought out by the former Governor Sinha in his Report to the President dated November 8, 1998. He said "that the silent and invidious demographic invasion of Assam may result in loss of the geostrategically vital districts of Lower Assam (on the border with Bangladesh). The influx of these illegal migrants is turning these districts into a Muslim majority region. It will then only be a matter of time when a demand for their merger with Bangladesh may be made. The rapid growth of international Islamic fundamentalism may provide the driving force for this demand......... Loss of Lower Assam (the area close to Bangladesh border) will severe the entire land mass of North East from the rest of India and the rich natural resources of the region will be lost to the Nation".[18]

The China factor

Meanwhile the China factor has also come into play. Ever since 1962 China has been doggedly claiming that Arunachal Pradesh is an integral part of the Tibet Region of the People's Republic of China. It has refused to accept the McMahon line as the boundary between the two countries. The Chinese say that this line was arbitrarily drawn by the British. China is doing this probably because it hopes to acquire the oil and other natural resources of Arunachal Pradesh. Recently, China protested against the Indian Prime Minister's as also the Dalai Lama's visits to Arunachal Pradesh. It has refused Chinese visas to many people including the Chief Minister of Arunachal Pradesh and the G.O.C.-in-C of the Western Command.

According to media report China has positioned more troops and ballistic missiles on the Arunachal border. To be more specific "China has moved new advanced longer range CSS-5 missiles close to the borders with India and developed contingency plans to shift airborne forces at short notice to the region", according to Pentagon. This note presented to the US Congress is reported to have concluded that "despite increased political and economic relations over the years between China and India, tensions remain along their shared 4,057 kms. border most notably over Arunachal Pradesh, which China asserts as part of Tibet and therefore China and over the Aksai Chin region at the western end of the Tibetan plateau".[19] China is also reported to be developing an electronic spy network which has "infiltrated Indian and other nations' government offices around the world". These are sinister developments. The legitimate question to ask is how far India is prepared to meet the challenges ? Is India better prepared than in 1962? Only the Central and the State Governments can answer these questions. One thing, however, is certain: the poorer people in Arunachal Pradesh as also some of the other states have not gained much during the past half a century in terms of economic development and they are not nearer the Indian main stream. The thousands of crores which the Central Government spent mainly enrich the local politicians, outside bureaucrats, insurgent outfits, upcountry businessmen, unscrupulous contractors and their cohorts. Not much percolated down the poorer section of the tribal people and not much development took place in the interior. It is high time that a proper enquiry is instituted, supported by special audit by CAG as well as social audit, to find where the money has actually gone during the past half a century.

While our politicians and bureaucrats seem to be smug in the belief that the Chinese and the Bangladeshi questions are separate it is not unlikely that China will let Bangladesh grab the other states of NE or allow Bangladesh to set up their dream "Swadhin Muslim Bangabhumi" in the NE and, in the bargain, itself occupy Arunachal Pradesh. This fear is real. In the context of Indian history such a situation seems to be quite probable.

Endnotes

1. The figures have been taken from The Assam Government publications.
2. Detailed figures are available in Jogesh Chandra Bhuyan, "Illegal Migration from Bangladesh and the Demographic Change in the North-East Region", in BB Kumar edited *Illegal Migration From Bangladesh,* Astha Bharati, Concept Publishing Company, New Delhi, 2006.

3. Lt. Gen. (Retd.) SK Sinha, *Guarding India's Integrity,* Manas Publications, New Delhi, 2009.
4. Jogesh Chandra Bhuyan. See reference at 2 above.
5. "Ishani", November 15, 2008. A magazine published by Nagaland Gandhi Ashram, Guwahati, 2008.
6. For details see BB Hazarika, *Political Life in Assam During the 19th Century,* Gian Publishing House, Delhi, 1987.
7. Dr. Nirode Kumar Barua (Cologne, Germany). *Ejon Satyagrahir Rajniti: Gopinath Bardoloi Aru Assam. Tetiya aru Etiya,* (Politics of a Satyagrahi : Gopinath Bardoloi and Assam, Then and Now) Published by Birendra Nath Bardoloi, Ulubari, Guwahati, 2010. The English translation is now under print.
8. Mrinal Hazarika, President, ULFA (Pro-talk). In his Assamese thesis on the Foreigners' Issue (2009) has given detailed views on the PIP scheme. The Monifesto of Hazarika's organization in English (2009) gives an outline of their proposed discussion with Government.
9. Nehru, BK *Nice Guys Finish Second,* Penguin Book, India, 1986.
10. Onkareswar Pandey, *ISI and New Wave of Islamic Militancy in the North East.* In BB Kumar edited *Illegal Migration From Bangladesh.* Astha Bharati, Delhi, 2006.
11. Lt. Gen. (Retd.), SK Sinha. Op. cit.
12. Lt. Gen. (Retd.) SK Sinha. Op. cit.
13. This was included in Zulfikar Ali Bhutto's book *The Myth of Independence.* See Onkareswar Pandey. Op. cit.
14. Onkareswar Pandey. Op. cit.
15. Kumar, BB edited *Illegal Migration from Bangladesh,* Astha Bharati, New Delhi. 2006. In Chapter 6 of this book DN Bezbarua writes that "there is also a strong demand within Bangladesh on the basis of what the Bangladesh intellectuals call "lebensraum" or living space and they seem to put it across as if they have a right to the living space that is available around Bangladesh". Bezbarua gives names of the intellectuals and also excerpts from their writing. Another writer Onkareswar Pandey, in Chapter 12 of the same compilation, quotes Muhammad Ali Jinnah, Zulfiquar Ali

Bhutto, Shaikh Mujib-ur-Rahman, Moinul Haque Choudhury and others to show how these Muslim leaders wanted Assam to be included in Pakistan through immigration. *Also see* EN Rammohan, *Lebensraum in the East* in Jaideep Saikia edited *Frontier in Flames.* Penguin, Books, Delhi, 2007.

16. The figures are from the Government of Assam publications.
17. Kumar, BB *Introduction to Illegal Migration from Bangladesh,* Astha Bharati and Concept Publishing Company, Delhi, 2006.
18. Lt. Gen. SK Sinha. Op. cit. *Also see* Prakash Singh, "Bangladeshi Immigration : Are We Heading for Another Partition?". In BB Kumar edited *Illegal Migration from Bangladesh,* Astha Bharati and Concept Publishing Company, New Delhi, 2006.
19. *The Economic Times* issue dated August 18, 2010.

CHAPTER – 4

Is Economic Backwardness the Cause of Insurgency in Assam?

The Assamese Mindset

The present unrest in Assam is a manifestation of the Assamese mindset which developed through a long history of two centuries of neglect and perceived discrimination. The roots have to be traced back to the Burmese invasion in early nineteenth century which culminated in the Yandaboo Treaty of February 24, 1826, since Assam came under British rule.

Ahom Period

During the long 600 years of Ahom Rule (1228-1826) the Brahmaputra valley was a comparatively peaceful area. Politically the Ahoms had united almost the entire valley as has been explained in Chapter 1. They subjugated the smaller potentates who used to engage themselves in sporadic internecine wars. The Ahoms never imposed their own language, religion or social practices on the indigenous people of Assam. Rather they allowed themselves to be absorbed in the greater Assamese nationality. What is more, they made the Assamese into a composite race during their rule through a process of historical fusion, integration and assimilation. The great historian Dr. HK Borpujari sums up the situation in the following words, "Free from caste prejudices and untouchability, they (the Ahoms) succeeded in assimilating different racial elements and cultural strains into a single national unit which had enabled them to repel the repeated invasions of the foreigners".[1]

It is true that there was some exploitation and occasional state oppression on the common people during the Ahom rule. But by and large the people were left to themselves. The people were happy and content. The villagers were called *paiks* who had to render physical labour and personal services to the king. Only the noblemen, priests and high caste people were exempted. In their turn the nobles had their own separate groups of bonded labour. The *paiks* were divided into '*gots*' of 3 or 4 people. About 3000 to 6000 *paiks* constituted a '*khel*' or fraternity.

The process of integration was further advanced by Sri Sankardeva and his principal disciple Sri Madhavdeva who spread the teachings of the ancient Indian epics and scriptures in simple Assamese to the masses. They brought about a revolution which elevated the Assamese people to great heights of social and cultural achievements. To quote Dr. Borpujari again "contributory factor to the fusion of different ethnic elements has been attributed to the advent of Sankardeva (1449-1568), the founder of neo-Vaisnavism, with its emphasis on anti-caste or classless society".

The British Period

It is against this backdrop of a near idyllic situation that the Burmese troops invaded Assam in 1817. They unleashed their fury on the population which was unheard of in the past. Thousands were killed or maimed, houses were torched and paddy fields destroyed. People fled their homes and hearth. Villages were deserted and the population decimated. It continued through three Burmese invasions for eight years until the British intervened and brought the Burmese marauders under control. The British forced the Burmese to sign the Yandaboo Treaty and annexed Assam.

Comparative peace prevailed thereafter. There were, however, a few revolts. The Ahom prince Gomadhar Konwar revolted soon after the British takeover. Another revolt resulted in the execution of Maniram Dewan and Peoli Phookan who were leaders of the Assamese middle class. The Assamese became dissatisfied with the British and the Bengalees when at the instigation of the Bengalee clerks Bengalee was introduced as the official language of the courts and schools in 1837 as has been mentioned in the previous Chapter. This infuriated the people and an agitation was mounted by the middle class through petitions and memorandums until 1873 when Assamese was restored to its due status mainly through the intervention of the American missionaries. This, however, left a deep scar in the Assamese mindset so that throughout the nineteenth and the twentieth centuries anti-Bengalee feelings dominated the political and social scenes in the state.

Beside the Bengalee clerks the British also imported the Marwari businessmen, the indentured labourers from Bihar, Orissa and Madhya Pradesh, the Nepali troops for the mercenary Army, and ultimately the Muslim cultivators from the districts forming present Bangladesh. "The result of such a large scale influx began to shake the foundation of Assamese social structure by breaking its homogeneity. This had its impact on the social, cultural and economic life of the people. The migrants were poised for taking almost all the benefits of the new opportunities created by the establishment of tea industry and commerce, the expansion of land use and the expansions of employment in Government services and in professions".[2] The influx of Bangladeshis continued unabated throughout the twentieth century. These developments had a profound effect on the Assamese mindset.

Another development was the economic exploitation of the people. The British introduced a plethora of taxes.

Beside the land revenue, which was increased several times during the early days of British occupation, license tax for cutting timber, reeds etc, income tax, stamp duties and other such taxes were imposed on a people who were not familiar with such imposts. The people organized *"raijmels"* (people's assemblies) and protested. These protests found their manifestations in the Phulaguri Dhawa (war) of September-October, 1861 and the *Patharughatar Ran* (war) of January, 1894, beside other smaller incidents.

Freedom Movement and Partition

Meanwhile, the spread of English education brought the Assamese closer to the people of other provinces of British India. They joined the national movements. Later, Gandhiji's teachings drew a large number of people into the vortex of non-violent freedom movement. This also affected the Assamese mindset and made it anti-Brtitish.

On the eve of partition of the country, the Assamese were agitated over the Cabinet Mission plan to tag Assam with Bengal in group "C" and thus to virtually push it to Pakistan. The Congress Working Committee's resolution of August 10, 1946, accepting the Cabinet Mission's plan infuriated the Assamese. Led by Bharat Ratna Gopinath Bordoloi, the then Prime Minister of Assam, an all-out agitation was mounted which had the tacit support of Gandhiji. Later, the plan was abandoned and Assam was not separated from India. But the scars remained. The Assamese could never forget how they were almost betrayed and pushed into Pakistan.

Refinery Movement

Soon after independence KD Malavyia, the then Union Petroleum Minister, prepared the scheme for taking crude oil from Assam by a 700 mile-long (1120 kms) pipeline to be refined and processed in Barauni. The whole of Assam rose in protest against the move. But the Union Government doggedly went ahead with the plan and Assam was temporarily silenced by the grant of a toy refinery at Guwahati. There were further popular refinery movements when attempts were made to take out more crude oil from Assam. This was solved by the setting up of the Bongaigaon refinery. These unwise actions of the Central Government, ignoring the sentiments of the people of Assam, had such a damaging psychological effect that the Assamese people have ever since continued to accuse the Centre of colonial exploitation. This type of situation has been created on each of the later occasions. What is more the Assamese people now believe that the Centre would not give any industry or institution to Assam without prolonged agitation.

After forty years of observing and dealing with the Union Ministries at different levels I personally feel that the majority of Indian politicians have now come to reconcile with the fact that Assam and the North East can no longer be ignored or taken for granted. The top bureaucracy, however, have not yet changed their fixed idea that any industry or institution given to the NE carries the risk of being lost in war or insurgency. They are yet to come out of the syndrome which impelled Jawaharlal Nehru to broadcast his farewell speech to Assam in the 1962 war when the Chinese troops crossed Bomdila. The most recent example of taking the NE for granted is the Central Government's representative Padmanabhayya's deal with Muivah over the Naga ceasefire in which he agreed to NSCN's demand for "Nagalim". This would have meant inclusion of territories from Assam and Manipur in Nagaland. This resulted in violent agitation and death of 100 people in Manipur. Assam narrowly escaped from another holocaust on this occasion because the Assam Chief Minister Tarun Gogoi promptly rejected the proposal.

Assam Movement

It is against this background that the Assamese mindset was swayed by the six year long assam Agitation (1979-1985) over the foreigner's issue. It was the culmination of nearly one and a half century of grievances and sulking. The Assamese were terrified that their very existence was at stake. The depth of feeling can be gauged only by those who have dealt with the agitation and had been the eyewitnesses.

Throughout the nineteenth century, since the Yandaboo Treaty of 1826, and during most part of the twentieth century Assam enjoyed comparative peace because all the agitations were non-violent except for the *Phulaguri* and the *Patharughat* incidents and the occasional language and communal riots particularly in the 1960s. However, the situation changed dramatically towards the late 1980s when the United Liberation Front of Assam (ULFA), which made its appearance in 1979, indulged in continuous violence, extortion, kidnapping and terrorism. The insurgent activities reached a crescendo all over the Brahmaputra valley by 1990 and the Army had to be called in after dismissing the first Assam Gana Parishad (AGP) Government some of whose members were alleged to have been either directly or indirectly connected with ULFA. Meanwhile, the Bodo outfits spread their tentacles particularly in the northern parts. The two hill districts of Karbi Anglong and North Cachar Hills spawned their own brand of insurgents. The Naga outfits, started more than half a century ago, continued their forays in Upper Assam.

Insurgency

The new developments completely disrupted the traditional peace. After a decade and a half of strong action, surrenders and occasional discussions about peace talks, insurgency in Assam appear to have subsided to some extent. Most of the outfits have lost their ideological content and forfeited their local support base. The Assamese people have become disillusioned both with AGP, whose inefficiency, corruption and scandals have surpassed all past records, and ULFA, which by aligning itself with the Pakistani ISI as well as Bangladesh and by indulging in indiscriminate killings and lootings have terrorized all residents of Assam including the indigenous people for whom the future now looks bleak and uncertain. There was a ceasefire followed by peace talks at the instance of the Gyanpith Award winner Indira (aka Mamoni) Roisam Goswami. But no concrete results emerged. The peace talks failed. In late 2009 all the ULFA leaders including the chairman Arabinda Rajkhowa were taken into custody. Only the commander-in-chief Paresh Barua remained outside. But the backbone of ULFA was broken. Another peace effort under the leadership of Dr. Hiren Gohain is now on. The Government of India's interlocutor PC Haldar is also making efforts to make ULFA come around for talks. It is against this backdrop that an attempt is made in this Chapter to analyse the economic scenario in order to show that economic development can bring peace back to the troubled land.

Economic Growth in Assam since Independence

If visual impressions are any guide one would say that the economic condition of the common people of Assam has not substantially improved during the past half a century after independence at least in the rural areas where 87 percent of the people live. It is true that a burgeoning middle class has emerged out of the Government's spending on development projects and programmes. This middle class, however, is more discernible in the urban areas. They form only a small proportion of the rural population. According to an Assam Government survey made some time ago the rural below poverty line (BPL) families in the state were 59.43 percent in 1998-99 as against 45.01 percent in 1993-94. This is probably an over-estimation. The Government of India's estimate of BPL population of Assam is 36.09 percent against an all India average of 26.10 percent. The percentage of BPL people is reported to have declined in 2004. The reduction was first reported to be by as much as 21 percentile points. But later the Suresh Tendulkar Committee put the figure of BPL people in Assam at 34.5 percent. But the increase in terms of absolute number continues.[3] That is rather unfortunate.

It would be wrong, however, to surmise that Assam has not progressed at all during this period. In fact, it did share in the common prosperity of the country to some extent but lagged behind the national average due to a variety of reasons. The major one, of course, has been the tremendous spurt in population mainly due to a continuous and unrelenting immigration from outside the state.

In 1951, Assam's population was 88.30 lakhs. By 2001 it has gone up to 266.38 lakhs. The density of population has gone up from 102 per sq. km. in 1951 to 340 per sq. km in 2001. Again, while Assam's population increased by almost 3 times during 1951-1999, the total cropped area increased only by 1.56 times from 25,17,058 hectares in 1951 to 39,44,000 hectares in 1991. The food production, including cereals and oil seeds, went up from 16,60,343 tonnes in 1958-59 to 40,42,000 tonnes in 1999-2000 and to 42.24 lakh tonnes in 2008-09. It is expected to reach 46.12 lakh tonnes by 2009-11. The yields of most crops did not show much improvement. In 1958-59, for example, the yield per acre of winter paddy was 408 kilograms. By 1999-2000 it increased to only 604.6

kilograms. Further improvements in both production and productivity have been claimed during the past one decade. In case of pulses production has increased to 0.88 lakh tonnes by 2009-10. Similarly, oil seeds production has gone up to 1.88 lakh tonnes and sugar-cane to 11.61 lakh tonnes by 2009-10.

However, several hundred crores of rupees worth of foodgrains, particularly edible oils, sugar, wheat and wheat products, etc., have to be imported to Assam from outside every year. Similar is the case with fish. In spite of the fact that Assam abounds in large rivers, lakes and ponds crores of rupees worth of fish have to be imported from outside. Substantial quantities of eggs and poultry are also imported every year. The amount of money outflow on account of such imports had been estimated by the LC Jain Committee at Rs. 700 crores.[4] A recent government estimate puts the import bill at Rs. 2,095 crores. Since it did not include meat, fish, poultry, etc., a realistic estimate today will be about Rs. 3500 crores.

As far as industries are concerned, tea happened to be the only major industry in 1947. The total production of tea in 1947 was only 134.91 million kilograms. The figure has now gone up to 486 in 2007-08. In 1970, a tea auction centre was established at Guwahati which had become the largest CTC tea auction centre in the world since the last few years. It is now selling about 150 million kilograms of tea every year valued at nearly Rs. 1500 crores. There was a small oil refinery at Digboi in 1947. During the past few decades refineries have come up in Guwahati and Bongaigaon. A new one has gone into production in Numaligarh a few years ago.

For proper utilization of associated gas coming out with oil as also natural gas, a medium sized Gas Cracker project is being set up at Lepetkata in Dibrugarh district. Work has started on three Growth Centres in Goalpara, Kamrup and Sonitpur districts. An Export

Promotion Industrial Park at Amingaon has come up recently. Quite a few industrial estates and small and medium units have been set up all over the state. Subsidies and concessions are also available to the entrepreneurs. Unfortunately, however, industrial sickness is rampant. Moreover, the efforts made so far are grossly inadequate to take care of more than 22 lakhs who have no gainful employment today and the lakhs of youths who are expected to join the work force in the immediate future.

Some advances have been recorded in the infrastructure sector. In 1954 the total electricity generated was only 8.35 million kwh. By 2007-08 it went up to 1541.317 million kwh. While in 1958 only 28 towns and villages had been electrified by 2007 the number increased to 14,516. The percentage of villages electrified stood at 57.78. In 1958 there were 1173 kilometres of National Highways and 12002 kilometres of other PWD roads. By 2007-08 the lengths increased to 2754 kilometres and 37,700 kilometres respectively. In the case of the Railways there were 1726 route kilometers of metre-gauge lines in 1958. The length has increased to 2283.71 route kilometers of both metre-guage and broad-guage lines in 2007-08. In 1954 there were only 496 post offices. The number increased to 4006 by 2007-08. In 1960 there were 173 telegraph offices and 20 telephone exchanges. By 2007-08 their numbers increased to 448 and 598 respectively. As on June 30 2007 the landline connections increased to 4,60,344, WLL to 84,340 and mobile connections to 6,00,377. The number of mobile connections is increasing daily. In the case of bank branches there has been a phenomenal increase from 2 in 1947 to 1317 by March 2008. Progress has been recorded in the health sector also. In 1957 there were 57 hospitals and 504 dispensaries and a total of 2342 hospital beds. By 1999-2000 the number increased to 161 Government hospitals, 610 primary health centres, 323 dispensaries, 268 rural welfare centres and 5109 sub-centres. The number of hospital beds increased to 12868. In recent years these numbers have gone up tremendously. There was a single medical college. There are now 3 medical colleges beside colleges of Pharmacology, Dentistry, Nursing, Ayurvedic and Homoeopathic medicine. One more medical college has started functioning recently. Another two will be ready soon. Scores of para-medical institutions have come up in the private sectors. However, health care arrangements are not yet fully geared to meet the standards of modern times.

The most significant advances have been registered in the field of education. In 1958 there were 521 high schools with 894283 students, 1689 middle schools with 161587 students and 14178 primary schools with 1706815 students. In 2007 the numbers increased to 620 higher secondary schools (plus 209 Junior Colleges) with 1,64,685 students, 5052 high schools with 6,39,248 students, 11,347 middle/senior basic schools with 13,26,735 students, 30,094 primary/junior basic schools with 32,45,754 students and 432 pre-primary schools with 23,240 students. These numbers are increasing. Besides there are thousands of private and English medium schools with very high emoluments. The numbers of Universities have gone up to 5 in 1996 from 1 in 1950. Several more have come up recently increasing the number to 12 as in 2010. There were only 29 degree colleges in 1958. Their number has increased to 312 in 1996. This has increased to more than 500 by now. Similarly the number of engineering colleges increased from 1 in 1958 to 3 in 1996. Scores of such colleges and other technical institutions have come up recently in the private sector. There is an Institute of Technology at Guwahati also although not many students from the State get admission. The percentage of literacy has gone up from 18.1 in 1951 to 64 in 2001. It has further increased in the aftermath of the Sarva Sikhsha Abhiyan.

The Middle Class

In terms of consumer goods the creature comfort has increased tremendously specially for the burgeoning middle class. There were, for example, only 12710 radio sets in 1953-54. Today millions of transistor sets proliferate even in the remotest areas side by side with television sets and household video and audio cassette recorders and players. While in 1950-51 there were only 29185 motor vehicles in the state by March, 2008 the number increased to 1165210. The number is increasing every month, almost every day. In Guwahati city alone more than 4000 vehicles are registered every month. Most middle class families have refrigerators. Many have washing machines and cooking ranges. They send their children to English medium schools and to colleges and universities outside the state. The luckier ones go abroad. Most middle-class families now have their relatives abroad mainly in the information technology companies and institutions.

What is reprehensible, however, is the fact that a sizeable proportion of the population is still reeling under grinding poverty and squalor. The percentage of BPL families in Assam will not be less than 40 although the State Government figure is higher and the Planning Commission allocations are based on a lower figure. The Suresh Tendulkar Committee appointed recently has fixed the BPL ratio of Assam at 34.4 percent. The other aspect is the comparatively lower development in Assam compared to the all India average. Assam is at the bottom of all states except Bihar so far as the per capita income is concerned.

An Analysis of Present Economic Scenario in Assam

While preparing Assam's seventh five-year plan in 1984-85, as the Planning and Development Commissioner,

I had carried out considerable research with the object of unravelling the basic trends of economic development process in Assam during the previous few decades. One outcome of this research was the development of a planning model, which could postulate the different rates of growth per annum, that will achieve corresponding reduction in the gap between the state's per capita income and the national average and also project the period during which the gap could be bridged.

Rate of Development

This research brought out, for the first time, that during the entire period of planned development the rate of economic growth in Assam was much slower compared to the national average. Secondly, at constant 1970-71 prices, Assam's per capita income was Rs. 50.04 higher in 1950-51 than the average per capita income of India. However, it started lagging behind since the late 1960s and by the year 1984-85, Assam's per capita income became Rs. 212.9 lower than the all India average. This fact now looks obvious and is often quoted by economists, politicians and social leaders. But no one had an inkling about it earlier. Thirdly, all along the period of planned development the per capita plan expenditure per annum in Assam upto the sixth five-year plan was lower than the national average. Only after the seventh plan, the expenditure picked up slightly.[5]

When Hiteswar Saikia, the then Chief Minister, took the model and the graphs to late Indira Gandhi she got a real shock. She told us that while she had always known that Assam was backward she could never imagine that it had been better off than the average of India in the year 1950 and had slided down so much in 35 years of planned development. That year Assam's central assistance went up by an additional Rs. 100 crores. This was quite a considerable sum in those days. However, this initiative was never followed up and nothing at all was done to provide the level of investment required to lift up the rate of economic development in Assam as postulated by the model. Meanwhile, insurgency and political problems complicated the scene and Government attention was diverted to other matters.

After retirement from service, in early 1995, I reworked the time series of per capita income at constant 1980-81 prices and found that there was no basic change in the trends seen earlier. The newly worked out series showed that while in 1950-51 Assam's per capita income was Rs. 40 higher in real terms than the national average, by 1992-93 the figure had lagged behind so much that it became Rs. 271 less than the national average.[6]

Inter-regional Disparity

When we make an inter-regional comparison in terms of per capita income, the differences appear to be glaring. In 1998-99, for example, while Assam had a per capita income of Rs. 8,700 the national average was Rs. 14,712. The highest of all States was that of Delhi which was Rs. 27,693. Maharashtra's figure was Rs. 22,763. What is significant is the fact that Assam is worse off than some of the North Eastern States also.

The current figures available on this subject would warrant a relook at the situation during the past one decade with the 1993-94 price index as the base. The published figures show that while the all India average of per capita income (pci) was Rs. 7690 in 1993-94, Assam's figure was Rs. 5715, that of Punjab was Rs. 12,710 and of Maharashtra Rs. 12183. The small states of Chandigarh, Delhi and Goa were far better off. But these states cannot be compared with the bigger states among which Punjab and Maharashtra were better off than the rest. In 2003-04, that is, eleven years later, at constant 1993-94 prices the figures stood at Rs. 11,799 all India,

Rs. 6,520 Assam, Rs. 15,800 Punjab and Rs. 16,479 Maharashtra. This means that while the all India pci increased by Rs. 4,109 Assam's pci increased by only Rs. 805. During the same period Maharashtra's pci increased by Rs. 4,296 and Punjab's pci increased by Rs. 3,090. The highest increase of Rs. 6,983 was, however, recorded by Gujarat from Rs. 9,796 in 1993-94 to Rs. 16,779 in 2003-04. The latest figures as given in the Assam Budget for 2010-11 shows that Assam's per capita income for 2008-09 was Rs. 16,272 at 1999-2000 prices and Rs. 23,993 at current prices. As against this the all-India average was Rs. 37,490 at current prices. The highest of the states that are better off was that of Haryana (Rs. 67,891) followed by Punjab (Rs. 50,558). It is very unfortunate that Assam lagged behind so badly in spite of the facts that our politicians and planners had been properly warned about it and that the Government of India and the Planning Commission were aware of it.

According to United Nations Development Programme (UNDP) in terms of Human Development Index (HDI), which gives a better insight into economic and social development, India's rank was found to be 128 among 174 countries. The value of HDI for India worked out to be 0.563 against Canada's 0.935, which happened to be the highest of all countries.[7] Among the Indian States the highest was that of Kerala being 0.603 against Assam's value of 0.379.[8]

The then Prime Minister, Indira Gandhi, was concerned about the disparity of income distribution and in her concluding address in the National Development Council's meeting held on July 12-13, 1984, she made the following significant remarks: "We are actually aware that India as a nation cannot remain together if disparities in income and living conditions of different regions, different States, different communities, tribes and castes are not removed. We look at the Centre-State relationship also in this perspective. Balanced all-round development, irrespective of the resource capabilities of the units has been one of the major objectives of our plan".[9]

Grinding poverty is writ large on the faces of the poor in Assam, particularly in the rural areas. Emaciated bodies and anaemic looks, protruding bellies and thin limbs, worn out clothes and dilapidated shelters, all point to deprivation.

Natural Disasters

Frequent natural disasters, particularly several waves of floods each year, cause further deprivation to a large portion of the state's already impoverished population and also cause depletion of resources. The funds available for relief and rehabilitation are so meagre that it never becomes possible to make up the loss.[10]

Women and Children

The condition of women and children is much worse. According to an Assam Government estimate out of a total state population of 266 lakhs, as many as 55 lakhs children belong to the BPL families. This may be slightly exaggerated. But the fact that the position is alarming should cause concern.

The life expectancy at birth in Assam is low. Against the national average of 63.5 years, Assam's figures are 59.3 years for females and 58.6 years for males. The infant mortality rate (IMR) in Assam is 66 against the national average of 55 per thousand births. The figure is reported to have come down to 46 in 2009 for Assam. The maternal mortality rate (MMR) is also high being 450 per 1,00,000 births in Assam (according to latest estimate of the State Government) against 195 for Kerala and 408 for the country as a whole. [11&12] In 2009, however, the rate has been brought down to 330 according to the Budget speech for 2010-11.

Viewed against the position obtaining in the developed countries the situation looks pretty bad indeed. In Japan the life expectancy at birth is 82.7 years, in Canada it is 80.6 years. The IMR is only 4 in Japan and 6 in Canada per thousand births. Similarly, the MMR is only 8 in Japan and 5 in Sweden and Israel out of 1,00,000 births.[13]

Literacy

As far as literacy is concerned the national average for India is 65 percent according to the 2001 census. Assam's figure is 64 percent. But female literacy in Assam is still very low being 56 percent against male literacy of 72 percent. As a result of the implementation of Sarva Sikhsa Abhiyan the rate of literacy has gone up during the past few years. What should cause worry is the school dropout ratio in Assam, which is quite high being 72.3 percent for girls and 68.3 percent for boys in classes I-VIII. Slight improvement has been noticed after the implementation of the mid-day meal programme.

Certain other indicators suggest that the situation in Assam is not very encouraging. A recent government report mentions about the unhealthy sanitary conditions, lack of safe drinking water and prevalence of malnutrition causing health problems. It also mentions about more than 50 percent of the pregnant women suffering from malnutrition and the low birth weight babies being as high as 37.3 percent.

An earlier study of the national nutrition profile conducted by the Food and Nutrition Board found that 32.9 percent of the adults in India suffer from chronic energy deficiency. As many as 49.2 percent of the children below 5 years of age are underweight and 20.3 percent are severely underweight. The growth of 61.2 percent of such children in Assam is stunted while that of 32.6 percent is severely stunted. Recently, a "state hunger index" has been prepared. This shows that Assam's hunger index score is 19.83 against the all-India score of 23.30. It also shows Assam's "prevalence of calorie under nourishment" as 14.6 percent against 20 percent of India. Assam's proportion of underweight children below 5 years is 36.4 percent against India's 42.5 percent. The under 5 mortality has been estimated as 8.5 percent for Assam against 7.4 percent of the country as a whole.[13]

A UNDP report showed that the percentage of households with drinking water from pump/pipe in Assam is 43.2 against the country's average of 68.2 and Punjab's 98.6. The households with access to sanitation facilities are 49.6 percent in Assam against 98.3 of Mizoram and 83.1 of Manipur. A host of other connected data may be quoted to show how Assam is lagging behind compared to not only the advanced states but also the small states of the North East.

Insurgency and Development

The historical events which influenced the formation of the present Assamese mindset have been discussed in sections 1 to 7. The economic situation has been traced since independence in sections 8 and 9. The present economic scenario has been analysed in sections 10 to 15. In the last few sections it is proposed to examine the link between insurgency and economic development.

Central Initiative for Development

One factor which is not well known and is hardly appreciated is that during the nineteenth century, pioneering work had been done in respect of several industries in Assam and it was only since the middle of the twentieth century that Assam started lagging behind. To quote the former Prime Minister Deve Gowda, "Assam was in the forefront of economic development of the country 100-150 years ago. It was a pioneering State and enterprising entrepreneurs invested in development of tea-plantations, oil, coal mining, railways and inland waterways. However, in the recent years investors have shunned these areas, because some of these States turned inward looking, while others have been afflicted by militancy and terrorism. This has set in a vicious cycle of terrorism, discouraging investments and economic development, leading to growing unemployment, which in turn provided recruits to militancy".

Deve Gowda said this in a press statement on October 27, 1996 while announcing the famous package for economic development of NE Region after his seven-day tour of all the seven States. This was the first time that a Prime Minister made clear the Centre's intention to take up a concrete and comprehensive package of projects for each of the seven States. These projects were identified and the State-wise lists were appended to the statement.

Committees and Studies

However, the emotional involvement of all sections of people of the State of Assam was brought out very clearly only by LC Jain in his report on Clause Seven of the Assam Accord. The report in the very first paragraph said, "Our entire thinking has been influenced by one major factor : a fairly well informed and fervent demand for development from the people at large - students, political parties, women's groups, voluntary organizations, economists, ministers, administrators, entrepreneurs - with whom we had the privilege of interacting. This magnitude of popular awareness and interest in development is a great social force. Constructively used, it can be the most precious capital for the development of Assam".[14]

Several other committees were set up and quite a few studies were commissioned on the same matter. Hundreds of valuable recommendations made by them are now gathering dust in the cupboards of the North East Council and the Secretariates of different States. One principal study has been that of the high level Commission appointed by the Planning Commission in 1996 under the Chairmanship of SP Shukla, member, Planning Commission, to critically examine the backlogs in respect of basic minimum services and the gaps in infrastructure sectors essential for development of the States in NE Region. In their 1997 report the Commission observed that there was a "two way deficit of understanding with the rest of the country" and that "the development of the tranquility in the Northeast is also a national security interest and can offer regional solutions to national problems". It then recommended that "the country must assist the Northeast to realize its full potential and avail of the emerging opportunities within and around it." The Commission felt that "the people of the Northeast cannot remain cocooned and wish to take their places as full and equal partners, contributing to the great enterprise that is Project India. It is right not to want to be swamped by Indians from outside the region, even less by an influx of foreigners. But the region does not need to fear 'outsiders' and lapse into 'localism'. Violence, insurgency and easy money are no solution to any problem, real or imagined. These eruptions and the bandhs, extortion, kidnappings, leakage, and the sulking and cynical indifference they have engendered in sections of the populace, can only delay and could even deny the peace, progress and prosperity that everybody seeks".[15]

Similar observations have been made by other Committees and Commissions. Unfortunately, however, most of the recommendations were not implemented. Some funds were made available for a number of schemes and projects by the Central Government under the Prime Minister's package. Funds also flowed to the States through regular schemes and programmes, particularly for rural development, in addition to other usual funds under the annual plans. But in every State of NE Region, plenty of allegations and complaints have surfaced about the misuse of funds and corruption. Media reports suggest that major portions of the funds are siphoned off by bureaucrats, politicians, bank managers, contractors and their cohorts. The poor people get very little, sometimes nothing.

Distortions in Planned Development

One use of such diverted funds is seen in the building boom particularly in the urban areas. According to a survey made sometime ago by the Federation of Industries and Commerce of North Eastern Region (FINER), in Guwahati city alone, 604 multi-storied buildings, which house residential and commercial apartments, have come up during 1995-2000. These involved an investment of Rs. 1200 crores. In the next ten years thousand of such apartment complexes have come up. The FINER survey found that 40 new superior class restaurants, beside the ones which are part of bigger hotels, have come up in Guwahati during the same period. Hundreds of more such restaurants will come up during the next ten years including branches of national restaurant and hotel chains. Guwahatians were estimated to spend about Rs. 1.30 crores in a month on eating out. Now probably the figure will be a hundred times more. The FINER survey also shows that sectors like transportation, hotels, tourism, greeting cards, healthcare, courier services, travel agencies and computer education have been growing at a phenomenal pace in Assam in the last three-four years. There has also been a "manifold" increase in "the sale of such items as colour televisions, music systems, refrigerators and washing machines". Mobile telephones and computers are recent additions. This has been the result of a rise in the "disposable income, at least among the urban population and a section of the rural population of the State in recent years".[16] My personal belief is that such a high level of investment and conspicuous consumptions have been provided by the funds siphoned off from development projects and schemes as already indicated. Besides, as the FINER survey has found, the World Bank assisted projects and the amounts flowing out of the Prime Minister's package have added fuel to this boom. More money is coming from the Asian Development Bank and other multinational institutions also.

Money to Insurgents

Substantial amounts have also been flowing to the insurgents. The channels through which these funds flow are well-known. Politicians, bureaucrats, bank executives, tea-planters, contractors and others who handle money in Government establishments and commercial and industrial houses have bought their own and their colleagues' security by passing on to insurgents a portion of their ill-gotten money. In the past, many Central leaders had warned the State Governments of the region against such payments to insurgent organizations. On June 14, 2001, the then Union Rural Development Minister, Venkaiah Naidu after the meeting with Rural Development Ministers of NE States at Shillong, warned that "the Centre would stop disbursing rural development funds to those States, where a bulk of the funds go to the coffers of the extremist outfits".[17]

As far as the State Governments in NE Region are concerned, security related expenditure has impaired their ability to finance development works to some extent. A recent report of a Committee on IRDP in NE States also mentioned "an upsurge in insurgency in Assam" as responsible for "practically no developmental activities in rural areas" and a simultaneous flight of capital from the rural areas to urban areas as the former were less secured than the latter.[18] This has impoverished the rural areas.

The general belief that insurgency is fuelled by economic backwardness, therefore, has some basis although it would be totally inappropriate to assume that there is a direct link between insurgency and economic backwardness.[19] Moreover, as the Shukla Commission opined, "It would be simplistic to believe that development by itself can end insurgency and restore tranquility. Yet it constitutes a most important element in that task and an effective entry point for dealing with complex problems and historical neglect, rapid transition and social change. The extraordinary ethno-geographic and bio-geographic diversity of the Region precludes uniform solutions as different communities are at varying stages of growth".[20]

Unemployment

In Assam the tremendous unemployment due to lack of development over a long period, is reflected by the number of jobless, which today has reached 2.2 million mark constituting about a tenth of the population. More than 70 percent of them are educated. They provide the reservoir of manpower from which the various insurgent outfits easily recruit their volunteers. Even the families of these volunteers do not object because of the lure of financial compensation which, though not handsome (as some sections of media tend to make out), is not meagre either. The leaders alone are reported to be leading a luxurious life. But all of them have now the added attraction of employment and easy money after surrender.

I personally feel that each of the insurgent outfits in the region was initially raised from among people who harboured feeling of neglect and "colonial exploitation" or who strongly resented certain perceived wrongs to the particular community or sub-region they belonged to. The outfits then gained strength through clandestine support of politicians and overground frontal organizations and with funds procured mainly by extortion. The ULFA, for example, was able to become such a big organization primarily because of the tacit support of the first AGP Government which the former Assam Governor DD Thakur described as "one of the classic example of culpable inaction on the part of a State Government". Actually a parallel ULFA government was running in Assam during those days.

Summing UP

To sum up, economic backwardness is one of the causes of insurgency in Assam. The Assamese mindset developed during the past two centuries has added fuel to it. It would be wrong, however, to say that lack of economic development is the sole cause of insurgency nor can it be said that lack of economic development is the only consequence of Centre's neglect. While trying to achieve material progress, rampant corruption by the bureaucrats, politicians etc., manning the delivery system, stands as the stumbling block. In such a milieu the only way out is to obtain people's participation at all levels and particularly through Panchayati Raj and urban local government institutions and carry out all development work through these institutions in a transparent manner with full co-operation of the local public.

It is against this background that future plans for economic development of Assam must be drawn up. The growth rate for Assam will have to be stepped up to 10 to 15 percent per annum against the proposed national growth rate of 8 to 9 percent if the State is to catch up with the national average per capita income. Bihar's annual growth rate is reported to have gone up to 16 percent. If that is true there should be no reason why Assam cannot match it. This will be a stupendous task which will need tremendous investments particularly in agriculture, industry and infrastructure sectors. Proper utilization of the substantial funds allocated by the Government of India for rural development will also have to be ensured. The role which micro-credit can play in poverty alleviation has now been appreciated by the Government of India by introducing self help groups similar to the Bangladesh experiment. Assam must take advantage of it. For this purpose, the delivery system will have to be strengthened and geared up so that projects, schemes and programmes are effectively implemented for the benefit of the people.

Endnotes

1. Barpujari, HK, *The Comprehensive History of Assam*, Volume Three, Publication Board, Assam Guwahati, 1993. The date when Chaolung Sukapha set up Ahom hegemony over Assam is not clear. However, 1228 has been mentioned in an article by Kiron Kumar Gogoi in the *Amar Asom* dated May 3, 2007, Guwahati.
2. Hazarika, BB, *Political Life in Assam during the 19th Century*, Gian Publishing House, Delhi, 1987.
3. Das, HN *Poverty Alleviation Through Agricultural Growth in Assam*, Rural Prosperity and Agriculture Policies and Strategies, National Institute of Rural Development, Hyderabad, September, 2000. For the "State Hunger Inde.." see Dr. Jayati Ghose, *The Political Economy of Hunger in 21st Century India*, 6th Brajamohan Sarma Memorial Annual Lecture, Guwahati, 02.10.2010.
4. Jain, LC, *Report of the Committee on Clause Seven of Assam Accord*, Planning Commission, New Delhi, April, 1990.
5. Das, HN, *A New Paradigm of Development : Regional Imbalance and Assam, The Economic Times*, October 23, 1985.
6. Das, HN, *A Model for Assam's Development, The Sentinel* April, 24, 1995.
7. United Nations' Development Programme, *Human Development Report*, 2000, Oxford University Press. In the Report for 2009 not much improvement was recorded as the

value was 0.594 for India while the highest recorded was that for Australia at 0.966.

8. United Nations' Development Programme, *India : The Road of Human Development,* 1997, India Development Forum, Paris.
9. Planning Commission Minutes, probably not published.
10. Das, HN, *Financing Disaster Response,* India Disasters Report, Oxford University Press, New Delhi, 2000.
11. Government of India, *Economic Survey,* 2009-2010, New Delhi, February, 2010.
12. Government of Assam, *State Plan of Action for Children,* Guwahati, 1999.
13. United Nations Development Programme, *Human Development Reports, 2000 and 2009",* Oxford University Press.
14. Planning Commission, *High Level Commission Report to the Prime Minister,* Chaired by SP Shukla, 1997.
15. Federation of Industries and Commerce of North Eastern Region (FINER), *Assam's Economy. A fresh Perspective,* Guwahati, 2001.
16. *The Sentinel,* Guwahati, *Centre's Money is not for Militants : Venkaiah,* June 15, 2001.
17. Hon'ble Gauhati High Court Judgment in Civil Rule Nos. 23K, 2238, 2425 of 1990 and 11 of 1991, Report of Assam Governor dated 2.11.90, quoted in full.
18. Ministry of Rural Development, Government of India, *Report of the Committee on Credit Related Issues Under IRDP in North-Eastern States.* 2000.
19. Das, HN, *Reclaiming a Lost World, The Indian Express,* May 11, 1998.
20. Das, HN, *Grameen Bank of Bangladesh : Concept and Process,* North Eastern Institute of Bank Management, Guwahati, 1999. The second edition published by the Grameen Vikash Bank of Assam (2008) and the third edition by the State Institute of Rural Development, Guwahati (2009).

CHAPTER – 5

Economic Consequences of Terrorism in India's North-East

Violence and Destruction

Terrorists unleashed great violence and destruction in NE India during the second half of the twentieth century. Thousands of people have been killed all over NE in bomb blasts, grenade attacks and assassinations. Hundreds of crores of rupees worth of public and private property have been destroyed in these activities. This has affected the economy in several different ways. Families have been shattered due to death of earning members. Communities have been affected by the loss of markets and the disruption of communication. Economic activities were stunted by erosion of investor confidence. The entire growth process has been slow in NE in the past three decades. One main reason for this phenomenon is terrorist violence and destruction. However, it has also to be noted that this terrorism had its genesis in the agitations over economic backwardness and the fear of loss of ethnic identity.[1] In this chapter, it is proposed to examine the ways in which the economy of NE has been affected by terrorism. The analysis will be based mainly on the reports of incidents in the media.

Nagaland

The Nagas were the first to resort to terrorism. In Chapter-1 it has been explained that the Naga's non-violent movement began in 1918, when they formed the

Naga Club as a common platform for all Nagas to unite and to express their grievances to the British.[2] The Nagas started becoming violent after they formed the Naga National Council (NNC) in 1946 under the leadership of AZ Phizo.[3] Later they formed the National Socialist Council of Nagaland (NSCN). NSCN got divided into two groups - the Khaplang group and the Isaac Muivah group. There is now a ceasefire agreement with the Government of India but sporadic violence continues.

Since 1946 Naga terrorists have caused extensive damage to the region's economy by resorting to violence and destruction in Nagaland, Arunachal Pradesh, Assam and Manipur. During this period substantial funds for economic development have poured into the State of Nagaland from the Government of India. These funds have primarily benefited north Indian businessmen and contractors, Bangladeshi and Bihari labourers, Naga politicians and Naga and non-Naga bureaucrats and technocrats. Through them substantial portions of money went to the terrorists. But money was spent mainly by the State Government departments. The amount flowing to the local government organizations was rather limited.[4] The general impression is that the percentage of fund actually received by those for whom the schemes and programmes were intended is rather small.

Central Funds

Funds directed to other states of NE from New Delhi in recent years are also substantial. A media report makes the following shocking statement, "Surprisingly, shortage of funds is not the root cause of poverty in the region. The expenditure of [the] eight North East states is almost Rupees 30,000 crore a year - which means Rupees 10,000 per person per year is spent annually. In states like Arunachal Pradesh, Nagaland and Manipur more than 80 percent of the amount comes from New Delhi.

According to some estimate, as high [a sum] as Rupees 20,000 crore comes as a direct transfer from the Central Government to the North Eastern states".[5] This report on the present situation is revealing. But the point that needs to be emphasised is that in the past when NE needed funds, New Delhi rarely helped. With the advent of terrorism, however, New Delhi started directing massive funds for development. Such ad hoc and haphazard fund transfers failed to achieve cohesiveness of NE with the rest of India.

Assam

In Assam, almost two centuries of neglect and isolation, ever since the British occupation of the Brahmaputra valley in 1826, have produced a deep sense of ambivalence - there is resentment against mainstream India, but at the same time there is reluctance to abandon the Indian identity. After partition, Assam and NE got physically delinked from the rest of India. The only conduit which remained was the narrow 26-kilometre corridor through West Bengal. The rail link, hurriedly built after partition, has become the lifeline between NE and the Indian heartland. The geographical distance increased the feeling of isolation. A feeling of discrimination was also generated which fomented separatist movements and ultimately terrorism. The general feeling in NE is that its natural resources, particularly oil, has been continually extracted from this area and the region's rich forest wealth has been denuded for the benefit of the rest of India. But when a refinery or a gas cracker, based entirely on local natural resources, has to be built, New Delhi feels that NE is not suitable or is unsafe as the region is too near the international borders.[6]

Autonomous District Councils

Within Assam, many ethnic groups, particularly the Bodos, seek to consolidate their own identity. Each of these groups feels discriminated by the ethnic Assamese. As explained in Chapter II the Bodo Territorial Council (BTC), beside the two Autonomous District Councils of Karbi Anglong and Dima Hasao Hills were set up under the Sixth Schedule of the Indian Constitution to assuage the feelings of the tribal people. Recently, seven more councils for the plains tribes outside the Sixth Schedule have been set up. Ethnic trouble has led to the setting up of seven more Development Councils for seven ethnic groups. An additional two are also being set up. Hundreds of crores of rupees have been allocated to these councils. The allegation is that there is rampant corruption in these councils. The terrorists take advantage of this situation and force the council functionaries to disgorge substantial amounts of Government funds to the terrorist outfits. Therefore, neither has the political situation stabilized at the grassroots level nor has the economic conditions of tribal and ethnic groups improved. The situation is similar in other states of NE. Exact figures are not available, but terrorism has affected the economy of all the states of NE.

It has to be emphasized that terrorism in NE is carried out through well organized and heavily armed underground outfits. ULFA is one such outfit. It had declared certain economic policies in conjunction with the objective of making Assam politically and economically independent. A booklet which ULFA circulated some years ago on Assam's tea industry is a revealing document - it sought to provide an idea about how the industry could 'help' in the economic regeneration of Assam. In the early 1990s, ULFA cadres had taken a group of tea planters through a maze of roads in Dibrugarh district to a remote and abandoned tea estate bungalow, avowedly for holding discussion on the subject. The planters were blindfolded. What transpired has not been officially divulged. But the 'invitation letter' to the tea planters said that economic development of Assam would be discussed.[7] This meeting resulted in extortion of more money from the planters.

In practice, however, except for a few Robin Hood style adventures, ULFA has done nothing for the economic development of Assam. The organization's fellow travellers set up a few agriculture farms, but even these disappeared within a short time. On the other hand, ULFA has extorted substantial amounts of money from the tea barons as also from other industrial and business establishments in Assam. One of the tea companies listed an amount of Rs 1 crore on the balance sheet as security-related expenditure. The entire amount is believed to have been given to ULFA. Moreover, various sums of money were talked about as ransom amounts paid for the release of kidnapped tea executives. In return for such huge payments most tea gardens earned comparative respite from terrorist attacks. Not a single day's work was lost because ULFA exempted tea gardens from bandhs and strikes. As far as physical violence is concerned, a number of cases have been reported. But it is believed that the number could have been several times more if payments had not been made to the terrorist organizations. The murder of Surrendra Paul (brother of Lord Swaraj Paul) of the Assam Frontier Tea Company is an important tea industry related assassination. Paul was gunned down in upper Assam by ULFA for reportedly resisting their attempts at extortion.[8] He was also accused of discriminatory treatment against some of his Assamese employees.

Collusion of Industry

It would be of interest to note that there have been some cases of collusion and collaboration by tea industry executives with ULFA. In the case of Tata Tea, for example, the company's senior executives were alleged to have travelled in a clandestine manner to meet ULFA cadres in Bangkok. Tata Tea is also said to have provided travel and medical expenses for ULFA's cultural secretary, Pranati Deka, during her pregnancy. Deka gave birth to a child in a Mumbai hospital, the expenses for which were borne by Tata Tea. The issue of a possible nexus between Tata Tea and ULFA generated much controversy and certain arrests were made by the Government. It is generally opined that Tata Tea probably had to engineer linkages with ULFA under duress. But the episode highlighted the considerable influence wielded by ULFA in upper Assam and in the tea industry. It is also interesting to note that nothing has been done by the Government to pursue the police case against Tata Tea.[9] Earlier, in another episode, the general manager of Tata Tea had been kidnapped and kept in captivity for almost an year.

Other terrorist organizations, which were established later, have also been following ULFA's example of extortion by means of terror, threats, physical and mental violence and kidnappings. According to Nitin Gokhale, "Audited accounts revealed that even companies such as Williamson Magor had paid over Rs. one crore twice in 1994-95 and 1995-96 to the National Democratic Front of Bodoland, smaller companies such as Bhergaon tea estate paid up to Rs. 25 lakh (it faced kidnappings twice in two years)".[10]

The oil sector too has been badly affected by terrorist activities. Oil was the target of the Assam movement launched by the All Assam Students' Union (AASU) in 1979. AASU's most significant slogan was "*Tej dim, tel nidiu*" (we will give blood, not oil). When the oil blockade was launched by AASU, New Delhi got rather worried because till the 1980s, Assam supplied a substantial portion of India's oil requirement. The then Union Home Minister, Zail Singh, visited Assam in the wake of the oil blockade. During discussions with AASU, he made a special request to the leaders to lift the blockade. The manner in which he made his request seemed to imply that the students' organization could carry on with their agitation programmes, but they should lift the oil blockade because the national economy was getting hurt.[11]

An estimate prepared by a security agency will show the extent to which the oil industry has been affected by terrorism. In the last sixteen years there have been 1681 bomb explosions in Assam, many of which affected oil installations. Oil India Ltd. (OIL) and Oil and Natural Gas Corporation (ONGC) lost over Rs. 3500 crores in militant-related activities during the period. The oil industry was reported to be seriously considering a proposal to convert the oil pipelines in Assam into explosion resistant pipelines.[12]

Meanwhile, the explosions continue and the industry is incurring huge losses. A report in the media indicated that OIL spends Rs. 20 crores every year on security cover for its oil wells and other installations in Assam and that ONGC is reportedly going to raise a dedicated battalion of its own at an initial cost of Rs. 40 crores in order to guard its installations in Assam. The battalion's upkeep will cost an additional Rs. 20 crores per year.[13] Such expenditure impinges on the profits of these companies - money that would have otherwise gone to the Government of India coffers.

Governor's Report

In November 1990, the then Governor of Assam, Devi Das Thakur, in his report to the President of India, estimated that the amount extorted by ULFA, until the time of submitting the report, was more than Rs. 400 crores.[14] Similar indications about the huge sums extracted by other militant organizations are also available from media reports and from raids and seizures conducted by the army, police and paramilitary forces. Large sums of money are required to run terrorist organizations. ULFA's annual expenditure for running the organization headquarters alone, excluding the cost of arms and ammunitions, food and clothes of its huge armed battalions, seem to exceed Rs. 30 crores. The ULFA budget for 2001-02, for instance, presented at the ULFA general headquarters in Bhutan's Sukhni Basti on the 18th March 2001 gives a detailed break-up of expenditure on different items.[15] Today the expenditure must have gone up by several folds.

Government Funds to Insurgents

The major portion of such funds seems to have come indirectly from government sources. Terrorists can easily blackmail corrupt officials because they know the illegal activities of such officials, as also those of unscrupulous businessmen. Such people pay up easily. One senior ULFA cadre, who was the quartermaster in charge of a camp, revealed during interrogation that 'officials' and other 'important functionaries' who had earlier been paying money to ULFA were still working with government in different capacities. He claimed that many of them are still paying money to the outfit. The cadre also spoke of a businessman from Nalbari, who was paying regular extortion money to the outfit.[16]

It is often remarked that the Government of India is the main source of funds for the terrorist organizations in NE. It is also commonly believed that government, public sector and bank officials pay the terrorists from what they siphon off from provisions for development programmes and projects. Such funds also go to insurgents, in the same way, from out of allocations from the World Bank, the Asian Development Bank, the World Health Organization, the United Nations Development Programme and other multilateral and bilateral agencies. Officials pay them out of fear or as a result of threats, or because of blackmail. Rural development has been identified as a lucrative sector and it is estimated that as much as seventy per cent of all funds available to the Government of Assam under this head are systematically siphoned off by ULFA and surrendered ULFA (SULFA), contractors, civil servants as well as the politicians. Sources estimate that of the total Rs. 11.65 billion made available under this head, rural development, during the period, 1992-93 to February 1998, less than four billion rupees went into legitimate schemes. There is little evidence of projects executed on the ground that may support the claim that even a fraction of this amount was spent as "legitimate" expenditure.'[17]

NIA

There are many cases of payment of Government funds directly to the terrorist outfits. A number of Block Development Officers and other officers of Government have been arrested for payment of money to these outfits. The most glaring instance of an attempt at such payment was discovered by police on April 2, 2009 when four youths were arrested along with Rs. 1 crore in cash and some weapons on the Assam-Meghalaya border. Two of them were drivers. But the other two, Phajen Hojai and Bipul Kemprai, were members of the Jewel Garlosa faction of Dima Halam Daogah (DHDJ), popularly known as the Black Widow. DHDJ is probably the most dangerous and daring terrorist outfit. The youths confessed that they were taking the money for payment to DHDJ. The money had been withdrawn earlier from the Government Treasury at the instance of Mohit Hojai, chief executive member of the Dima Hasao Hills Autonomous District Council and RH Khan, Joint Director of the Social Welfare Department posted at Haflong, headquarters of Dima Hasao district. Both of them were arrested on May 30, 2009. Jewel Garlossa himself and his accomplice were arrested in Bangaluru on June 1, 2009. The Government of India has handed over these two cases for investigation by the National Investigation Agency (NIA). These two are in fact the very first cases taken up by NIA. In the course of investigation a number of *Benami* bank accounts have been unearthed and an amount of Rs. 13.45 crores was found hidden between two false walls in a garage belonging to RH Khan's relative at Guwahati.

Very serious allegations were made in a section of the media that either the state government directly or some important members of the party in power made a huge payment in cash to ULFA to persuade that outfit to allow the 33rd National Games in Guwahati in 2007. This allegation was neither proved nor probed. This type of misutilisation of Plan funds have distorted the national and state priorities. In fact, Plan funds meant for development have been diverted for destructive and anti-social purposes. The gravity of the situation can be discerned from the statement of a former union minister for rural development, Venkaiah Naidu, who once reportedly warned that the Government of India would stop disbursing rural development funds to those states where the bulk of the funds go to the coffers of extremist outfits.[18]

Business people who are subjected to periodical illegitimate 'taxation' by the terrorists have resorted to the practice of making up or recouping their losses (as a result of extortion) by creating artificial scarcities and consequently raising the prices of goods and commodities. The most affected by such illegitimate taxation are the people below the poverty line. Even BPL people, including those living in remote areas, are periodically made to pay 'goonda tax' out of their meagre earnings. These include peons, menials, daily-wage earners and *pan-bidi* shopkeepers. This situation has led to further impoverishment of these people.

Extortion by Police

Under the pretext of controlling the movement of terrorists a section of the police set up numerous checkpoints. In reality these double up as checkpoints for collecting large sums of money from truck drivers and such others. According to a past government estimate, there were as many as 184 such checkpoints in Assam at one point of time. A few years ago, several of these illegal checkpoints were demolished and the guilty police personnel involved in this illegal activity were transferred. Again these checkpoints have resurfaced and have actually proliferated. Extortion through checkpoints, especially in the case of truck drivers, has really become a nuisance. Many truck drivers refuse to come to Assam or to pass through Assam to go to other NE states primarily for this reason. Some unload their cargo at the border which is then picked up by trucks from Assam. Such practices not only cause delay but have resulted in unjustified increase in the prices of essential commodities brought from outside the state. Unfortunately, such practices still continue.

There has also been a flight of capital from Assam. This is clear from the steadily declining credit-deposit ratio of banks and the diversion of surplus funds and earnings by industrial establishments of the state to units outside in the name of diversification. Some tea companies have taken out surplus funds to units outside Assam. The credit-deposit ratio has declined from 50.20 percent as on 31 December, 1991 to 31 percent on 31 December, 2001 and 29.27 percent in 2003. There has been some increase since then so that the ratio has become 50.48

percent by March, 2008. A committee appointed under the integrated rural development programme of the Government of India even found a flight of capital from rural to urban areas of Assam due to the threat posed by the terrorists. The committee also found that 'an upsurge in insurgency in Assam' was responsible for "practically no developmental activities in rural areas".[19]

The flight of capital is menifest in Siliguri's unbelievable growth in recent times at the expense of Guwahati and other towns in Assam from where a number of traders and businessmen have partially shifted. Siliguri is geo-strategically located at the entry point to NE from the rest of India through the narrow 26 km corridor called the "chicken's neck". Taking away their capital stocks from Assam, many businessmen have set up shops in Siliguri. Consequently, West Bengal's tax collection is reported to be going up in Siliguri. Similarly, some industrial units from Assam are now shifting to Byrnihat area of Meghalaya due to threats particularly by the so-called syndicates of the Beltola area of Guwahati, many of which consist of SULFA or surrendered members of ULFA. These syndicates are extortion units, allegedly having official blessings, which levy 'goonda tax' from each commercial transaction and on every consignment of goods produced.

Destruction in Bodo Areas

Large-scale destruction of public and private properties – such as roads, bridges, buildings, schools, flora and fauna, factories, vehicles – by different Bodo terrorist outfits have had a telling effect on the economy. For quite some time, many Bodo-inhabited areas remained cut off and inaccessible due to destruction in the wake of violence following agitations by All Bodo Students Union and the Bodo terrorist organizations such as the National Democratic Front of Bodoland (NDFB) and the Bodo

Liberation Tigers (BLT). More than three lakh people were displaced and had to take shelter in refugee camps due to ethnic clashes in Bodo areas. There have been many instances of attempted ethnic cleansing. Some clashes have occurred as a result of psychological reaction due to forced stay for inordinately long periods in the refugee camps. These people were distraught because their houses were torched, their kins killed and their harvests destroyed. More importantly, their spirit was damaged beyond repair. The Bodos, Santhals, Koch-Rajbongshis and Bangladeshi Muslims suffered equally. There were periods when all economic activities had ceased in certain areas.

Destruction in Hill Districts

Similar destructions have taken place in the districts of Karbi Anglong and Dima Hasao, primarily due to similar problems created by Karbi and Dimasa terrorist organizations, as well as Naga terrorist organizations attempting to gain a foothold in the area in their quest for a greater Nagalim. It must also be mentioned that illegal tax collection by both factions of NSCN is organized and systematic. This applies to both Nagaland and Manipur. There is a virtual parallel economy in these two states. Almost everyone living in the areas under the influence of NSCN have to pay a certain percentage of earnings as illegal tax. Therefore, a portion of the development fund for Nagaland and Manipur go to the 'war-coffers' of NSCN. The NSCN also get paid for each terrorist that they train for other outfits. That is why NSCN is called the "mother of all terrorist outfits".

The Middle Class

In this connection one aspect of India's socio-economic structure needs attention. After the economic reform process was set in motion in the country in the 1990s, the rise of the Indian middle class has been accelerated. This class cannot be defined exactly, but can be known "culturally, through consumption patterns and psychographic".[20] They mainly belong to the services sector and have high disposable incomes.[21] The middle class in NE and Assam in particular, has benefited from money diverted from the allocations for development plans. This has been in the shape of bribes, kickbacks and illegal siphoning off of plan money. In the past two decades, terrorism in Assam has added fuel to the general trend of bribery and corruption among the middle class. Financial gain from terrorism has further enriched a section of the middle class and also added to their numbers.

Middle class businessmen often take their cash away to places outside the state and invest it in New Delhi, Jaipur, Ajmer, Jodhpur, Kolkata, Siliguri, Bangalore and Mumbai. They spend conspicuously. The wealth of the middle class is reflected by the artificial boom in Guwahati as revealed by a survey conducted by the Federation of Industries and Commerce of the North Eastern Region (FINER) and a later report.[22] In Guwahati city alone, over seven hundred apartment buildings have come up in the period 1997-2001, involving an investment of Rs. 1400 crores. Probably triple that number have come up later. Thousands of other commercial and residential buildings have also been constructed. The economically better off people in Guwahati used to spend Rs. 1.5 crore on 'eating out' in restaurants every month. That was in 2001. This figure has gone up substantially in recent years. This type of development has taken place in quite a few other towns in NE including Shillong, Silchar, Tinsukia, Aizawl and Kohima. It is true that a portion of the money has come from legal earnings. However, it is believed that the major portion of the spending has emanated from black money.

Conspicuous Consumption

A study by researchers of the New Delhi-based Institute for Conflict Management has revealed several ways in which funds have been diverted through corruption.[23] A series of articles in the media, particularly the *Telegraph,* showcased the interiors of residences where the affluent live in Guwahati city. The photographs accompanying the articles show elegant living rooms, kitchens and bedrooms. Some SULFA members seem to have spent on conspicuous consumption the huge sums of subsidy given to them by the government as also the loans advanced to them by banks at the time of their surrender which were meant for their rehabilitation through self-employment. They are reported to be having a hand in every type of economic activity from which they raise a 'tax'. In a report in the *Economic Times,* the following facts have been revealed: "Security-related expenditure in the North-East has been over Rs. 100 crore annually from 2000-01 onwards. A 10 to 20 percent of leakage of development fund in some states goes to militants. Militants in Nagaland and Manipur levy illegal tax on all business operations. Every government employee pays a part of his salary to militants. Some militant outfits charge an oil tanker Rs. 3,000 per trip, followed by trucks carrying cooking gas cylinders at Rs. 2,000, and those carrying cement at Rs. 1,000. They charge a truck Rs. 7,000 and a tourist bus Rs. 12,000 annually as 'permit fee' to operate".

In the general elections held in Nagaland in March, 2008, as many as 58 candidates were reported to be crorepaties. The figures were worked out jointly by a few NGOs and social activists in the "Nagaland Election Watch (NEW)" which has been described as "a first of its kind disclosure of criminal, financial and educational backgrounds of contestants".[24] In Meghalaya 27 candidates were reported to be crorepaties in the general elections held in March, 2008. In the general elections held in October, 2009, as many as 63 candidates were reported to be crorepaties in Arunachal Pradesh. One candidate declared his worth to be Rs. 209 crores. These are small tribal states which were poor till recently in terms of per capita income and wealth. Most families were poor and probably no one had even a few thousand of rupees. It would be relevant to enquire how these people made their crores. It would also be interesting to know how many thousands other people have become crorepaties out of money siphoned off by various means from Plan funds of the NE states. Most of these other crorepaties normally live outside NE Region. They however continue to pay the terrorist outfits in order to escape death and kidnapping.

The situation is uncannily similar in the other states of NE as well. In Manipur, for example, the terrorists have virtually stopped all economic activities in the evening hours. Between dusk and dawn, when the state takes a back seat, the terrorists take over. Besides the numerous bomb blasts, explosions and other destructive activities, they raise substantial amounts of money by devious means. Many Manipuri middle class families have temporarily shifted to places outside Manipur. The usual practice seems to be that the earning member remains behind while the others, especially the school and college-going children, live outside the state. In Guwahati there are several hundred such Manipuri families. A majority of Manipuri young men and women now prefer to study in colleges and universities outside the state.[25]

In Nagaland, the number of cases of destruction of property as well as killings have gone down considerably after the ceasefire. However, occasional killings by the two factions of NSCN, extortion and 'tax collection' continue. These practices have been institutionalized.

Rates of payment to the terrorist organizations are fixed and have to be made on a regular basis. No one can avoid such payment and no one is usually hurt unless there is a default in payment.

In Tripura, the situation has now become much better. Tripura's CPM Government has been able to implement development work at tremendous speed. They have also been able to control terrorism to a considerable extent. The cumulative annual rate of growth in Tripura is more than nine percent. Even corruption and diversion of development funds have been controlled to a great extent by the enlightened government of the present Chief Minister, Manik Sarkar. If Tripura can steer clear of terrorist activities, its growth rate will further accelerate in the near future.

In Arunachal Pradesh and Meghalaya terrorism seems to have lowered. Therefore, the economic consequences of terrorism are still peripheral. In Mizoram, after the terrorist activities of 1960s, there has been a modicum of peace. Mizoram has become so peaceful that the State Government is apprehending that it will miss out on New Delhi's largesse and packages given to terrorist infested states. It is good that New Delhi has provided Mizoram a 'peace bonus', in order to allay such misgivings.

Positive Result

The only positive result of terrorism has been that the Government of India has now developed a proactive outlook towards NE. It is taking active steps to assist economic development of NE. For this purpose the Government of India has created the non-lapsable pool from out of ten per cent of the budget allocations of a number of ministries and departments of the Government of India. This fund is to be spent for NE. The pool is carried forward from year to year and is not allowed to lapse at the end of a particular financial year. Grants out of this fund are made to projects and schemes recommended by the State Governments of NE. This will hopefully improve the economic situation and reverse the feeling of neglect, discrimination and colonial exploitation. However, if diversion of money continues to insurgent outfits, even these funds might dry up. No economic development can take place unless the misuse of such funds by politicians, bureaucrats, bank managers, contractors and their cohorts is stopped.

Endnotes

1. For a detailed analysis of the problem, see HN Das, "Ethnicity and Insurgency in the North Eastern Region of India". Aakrosh, (October 2004)
2. CL Imchen, *Naga Politics: Regionalism or Non-State Nation*. In *Regionalism in India*, ed. B. Pakem, Har Anand Publications, New Delhi, 1993.
3. Kaka D. Iralu, *Nagaland and India: The Blood and the Tears*. Publisher not mentioned. September, 2000.
4. Nagaland does not have Panchayati Raj. There are village councils which look after development works in different localities.
5. "East of Burden", *The Economic Times*, 12 November 2006. For details of fund requirements for a few recent terrorist activities in Mumbai, Madrid, London and New York see summary of former National Security Advisor MK Narayanan's lecture. He mentioned about Islamist militants' attempt to penetrate Mumbai and Chennai Stock Exchanges. *The Hindu*, February 17, 2007.
6. To see how neglect and discrimination have resulted in lower growth rate, depletion of non-renewable resources and continuous lowering of Assam's per capita income in comparison with the all-India average, refer to HN Das, "A New Paradigm of Development: Regional Imbalance and Assam," *The Economic Times*, 23 October 1985; and HN Das, "Model for Assam's Development," *The Sentinel*, 24 April 1995.

7. This booklet was widely circulated in the 1990s. Though the name of the writer is not mentioned, someone who knows the tea industry intimately must have written it. One of the 'invitees', HP Borooah (former Chairman of the Indian Tea Association), told me about the meeting. According to Wasbir Hussain ("Life and Times: Story of an Assamese Tea Baron", Guwahati, 2007) the tea planters reportedly had a harrowing time. A facsimile of the 'invitation letter' was published in an issue of the Kolkata edition of the newspaper *Business Standard.*
8. Paul was assassinated by ULFA on 9 April 1990 near Dibrugarh in Upper Assam.
9. For details of how the tea industry in Assam has suffered, see Nitin Gokhale, *The Hot Brew: Assam Tea Industry's Most Turbulent Decade, 1987-97*, Guwahati, Spectrum Books, 1998.
10. Gokhale, *Hot Brew*, p 81.
11. At that time, the AASU leaders were not completely conversant with spoken English. They required the aid of an interpreter. The Late Prof. KN Sharma of Guwahati University acted as their interpreter. The then Governor of Assam, LP Singh, felt that an officer from the government should act as the interpreter for the Union Home Minister during his meetings and visits to riot-affected areas. I was then the Commissioner for Lower Assam Division. I was asked to work as the government interpreter.
12. *Khabar*, Assamese daily from Guwahati, 10 October, 2006.
13. *The Economic Times*, 16 October, 2006.
14. The Honourable Gauhati High Court judgment in Civil Rules nos. 23k, 2238, 2425 of 1990 and no.11 of 1991. Report of Assam Governor, 26 November, 1990, quoted in full. It is no longer confidential.
15. Jaideep Saikia, "Revolutionaries or Warlords: ULFA's Organizational Profile," *Faultlines*, 9 July, 2001, p. 121-23.
16. "Still Paying the Boys," *The Sentinel*, 11 February, 2002.

17. Ajai Sahani, "The Terrorist Economy in India's Northeast: Preliminary Explorations", *Faultlines*, 8 April, 2001, p 139.
18. "Centre's Money is not for Militants: Venkaiah," *The Sentinel*, 15 June, 2001.
19. Report of the Committee on Credit Related Issues under IRDP in North Eastern States, 2001, Ministry of Rural Development, Government of India.
20. Bibek Debroy, "Class Conundrum: India's Middle Incomers Set to Touch 600 million by 2007 are Characterized by Contradictions," *Week*, 30 December, 2001.
21. For a definition and description of the middle class see BM Bhatia, *India's Middle Class: Role in Nation Building* New Delhi: Centre for Policy Research and Konark Publishers, 1994.
22. Federation of Industries and Commerce of North Eastern Region, *Assam's Economy: A Fresh Perspective,* 2001.
23. Ajai Sahani and J. George, "Security & Development in India's Northeast: An Alternative Perspective," *Faultlines* 4, February 2001; and Ajai Sahani: "The Terrorist Economy in India's Northeast: Preliminary Explorations," *Faultlines*, 8 April, 2001.
24. *The Assam Tribune,* Guwahati. March 5, 2008.
25. As President of the Government of India's Staff Selection Commission's Interview Board for the North East Region, I had to interview hundreds of young men and women from Manipur. Most of them had degrees from universities outside their state. The candidates said that fear of terrorists made them leave their state, although their familys financial situation would not normally permit such a course of action.

CHAPTER – 6

Administrative and Police Reforms for Curbing Insurgency

Administrative Reform

In order to control or even to curb insurgency, a number of measures are essential. Elaborate research has been done and many methods have been suggested. Organised states will have to take these measures. They must be devised specially to strike at the factors which cause insurgency so that by removing or reducing the potency of the factors, the base itself is taken away. Administrative reforms will be one of the means which will facilitate preparation for taking such measures. It is these administrative reforms which this Chapter seeks to address. The first step in this direction will be to identify the major causes which lead to insurgency. In doing that the base adopted is India and specially the NE Region of India including mainly Assam where insurgency has become both intensive and extensive.

As a prelude to the main discussion it is perhaps necessary to mention that ever since independence in 1947 the Indian intelligentia has been apprehensive about the capability of the administrative system left behind by the British empire to tackle the myriad of problems in a newly democratic country where economic development has been taken up in a planned manner. Needless to say that during the British times administration had only two functions - maintenance of law and order and the collection of revenue. There was hardly any concern with development. Even the link with trade and commerce became peripheral in the later half of British rule. There was one line of control. Everyone in the British Indian administration had his own allotted slot. Everyone knew his duties and responsibilities. So long as he functioned within the contours of his own job and continued to show loyalty to the British Raj no one questioned him nor troubled him. All this changed in independent India in a major way. However, these were essentially political changes. Most of these changes were brought about by the Constitution of 1950 and specially by the provisions enshrined in its Preamble, Fundamental Rights and Directive Principles. But the administrative system and the administrative culture did not change much in response to the political changes.

During the first three decades of independence, several reports including those of Girija Shankar Bajpai (1947), N. Gopalaswami Ayyangar (1949), AD Gorwala (1951), and Paul H. Appleby (1953 and 1956) made many important recommendations for administrative reforms. A majority of these were not implemented. The first Administrative Reforms Commission (ARC) was set up in January, 1966. This ARC submitted 20 reports containing 537 recommendations. Some of these were implemented in part or in full. In the next two decades (1970s and 1980s) some more reform measures were taken. In 1985 Rajiv Gandhi emphasized training and decentralization. As a sequence to this emphasis, reforms in Panchayati Raj Institutions (PRIs) and Urban Local Bodies (ULBs) were brought about. The Second Administrative Reforms Commission was appointed in August, 2005. It is in the process of submitting its reports part by part. Already six reports have been submitted. The last one was on local governance. This Commission's terms of reference do not include insurgency specifically. But it has been asked, among other matters, to "suggest a framework to strengthen administrative machinery to maintain public order conducive to social harmony and economic development". It has also been asked to consider "capacity building for conflict resolution"[1] In its Approach Paper on "Reforms in Governance and Administration" it has been emphasized that "there is increasing lawlessness in several pockets of the country and armed groups are resorting to violence with impunity for sectarian or ideological reasons. The state apparatus is generally perceived to be largely inefficient with functionaries serving no useful purpose".[2]

A review of the recommendations made and the measures taken so far would indicate that administrative reforms have not been commensurate with the requirements of the delivery system for economic development in a democratic country. Meanwhile insurgency spawned by economic backwardness, ethnic aspirations, feeling of neglect, high unemployment, class discrimination, religious bigotry and other causes has brought about unrest and even disturbances.

Economic Backwardness

Insurgency's fertile ground is where economic backwardness, inequality and inequity prevail. Added to these is high unemployment which makes the youths uneasy. These are the youths who are prone to join insurgent outfits without much introspection. A look at insurgency ridden Assam will exemplify the situation. In Assam the per capita income, which was higher than the national average, started falling since 1950. I had recorded this phenomenon when my research in the 1980s brought this fact into sharp relief.[3] The present position seems to be that compared to the all India per capita income of Rs. 37,490 at current prices Assam's per capita income is Rs. 23,993 in 2008-09. In 2009-10 it is expected to rise to Rs. 26,242 which is also low.[4] If this trend is allowed to continue it is apprehended that Assam will lag further behind other states of India in the future. The below poverty line (BPL) population in Assam was 36.1 percent compared to the all India average of 26 percent in 1999-2000. Assam's BPL population is supposed to have fallen to 15 percent in 2004-05 according to the results of the 61st round of survey of the National Sample Survey Organisation (NSSO). But that is not believable because a 21 percentile point fall in 5 years from 1999-2000 to 2004-05 is just not possible. More so when the all India average has been estimated to have fallen to 21, that is, by only 4 percentile points in that same period. There is something wrong with the estimates.[5] In any case poverty in Assam is still very acute because the same 61st round of NSSO has estimated that the calorific value of food consumed in Assam is much lower at 2143 kilocalories compared to the minimum required of 2400 kilocalories per person per day. After protest by several states the Government of India appointed an Expert Group with Prof. Suresh D. Tendulkar as Chairman. This Group's Report shows that the current BPL ratio in Assam is 34.4 percent against the all-India ratio of 37.2 percent.[6]

India has changed during the period since 1990-91 when economic reform started the process of liberalization, privatization and globalization. The per capita income is going up. The GDP growth rate has registered 8/9 percent annual increase during the past few years. It is expected to sustain that rate during the next few years. What is reprehensible, however, is the fact that as in the past the recent growth also has not been inclusive. In fact the inter-regional and inter-personal disparities have got rather accentuated in recent years. Backward states such as Assam and Bihar seem to have lagged behind. Many of the below poverty line people also have had the same fate.

India's Middle Class

During this period the most significant development has been the rise of the Indian middle class. This class has proliferated. They seem to be cornering most of the benefits of development. They have big houses and apartments. Plenty of sleek cars and household goods and accessories. They spend substantial amounts of money on foreign jaunts and tours inside the country. Their children go to expensive schools and even to institutions abroad. They can afford many things which their predecessors of two/three generations ago could not even dream of. This class is making conspicuous consumption in such a vulgar way that others feel poorer. This rich-poor divide is affecting social cohesion adversely.

Those who work in multinational organizations, those who are in legitimate professions and business particularly in the information technology and similar high paying sectors and those whose ancestors have left behind realty and equity shares have become well off. In fact as a result of realty values going up and sensex rising many people are making enormous capital gains and unearned incomes. But a majority seem to have become rich by siphoning off government funds in many different ways such as kickbacks, scams, defalcations, frauds and grafts. They have actually distorted the plan priorities by using such ill gotten money on less priority sectors such as realty, films, luxury food and clothing, expensive education, elaborate healthcare and consumer durables. The tell-tale signs are there for all to see in the cities and towns all over India. In NE, Guwahati and Shillong are now full of malls and shops, apartments and big houses, hotels and restaurants, multiplexes and other luxury establishments.[7] Even smaller towns like Aizawl, Silchar, Nagaon and Kohima are not far behind.

Unemployment

Meanwhile population increase throughout the second half of the twentieth century added millions of young people to the already unemployed multitudes. These unemployed youths created great unhappiness in society. Some of them joined the insurgent units due to frustration and dejection. Some joined because it provided them with purchasing power. In Assam at least such entry into insurgent outfits had become fashionable in the initial stages. It provided the youths with an identity. Even parents used to take pride in their offsprings joining the ULFA and other outfits. Most ULFA leaders collected enormous amounts through extortion. They became really rich. They are reported to be having property and investments in Bangladesh. Some surrendered ULFA cadres (SULFA) have retained their ill gotten money. They have built posh bungalows in Guwahati's water front. Many of them have started hotels and restaurants, shops and boutiques, apartment blocks and commercial malls. They are now big businesmen.

I have always advocated that insurgency has to be fought on several fronts. The first and foremost step in this direction, in my view, will be to remove the present regional disparity through a more inclusive growth.[8] This will mean that the disparity in per capita income, the number of people below the poverty line and the per capita daily intake of food between the better off states and the poorer states must be reduced at the earliest. This can be achieved through more intensive capital infusion, greater emphasis on human resource development and arrangements for ensuring proper implementation of development projects. The first and the foremost requirement will be to reform the administrative structure so that it becomes development savvy.

Decentralization of the Delivery System

It is the flawed delivery system which must be reformed first. As several reports and studies had shown the present delivery system is not capable of bringing about economic development to the grassroots level. I feel that certain specific administrative reforms have become necessary to refurbish the delivery system. This will entail inducting more motivated personnel into the concerned government departments such as rural development, agriculture, horticulture, fisheries, industry and specially the cottage and small scale industries departments. When in the sixtees of the twentieth century Community Development Blocks were at the height of their glory there was a tremendous enthusiasm created at the Bloc level and the delivery system appeared to have been reasonably propped up. But it started deteriorating in most states within a short time. What is needed is to revamp this machinery. One method would be to induct more Non Government Organizations (NGOs) and Community Based Organisations (CBOs). The functionaries of NGOs and CBOs will need to be properly motivated. As in Bangladesh, they will have to give more importance to the social service ideals while joining these organizations after graduating from the Universities.[9]

Complete decentralization of development administration is a sine qua non of economic advancement. Article 243 of the Constitution has laid down the enabling provisions and the administrative machinery for decentralization. The Eleventh Schedule has listed 29 items which should be transferred to the Panchayati Raj Institutions (PRIs). The Twelfth Schedule similarly lists the 18 items to be transferred to the Urban Local Bodies (ULBs). Based on these constitutional provisions the states have amended and expanded their respective Panchayat Acts and Municipal Acts. Some states have gone ahead and completed the process of decentralization. But many states are yet to fully implement the provisions. In these states the line departments are refusing to transfer or effectively transfer the powers to PRIs and ULBs. Centralized purchases and departmental control over enormous funds released by the Government of India are devices which are used to subvert the Constitutional provisions by these line departments. The most obnoxious is the continued pre-eminence of extra-constitutional administrative structures such as the District Rural Development Agencies (DRDAs) through which a major portion of rural development funds are still channelised. Similar is the case with City Development Authorities which are appointed on political considerations and are not elected bodies. These are also extra-statal authorities.

The task of administrative reform in this area will be to empower PRIs and ULBs in accordance with the Constitutional and statutory provisions by transfer of functions, functionaries and finances. This will achieve the objective of better and proper participation of the entire population in the process of governance and decision making. It is not possible to adequately exemplify that such a result will necessarily follow decentralization. But it can be expected that once the general mass people are involved in the decision making process and the unemployed are absorbed in the economic development activities there will be lesser attraction to join the insurgent outfits. This conviction is based on the fact that enormous financial resources are now available for rural development. It will, of course, be necessary to buttress the process by vigorous adherence to transparency so that corruption is lessened. Already the Right to Information Act has been promulgated with a quasi judicial infrastructure for enforcement of its penal sections. Secondly, provisions have been made for social audit particularly in the Mahatma Gandhi National Rural Employment Guarantee Act (MGNREGA). These have enhanced the possibilities of transparency. The Fiscal Responsibility and Budget Management Act has restricted the administration's powers to finance unnecessary expenditure through fiscal deficits.[10] In Assam an excellent document for Activity Mapping was prepared in 2007. But the concerned departments are yet to implement its suggestions by transfer of functions, functionaries and funds to PRIs and ULBs. Similarly the detailed recommendations of the Third Assam State Finance Commission (2006-11) are being allowed to lapse by passage of time. This is unfortunate.

Agitations over ethnic grievances often result in insurgency.[11] One of the methods applied to curb such insurgency is the devolution of more power to ethnic groups through innovative designing of administrative structures to meet, to the extent possible, the demands made on the central power. This has been tried in many countries. The most recent case is that of Ireland.

Emergence of Nation States

In fact, ethnicity has played a very important role in the public affairs of different countries as has been explained in Chapter-1. Actually, ever since the Congress of Vienna of 1815 failed to prop up the universal empires nation states have started emerging in Europe. The German and the Italian unifications of the nineteenth century were the results of this idealism. Again ethnicity was the basis of the new nation states which emerged particularly after the Holy Roman, the Ottoman and the British empires broke up, one after another. Ethnicity was also the basis of formation of many nation states in Asia and Africa. The most recent examples are the nation states which emerged after the break up of the erstwhile Soviet Union and Yugoslavia.

In Assam and the NE sub-national aspirations of ethnic groups have led to vivisections into very small political units. These units have been sustained by substantial central financial assistance during the past half a century. Co-ordination among the units has been sought to be achieved through the establishment of North East Council (NEC) under an Act of Parliament. It was actually popular agitation followed by insurgency which propelled the process of break up of Assam and the innovation of a maze of new and smaller political structures to meet, to the extent possible, the ethnic aspirations. However, many of the ethnic problems remained unresolved. These will have to be addressed in order to find a solution of the nagging problems.[12]

The Unified Command Structure

One important innovation in the process of dealing with insurgency is the Unified Command system. Some such structure already existed in Jammu and Kashmir even before 1990. But the structure had not been formalized. When Bajrang operation was started against ULFA in November, 1990, the Unified Command consisting of civil administration, police, CRP, BSF, Army and others was introduced in Assam with the Chief Secretary as the head. This Unified Command is an apex body which co-ordinates the activities of the security forces dealing with insurgency. I had found the Unified Command to be quite effective during the period I had headed it from November, 1990 to February, 1995 as Chief Secretary, Assam. In 1996 its structure was reformed and revamped. This created the impression in the media and in the minds of the general public that the Unified Command system started operation only in 1996. Most people forgot that it had existed since 1990. In our time we had our share of difficulties. There were differences also. But we established good and co-operative working ethos among the members.[13]

Two aspects of the Unified Command need mention. One is the sharing of intelligence. We used to have a system by which the intelligence officers would meet separately and evolve a joint strategy. This was necessary in the interest of secrecy. But they would always keep others informed even if it was after the operations had been carried out.[14]

The other is that all units, while going out on operations, must be accompanied by a local police officer. Many embarrassing incidents occur because in their hurry Army sometimes fail to take the assistance of local police. In these cases Army had to face allegations, and even prosecutions for human rights violations. The very principle on which the Unified Command had been established is defied when the procedure of joint operation is not followed.

Recently the Chief Minister has been put as the head of the Unified Command in place of the Chief Secretary. I personally feel that it was wrong to have put the political head of Government in charge of an essentially executive and operational command structure. The Chief Minister can review the decisions taken by the Unified Command if these are contrary to the interest of the State. He can also reverse any decision which is not in the interest of the public. Similarly he can always intervene if he finds that human rights have been violated by the security forces. In our political system the Chief Minister has enormous powers and wields considerable clout. The present arrangement therefore needs immediate reversal.

The most important participant in the Unified Command is the police. Police has an unenviable task in controlling insurgency. It is the local police who have the training and the experience to find out any unusual or surreptitious movement or any missing person or persons in the locality. It is they who get the first sense about any secret meetings or confabulations held in the locality. There is less possibility of detecting insurgents and terrorists without the full assistance and co-operation of the local police. No outside agency can ever replace or supplant local police in the search for insurgents. There are, of course, rare exceptions which prove the rule again.

The Role of Police

Police have been subjected to various pressures in recent times specially in insurgent infested states like Assam. During the first Asom Gana Parishad (AGP) regime in 1986-1990, it was suspected that a section of the local police force were covertly supporting ULFA. Some instances of assistance to the ultras were cited. There were other instances of leakages of information about Army movements. Complicity in cases of extortion were also alleged. During the second AGP government (1996-2001) the Chief Minister (Prafulla Mahanta) himself was alleged to have been involved in secret killings (*Gupt Hatya*). A judicial commission headed by former Supreme Court Justice KN Saikia enquired into a large number of cases of such secret killings. This Commission found complicity of Mahanta in the secret killings. Again, during the first AGP government period local public support to ULFA was extremely high. Police had difficulty in obtaining information and spotting insurgents in the rural areas where the local public did not co-operate with them. In the circumstances there were aberrations. Even then the overall performance of police cannot be said to have been all that bad.

For dealing with insurgents attention must be paid to recruitment of proper personnel for the police. Proper personnel will mean young men and women with good physical strength, better motivation and higher education. They must be intelligent enough to match the insurgents. It has to be emphasised that the ULFA cadres are not only educated but cunning too. Their leaders are good strategists with high organizational abilities. Many ex-service personnel have joined the insurgent outfits specially in the Bodo areas. These people had good training and experience. They were experts in sophisticated weapons and in gathering intelligence. While in the Army or the paramilitary forces they were motivated to fight against the external enemies. Later they used the same skills to help insurgent units. Police will need proper grooming in order to face these types of rebels. One special school for counter-insurgency training has been started in Mizoram. Another is proposed near Tezpur. More such institutions will be necessary.

Different commissions and committees on the police force and police law have recommended many reform measures for improving the functioning of the police forces. It is important that these recommendations are given due weightage and implemented. In Assam an Expert Committee was appointed with Justice (Retd) S. Haque as Chairman to examine the suitability of the draft Model Police Act prepared by the Soli Sorabjee Committee and in accordance with the Supreme Court's order dated September 22, 2006. This Committee recommended many measures for amendment of the draft "keeping in view the existing laws and rules and the prevailing law and order situation in the state in view of insurgency, socio economic and political changes, the special problems faced by the Assam Police personnel, among others". The Committee's suggestions have been incorporated in the amended Police Act.[15]

Another important requirement is to upgrade the weaponry of the police forces. Steps were taken in this direction sometime ago and AK 47 and AK 56 rifles were introduced. But a systematic approach is necessary so that the sections of the police force which are engaged in insurgency control duty are properly armed and equipped.

In this process their communication network will also need modernization. Militant outfits are reported to be well equipped with modern communication networks. Recently a few ULFA cadres were arrested who had in their possession cellphone sim cards of middle level Congress leaders. They must have obtained these fraudulently by false representation. There are also instances of ULFA using remote control equipments in many cases of bombings.

A suggestion has been made by the Second ARC to separate criminal justice and investigation from the law and order functions of police. I also believe that police will be able to deal with insurgents more adequately if this recommendation is accepted. Under the present system both these functions are suffering. Criminal cases are getting delayed because law and order has the higher priority. Insurgency is not getting immediate attention because manpower is not sufficient. That is why there are frequent demands to the Government of India for more paramilitary forces by the affected states.

Meanwhile, organised gangs of extortionists have proliferated at tremendous speed in the mega and metropolitan cities including Mumbai, Delhi and Kolkata and even in smaller cities like Guwahati. This has spread to the rural areas in Bihar where gangs of Ranbir Sena attack and kill the Dalits. Mao and Naxalite insurgents have terrorized many localities in quite a few states including Bihar and Andhra Pradesh. They have made their presence felt in the tea gardens of Assam. A very concentrated effort will be necessary to weed them out or to curb their nefarious activities. Senior police officers will have to be drafted to evolve a strategy in each case to deal with such insurgent groups.

Terror Funding

Terror funding has become big business. Something has to be done about hitting at the sources of these funds. In Assam, tea industry provided funds to ULFA and other outfits since the beginning of insurgency. Later collection of funds became much more organized. Kidnappings for ransom have been many. In Nagaland it is suspected that a percentage of salary is collected as "tax" by the insurgent units from all government employees. Police personnel will have to be empowered to take action in an intelligent manner to stop this menace. For this the vigilance machinery in all government departments and offices will have to be geared up. The Unlawful Activities (Prevention) Act deals, inter alia, with financing of terror. The provisions of the Prevention of Money Laundering Act, 2002, can also be used in appropriate cases. But it is the corrupt government officials and ministers who are susceptible to extortions by the insurgents. When a public functionary siphons off government money he cannot deny a part of it if demanded by the insurgents. In this area the reform required will have to be all embracing. A big fight against corruption will have to be mounted.[16]

Deployment of Army

Army has been deployed in insurgency ridden Nagaland for more than 50 years continuously. Army has fought with the rebels and decimated them. But the rebels revived again and grew in numbers. From time to time media would report this or that Army general claiming that the rebels have been "finished" only to be proved wrong immediately thereafter by a fresh spate of violence. It is not easy to control insurgency which has the support of the mass people. Even the former Chief Ministers of Nagaland (SC Jamir) and Manipur (Rishang Keishing) had been accused of complicity with the rebels while in office by no less a person than one of the

Governors.[17] In Assam Army has been deployed to control insurgency for almost 18 years continuously. Here also Army has not succeeded fully in spite of the fact that the general public is no longer supporting ULFA. Allegations of support for ULFA at the highest level of AGP government had been made by one of the Governors in his report to the President.[18]

It is generally believed that Army should not be kept engaged in support of civil authorities for long. In Assam, Manipur and Nagaland, the situation has become almost intolerable. Army has developed fatigue and civilians have developed great antipathy towards the personnel in khaki against whom there are plenty of complaints of human rights violations and atrocities on innocent persons. Reforms will have to be carried out to ensure that Army remains within the confines of their own duties and police is strengthened and modernized to deal with insurgents adequately. This might take time. But it is essential.

The Armed Forces Special Powers Act

Beside the police the Assam Rifles have some special police powers in the North East which enable them to deal with law and order situations. The Armed Forces (Special Powers) Act was promulgated in Assam and Manipur with effect from September 11, 1958. This Act was later extended to other States of NE. Under this Act the state governments have power to declare an area as "disturbed area" when the state government fails to maintain internal peace in that area. The Act empowers Army officers to arrest any person without a warrant if that person is suspected to be engaged in any crime. It also enables such an officer to enter into and search any suspected premises without warrant. What is more is the empowerment of the Army officers "to fire upon or otherwise use force, even causing death". This is draconian. This has been deprecated by civil society for a long time. Many protests and agitations have been organised on this issue including the group of Manipuri women baring themselves in front of the Kangla Fort of Imphal and the long hunger strike by Sharmila Chanu. A Committee headed by Justice (Retd) Jeevan Reddy had recommended the repeal of the Act after inserting certain provisions into the Unlawful Activities (Prevention) Act. The Second ARC also made similar recommendations. But the Defence Ministry seems to have rejected these recommendations because they felt that if the armed forces have to work in this area personal protection must be ensured to them.[19] I am convinced that this draconian piece of legislation should be repealed immediately in order to assuage the feelings of the local people and to restore the human face of Indian democracy. Personal protection for the armed forces personnel acting in good faith may be provided by some other legislation. But the draconian provisions must go.

Intelligence

One area where the Government has failed very badly is intelligence. There are mammoth organizations like Research and Analysis Wing (RAW) and others. But they have failed to gather the correct information at the right time. Even police have not been up to the mark. Many police informers have been killed mercilessly by the ultras. Many others live in mortal fear. Something drastic, something urgent has to be done about intelligence and the training and motivation of intelligence personnel. Organisations such as the Israeli MOSSAD might help in training intelligence officers.[20]

Insurgency causes terrible damage to the economy. Its tentacles have spread deep and affect even the poor people in a backward economy.[21] It is important that administrative reforms, among other measures, are carried out to help control and curb insurgency.

Endnotes

1. The terms of reference of the second Administrative Reforms Commission. No. 15 in the Schedule attached to Government of India, Ministry of Personnel, Public Grievances and Pensions, Department of Administrative Reforms and Public Grievances Resolution No. K-11022/9/2004-RC dated August 31, 2005.
2. Government of India. Department of Administrative Reforms and Public Grievances. "Reforms in Governance and Administration. An Approach Paper of the Second Administrative Reforms Commission". New Delhi.
3. Das, HN: "A New Paradigm of Development. Regional Imbalance and Assam". *The Economic Times*, October 23, 1985.
4. The figures have been taken from the (i) "Economic Survey 2006-07" published by the Government of India, Ministry of Finance, Economic Division, New Delhi. February, 2007. (ii) Government of Assam. "Budget Speech of Finance Minister, 2007-08". Guwahati, March 12, 2007, and (iii) Government of India, Ministry of Statistics and Programme Implementation, National Sample Survey Organization: "Level and Pattern of Consumer Expenditure, 2004-2005. NSS. 61st Round (July, 2004-June, 2005)". New Delhi, December, 2006.
5. According to the Planning Commission's latest estimate based on NSSO's 61st round referred to at 11 and published through PIB's Press Note dated March 21, 2007 the BPL percentage of Assam has improved to 15 in 2004-05 compared to 36.1 in 1999-2000. This is unbelievable and will need very careful reexamination. Even the 61st NSSO data, on which the above estimate is based, seems to be flawed. In a recent informal meeting I have expressed my reservations and apprehensions on this matter to Dr. Pranab Sen, Secretary of the Ministry. See HN Das, "Is Assam Richer Than Maharashtra", *The Assam Tribune*, July 27, 2008.
6. Government of India, Planning Commission, "Report of the Expert Group to Review the Methodology for Estimation of Poverty", November, 2009.

7. Many Books and research papers are available on India's Middle Class. The following appear to be helpful: BM Bhatia *India's Middle Class.* Centre for Policy Research, Konark Publishers, New Delhi, 1994. (ii) Claudia Cragg: *The New Maharajas,* Rupa and Company, 1996.

8. Das, HN: "Insurgency and Development, the Assam Experience". *Faultline,* Volume 10. Institute of Conflict Management, Bulwork Books, New Delhi 2002.

9. Das, HN: "Grameen Bank of Bangladesh, Concept and Process". North Eastern Institute of Bank Management (now called Indian Institute of Bank Management) Guwahati, 1999. The second edition was published in 2008 by the Assam Gramin Vikash Bank, Guwahati. The third edition has been published in 2010 by the State Institute of Rural Development, Guwahati.

10. Das HN : "Good Governance in Assam : the need for Fiscal Responsibility Legislation". Dialogue. Vol. 5. No. 4. April-June, 2004. New Delhi.

11. Das, HN: "Ethnicity and Insurgency in North Eastern Region of India". Aakrosh. Asian Journal of Terrorism and Internal Conflicts. Vol. 7. No. 25. October, 2004. New Delhi.

12. For opposing views see : (i) BD Sarma : "Ethnicity and Self Governance in the North East", and (ii) Patricia Mukhim : "Negotiating Ethnic Identity in a Democracy". Both the articles were published in BB Kumar edited *Problems of Ethnicity in the North East India.* Astha Bharati, Delhi and Concept Publishing Company, New Delhi. 2007.

13. This became possible because of excellent personal relationships that existed among the seniormost officers who manned the Unified Command. From the Army I had very mature and enlightened officers to work with who actively participated in the deliberations. These included Lt. Gen (Retd) Ajay Singh, the present Governor of Assam. He was then the General Officer Commanding 4 Core at Tezpur.

14. As per laid down procedure all information had to be shared among the participants of the Unified Command. Once an Army detachment achieved a major breakthrough and probably wanted to take the credit for itself. So the Army officials informed the Eastern Army Commander at Kolkata

who came poste haste to Guwahati within a few hours. Meanwhile the ubiquitous local police got the information and then the report came up to the Chief Secretary through the usual channels. I tried to verify the information with the Army but could not get any confirmation at all. So I apprised the Chief Minister (Hiteswar Saikia) about it but told him that the news was yet to be confirmed. Meanwhile the Army released the news to the Press. But the Army's "one upmanship" did not work because the Chief Minister did not heed my warning and had spoken to the media first.

15. The Government of Assam's Expert Committee submitted its report in March 2007. This Committee reviewed and examined the Police Act, 1861 and made valuable suggestions. TL Baruah who had worked with me as Home Commissioner and Secretary for a long time during the worst days of ULFA insurgency was one of the important members of the Committee.

16. KL Malhotra, *Facets of Vigilance*, Himalayan Publishers, Delhi. 1988. It deals with proceedings on and punishment of government employees.

17. BB Kumar: "Ethnicity and Insurgency in India's North East," in *Problems of Ethnicity in North East India*. Astha Bharati and Concept Publishing Company, New Delhi, 2007. Also see : (i) Ved Marwah: *Úncivil Wars, Pathology of Terrorism in India.* Centre for Policy Research, Harper Collins Publishers. New Delhi. 1995. (ii) Vijay Karan: *War by Stealth, Terrorism in India.* Viking, New Delhi, 1997.

18. The Hon'ble Gauhati High Court Judgment in Civil Rule Nos. 23k, 2238, 2425 of 1990 and 11 of 1991. In this judgment the Report of Assam Governor dated 26.11.90 to the President was quoted in full.

19. For both the Second ARC recommendations on this point and the Defence Minister A K Antony's reaction see the issue of *The Hindu* dated June 27, 2007.

20. There are many writers on terrorism and insurgency like John Simpson, Anthony Summers, John Buchan, Michael R. Besthloss, Strobe Gabott, Erskine Childers, William Le Queux, Stephen Dorril, Ronald Kessler, Peter Hopking and others. About MOSSAD there are many books. But the following

may be helpful: Victor Ostrovsky and Claire Hoy, *By Way of Deception*. St. Martin's Press. New York. 1990. About British Intelligence the following is suggested: Robert Fleming with Hugh Miller. *Scotland Yard*, Michacl Joseph, London, 1994.

21. Das, H N: "Economic Consequences of Insurgency in Assam." *The Indian Police Journal*. Vol. L. No. 1. Jan- March, 2003, New Delhi.

PART - II

RELATED ESSAYS

CHAPTER – 7

Intelligence for National Security

Sitting in the breakfast room of the Harrington Hotel, only a few blocks away from the White House in Washington DC, I looked across the street through the plate glass window and saw for the first time the huge, ugly, monstrous and dreadful office building of the Federal Bureau of Investigation (FBI). This building has been named after J. Edgar Hoover. The FBI existed in different forms ever since July 26, 1908 when the US Attorney General Charles J. Bonaparte set up a permanent investigation team and then in 1909 named it the Bureau of Investigation. The name FBI was given in 1935. The FBI assumed power, clout and importance during the long period from 1924 to 1972 when its greatest Director, John Edgar Hoover was in office. It is said of Hoover that he "held more power in the United States, for longer, than any man in history. The creator of FBI and its Director for nearly fifty years, he played a key role in most of the great tragedies and scandals of our century. When he died in 1972, he was acclaimed as an American hero". But painstaking research has revealed that Hoover misused his power quite often. Among the allegations against him were that he "used his intimate knowledge of John F Kennedy's sex life to ensure that Lyndon Johnson became Vice President; suppressed evidence about Kennedy's assassination; was a secret homosexual, said to have enjoyed dressing up as a woman; was blackmailed by the Mafia; was a compulsive racist, tormented by the notion that he himself had black blood; died, on the eve of Watergate, holding some of President Nixon's darkest secrets" said Anthony Summers in his book entitled "The Secret Life of J. Edgar Hoover". Summers also made the damaging comment that "J. Edgar Hoover believed he could use his power to silence newspapers, to crush individual writers and thinkers, and to smother truth".

My look at the J. Edgar Hoover Building, FBI's head-quarters, on the warm morning of June 18, 2008 confirmed what I had read long ago in Ronald Kessler's monumental book entitled "The FBI". This is one of the scores of books on terrorism, anti-terrorism, espionage, spying and intelligence generally which I had read, browsed over and glanced through when I was Chairman of the Unified Command in my capacity as the Chief Secretary, Assam. I had then learnt that the FBI keeps dossiers on all important persons and all potential troublemakers through hundreds of offices in the USA and outside and thousands of agents spread all over the world. It has been said of the FBI that "no institution can obtain so much information and penetrate so deeply into private lives. And no institution plays a greater role in safeguarding America's freedom - or potentially threatening it". The FBI has become "the most important and powerful law enforcement agency in the world".

The USA has another organization, which is of equal importance. It is the Central Intelligence Agency (CIA), which was created in 1947, by the National Security Act. It is specially entrusted to deal with all foreign intelligence operations. The CIA is an independent agency "responsible for providing national security intelligence to senior US policymakers". The CIA has four basic components as follows: "the National Clandestine Service, the Directorate of Intelligence, the Directorate of Science and Technology and the Directorate of Support". In addition, CIA staffers also "deal with public affairs, human resources, mission innovation, protocol, congressional affairs, legal issues, information management and internal oversight".

In order to "accomplish its mission, the CIA engages in research, development and deployment of high leverage technology for intelligence purposes. As a separate agency, CIA serves as an independent source of analysis on topics of concern and also works closely with other organizations in the Intelligence Community to ensure that the intelligence consumer - whether Washington policymaker or battlefield commander - receives the best intelligence possible".

The Director of CIA is nominated by the President with the advice and consent of the US Senate. The present Director is Leon E. Panetta since February 13, 2009. The Director of CIA reports to the Director of National Intelligence. Over the decades CIA has become very prominent and important. It is feared and hated all over the world. It has been linked to scores of sinister happenings in many places. But it is the CIA which has helped the President and the other top functionaries of the US Government to take decisions on important matters of state.

In the United Kingdom, the headquarters of the Metropolitan London Police is called the Scotland Yard. It is housed in an elegant Victorian building near the Whitehall (seat of UK Government). I was fascinated by the big and eternally rotating metal wheel in front of the Scotland Yard, which is really a beautiful piece of sculpture. The Criminal Investigation Department (CID) functions out of Scotland Yard. It has achieved great expertise in collection and analysis of intelligence.

However, the real intelligence work is done in the UK by the Secret Intelligence Services (SIS). As the UK's secret service, "SIS provides the British Government with a global covert capability to promote and defend the national security and economic well being of the United Kingdom". While the Security Service (MI5) is "responsible for protecting the United Kingdom against threat to national security", the Secret Intelligence Service, generally known as MI6, which originated long ago in 1909, is the United Kingdom's external intelligence agency. MI5, the Government Communications Headquarters (GCHQ) and MI6 together form the intelligence network of the country. It is believed that in spite of safeguards to individual liberty these organizations have successfully committed "secret surveillance of the public" and that their activities include "the use of informers, infiltrators, wire tapping, checking on Bank accounts and opening mail". These intrusions are so pervasive that Stephen Dorril dedicated his famous book "The Silent Conspiracy : Inside the Intelligence Services in the 1990s" to 'the British Telecom engineer' who turned up and 'repaired' the unreported and non-existent fault on my telephone". Dorril then wrote, "May he find a more worthwhile occupation".

The most dreaded secret service organization that ever existed was the KGB or Komitet Gosudarstvennoi Bezopasnosti meaning Committee for State Security. It disappeared with the breakdown of the Soviet Union. While the secret police was Stalin's weapon of mass terror, during Khrusehev to Gorbachev period the "KGB was the party's "sword and shield" that "protected Soviet society from free speech, association and expression". The KGB meddled with politics and had a status higher than any of the Ministries in the Soviet Government. The KGB is reported to have carried out many executions at the behest of political functionaries. The KGB had many predecessors such as Okhrana, Chekra, GPU, OGPU, NKVB, NKGB and MVD. These were dreaded organizations. The KGB is now abolished and its old headquarters, a beautiful building, near Kremlin has been transformed into a Museum. While in Moscow I have had a good look at the building but could not find the time to visit the Museum, which is open to public. Vladimir Solovyov and Elena Klepikova in their, "Inside the Kremlin" give glimpses of the KGB's and the erstwhile Communist Party of Soviet Union's clandestine activities. The present Prime Minister, Vladimir Putin, who happens to be the most popular Russian politician, was head of KGB for some time. "The KGB's heirs are spin offs of two of its divisions: the First Chief Directorate became the Russian Foreign Intelligence Service (SVR) and the Second Chief Directorate became the Russian Security Ministry (MBR)".

The most efficient security and intelligence organization in the world is believed to be the Israeli one - MOSSAD or the Institute for Intelligence and Special Operations. It's motto is : "By way of deception, thou shalt do war". (Claire Hoy & Victor Ostrovsky : "By way of Deception : An Insider's Devastating Expose of the MOSSAD").

There are many secret service organizations in different countries. The Pakistani Inter Services Intelligence (ISI) and the Bangladesh Directorate General of Forces Intelligence (DGFI) are well known in India. Their sinister activities have caused great harm to Indian organizations inside the country and abroad. My object in writing this essay is to provide a basic, non-technical and non-controversial introduction to some of the internationally active secret service organizations to the general public in the context of Government of India's launching of the National Intelligence Agency (NIA).

CHAPTER – 8

The National Investigation Agency

In the wake of the mayhem unleashed in Mumbai on November 26-28, 2008 by a group of 10 Pakistani terrorists, which left 173 dead and 288 injured beside substantial damage to property, the National Investigation Agency (NIA) was launched on January 1, 2009. A day earlier the President of India had given assent to the National Investigation Agency Act, 2008 and the Unlawful Activities (Prevention) Amendment Act, 2008. The NIA has very wide powers. In most ways it is similar to the Federal Bureau of Investigation (FBI) of the United States of America.

On June 1, 2009, the Government of India decided to hand over two cases involving the alleged attempt by the Chief Executive Member (CEM), Mohit Hojai, of the North Cachar Hills (now called Dima Hasao) Autonomous District Council (NCHADC) to transfer Government funds, amounting to Rs. 1 crore, to the Jewel Garlosa faction of the Dima Halam Daogah (DHDJ), popularly known as the Black Widow. Earlier, on April 2, 2009, four youths had been arrested along with the money and some arms in the Assam-Meghalaya border. Two of them, Phajen Hojai and Bipul Kemprai were members of DHDJ and the other two were drivers.

The need for a federal agency to deal with cases of terrorism has been debated for a long time. It was realized that the maze of organizations that are working in the field of intelligence in India today are inadequate and lack proper co-ordination, if not efficiency and effectiveness. For co-ordination there is a National Security Council (NSC) with intellectuals and private functionaries as members and a Secretariat with three Deputy NSAs.

The other outfits which provide inputs to the NSA include the Intelligence Bureau (IB) which has offices in all cities and major towns and representatives abroad. It is the prime agency which collects information on terrorist activities.

Then there is the Research and Analysis Wing (R&AW), which like CIA in the USA and ISI in Pakistan, is concerned with India's external intelligence. There have been complaints that R&AW is inadequately manned and scantily funded. An Aviation Research Centre (ARC) is attached to R&AW. Besides, for collection and dissemination of data received from the satellites and other installations in space an outfit called the National Technical Research Organization (NTRO) has special responsibility. In the case of the defence services the Defence Intelligence Agency (DIA) collects inputs received from the Army, Air Force and Navy and supplies the filtered intelligence to the services. The Government of India also has the inputs from the Department of Revenue Intelligence (DRI), which gathers intelligence mainly on infringements of fiscal laws.

In the states there are various Special Branches (SB) and other intelligence outfits, which are suspected to be highly politicalised. However, these organizations can be prolific information collectors since they are close to the people and work in every hamlet, village, town and city. For this purpose the Criminal Investigation Department (CID) can also be of great help.

However, the existence of all these organizations and their continuously churning out reports has not ensured perfection in collection and dissemination of intelligence. That is why only 10 well-armed Pakistani terrorists could hold Mumbai to ransom and cause so much damage.

According to media assessment "intelligence failure, ill equipped forces, lack of co-ordination and apathy" had shown that "everything that could go wrong went in Mumbai" (*India Today*, December 15, 2008). There was no definite information that the Pakistanis were coming. They had a free passage by the sea route from Karachi to Mumbai. After they landed police did not react immediately. Information given by local residents was ignored. In the encounters a number of policemen unnecessarily lost their lives. It took 59 hours to clear Taj Hotel.

There were many commendable aspects of the operations by the Indian police and armed forces in Mumbai including specialized outfits such as the National Security Guards (NSG). But a co-ordinated approach was lacking. The absence of a full-fledged organization to take over investigation of and action on terror related cases was felt. Moreover, the strategy was not in place. In this regard what Barack Obama had said, as President-elect, is significant. He opined that "when you see what happened in Mumbai, that potentially points to a new strategy", (*Economic Times*, December 17, 2008).

In this context the launching of the NIA is the most important step taken by the Government of India. Actually, such an organization had been planned for quite some time. The Second Administrative Reforms Commission had recommended that "dealing with the menace of terrorism would require a comprehensive strategy in which different stakeholders, the Government, political parties, security agencies, civil society and media, would have an important role to play". According to the Commission political consensus, good governance and socio-economic development, respect for rule of law, countering the subversive activities of the terrorists, providing the appropriate legal framework and capacity building should be the elements of such a "multi-pronged strategy". It also recommended that "there should be convergence and co-ordination in the intelligence set up at the national level". The Commission recommended "the creation of a specialized division in the CBI to investigate terror offences". It further recommended "the enactment of a law using the 'residuary powers' and Entry 8, List I, to define the constitution of CBI, its structure and jurisdiction" and that "the changes made in the Delhi Special Police Establishment Act in 2003 should also be incorporated in the new law". It may be recalled that CBI had been constituted under the Delhi law.

However this time the Government of India did not follow the ARC recommendations. In my view the Government of India did better because reorganization of CBI would have been some kind of a patchwork. The NIA is a fresh beginning. Such a decision was facilitated by the long debate on the matter. In fact, soon after the serial terror attacks in Bangalore and Ahmedabad, which claimed 50 lives, a high level meeting was held on August 8, 2008, which was attended by the State Chief Secretaries and DGPs. It proposed the setting up of "a federal crime fighting agency" and the strengthening of "intelligence gathering mechanism at the grassroot level". The Chief Ministers did not attend the meeting. Some of them opposed the proposal on the specious reasoning that law and order is a state subject and that the Government of India should not interfere in this matter. This plea was rejected.

On September 17, 2008 addressing the Governors' Conference, the Prime Minister asserted that although Indian security and intelligence agencies had averted a few terrorist attacks, inspired by Pakistan, the blasts at Jaipur, Bangalore, Ahmedabad, Surat and Delhi could take place because "there are still vast gaps in intelligence". He mentioned the needs for amendment of the law relating to terrorist activities and for setting up of a new investigation agency. He emphasized "the need for ensuring better co-ordination and integration among the existing agencies for devising an effective counter terrorism strategy".

Under the newly passed law the NIA will take up investigation of cases, which are referred to it. A two-judge committee will decide, within seven working days, the cases to be referred to the NIA. The Government's decision on the cases will also be taken in as many days.

Beside law and NIA, work has started on 20 anti-terrorist and counter insurgency schools. Moreover, the Multi Agency Centre (MAC), acting as a nodal agency on all terror-related intelligence, has become operational around the clock. What is significant is that "MAC has to share inputs with all intelligence agencies, including agencies of State Governments and Union Territories and vice versa". Subsidiaries of MAC will be established in all state capitals. The Union Home Minister is reported to have expressed the view that there would be "distinct improvement" in the "gathering and sharing of intelligence relating to terrorism, terrorist threats and terrorist offences". NSG hubs are being established in four cities. More such hubs will be established in other cities. (*Economic Times,* January 1, 2009).

NIA has started working on two Assam cases. These are the first cases to be taken up by the NIA. As the Union Home Ministry release dated June 1, 2009 said, "preliminary investigations have revealed that the funds (seized from the arrested insurgents) were meant for an underground/insurgent group for procurement of arms and ammunitions and other terrorist related activities... Having regard to the nature of the cases.... and the offences involved therein, the Central Government..... decided to direct the NIA to take over the investigation of these cases in exercise of the powers under Section 6 (5) of the NIA Act".

It may be recalled that momentous events have taken place in the NCHADC areas since April, 2009. Beside the recovery of the money and the arrest of the insurgents, the CEM has been arrested on May 30, 2009 along with the Joint Director of the Social Welfare Department, RH Khan, who is alleged to have master minded the withdrawal from the Bank and the subsequent transfer of government funds to the insurgents. In a press conference held on May 30, 2009 the Assam Chief Minister had admitted that development funds had been diverted to the insurgents. The second most important event was the arrest of the DHDJ chief Jewel Garlosa himself along with two of his accomplices (Ahshringdaw Warisa and Samir Ahmed) from their hideouts in Bangaluru on June 4, 2009. Meanwhile, DHDJ's Foreign Secretary, Frankie Dimasa, was killed in an encounter in Guwahati. He was making arrangements for DHDJ's shifting their base to Bangladesh. These two events inflicted a deathblow on DHDJ, which had been formed in 2006 after breaking away from the original DHD (Nunisa Group). The latter had declared a ceasefire in that year. The DHDJ had stopped the construction work on the East-West corridor and the railway track conversion into broad guage in NCHADC and nearby areas, killed 70 odd innocent people and 35 security personnel and harassed scores of company executives and engineers through kidnappings and extortations. The DHDJ, now under its Deputy Commander-in-Chief, Denial Garlosa, has declared a unilateral ceasefire with effect from June 7, 2009. But the police suspect this to be a strategy to gain time to reorganize the DHDJ cadres. Therefore, the Chief Minister has rejected the proposal.

What is significant, however, is the fact that the two cases were suo moto handed over under section 6 (5) of the NIA Act, 2008. This has been interpreted by some as a snub to the State Government of Assam because the alternative procedure of registering a case in the relevant police station and then the State Government moving the Central Government to hand over to the NIA would have looked more decent.

The NIA has been given very wide powers of investigation. In the NIA Act there is provision for Special Courts for trial in such cases. Under Section 6 (9) "a State Government shall extend all assistance to NIA for investigation of terror related offences." So the State Governments cannot put any hurdles in the path of the NIA.

Under the Unlawful Activities (Prevention) Act, 1967, after its amendment in 2008, an accused can be detained without trial for 180 days. This Act has defined "terror acts" to include "use of bombs, dynamite, poisons or noxious gases, biological, radioactive, nuclear substances". Punishment upto 10 years imprisonment for "aiding, abetting or committing a terrorist act" has been provided. Similarly, for "funding terror activities, organizing training camps and recruiting persons for committing terror acts" the imprisonment can be upto five years. A draconian provision has also been added. It is that the "court shall presume, unless the contrary is shown, that the accused has committed the offence". The NIA will have all the powers invested in it by the NIA Act, 2008 and the procedure and punishment prescribed in the Unlawful Activities (Prevention) Act, 1967, as amended in 2008, should be able to assist the Central and the State Governments to control terrorist activities in India and prevent a replication of the Mumbai attack.

CHAPTER – 9

Guarding India's Integrity

Lt. Gen. (Retd.) SK Sinha PVSM, former Governor of Assam and Jammu and Kashmir, has penned a most remarkable book titled "Guarding India's Integrity", published by Manas Publications, New Delhi, it contains two forewords - one by the former President APJ Abdul Kalam and the other by the former Prime Minister Inder Kumar Gujral. Within the confines of 375 pages, Sinha has written very ably and concisely about his experiences. In the chapter on "Mission Assam" Sinha gives a panorama of the recent events particularly during his tenure of office and in the background of the troubled times of the past few decades. Similar is the case with the chapters on Jammu and Kashmir - "Paradise in Peril: Kashmir Imbroglio" and "Amarnath Controversy and After". The omnibus chapter "Interlude" contains Sinha's thoughts and impressions during the time he was free of any major assignments.

Those of us who were connected with the affairs of Assam would remember that among the Governors in the recent past the most pro-active ones were BK Nehru, LP Singh and SK Sinha. All of them were retired Government officers. Nehru made strong representations of the State's problems to the Centre but failed to achieve any success. Singh tried to bring about cohesion among the sub-federating units through the North-Eastern Council. His success was partial.

Sinha focused on the problem of identity of the indigenous people. He could not persuade the Centre to take any effective steps. But he could convince some of the mainstream leaders that the Assam problems were real and that the enormous and unrelenting infiltration of Bangladeshis into Assam was making the Assamese people a minority in their own land. Where he immensely succeeded was in giving stature and status to the local heroes in the all India scene. The trinity of Sankardeva, Lachit Barphukan and Gopinath Bordoloi, "the three highly revered icons of the Assamese people", received his special attention, and he decided to "promote awareness about them in the whole country". It is only since Sinha's time that the Governors and Chief Ministers of Assam have taken their oaths below the painting of Sankardeva in the Durbar hall of the Rajbhawan. Similarly it was through Sinha's efforts that Lachit Barphukan's military strategy has come to be well appreciated by every commissioned officer of the Indian Army. Gopinath Bordoloi's elevation by the posthumous conferment of Bharat Ratna and the naming of the Guwahati Airport after Bordoloi are also Sinha's achievements which the Assamese people will remember long.

Actually Sinha has been familiar with the State ever since he was posted at Palasbari as a nineteen-year old subaltern in the Indian Army. Like many young people coming to the verdant Brahmaputra valley he fell in love with the landscape. But, unlike most other Army officers, Sinha established an empathy with the local people which, after four more tenures in the State, flowered into deep love and respect for different ethnic groups. Therefore, as Governor he spared no pains to fight, in his own inimitable way, to solve the local problems. He encountered many hurdles and had to go through very difficult processes. But he managed to achieve success in some of his ventures although he had his "share of failures" as he himself has admitted. All of this he did because of his "deep attachment for the people of Assam" and also because he "strongly felt that it was in our national interest to get the alienated people of Assam into the national mainstream".

His greatest contribution to the State is his famous 42 page special report personally submitted on November 8, 1998 to President KR Narayanan at Guwahati on illegal migration from Bangladesh. This report was "based entirely on security and demography considerations. It was in the interest of the people of Assam, irrespective of their religion and also in the interest of national security". According to Sinha, "there were some senior and respected Assamese Muslims who had agreed with my views". Sinha has rightly claimed that "it was a matter of great satisfaction to me that the Supreme Court gave a landmark verdict upholding my recommendation on repealing the controversial IMDT Act, 1983 and quoting extensively from my report on the subject to the President". The case in the Supreme Court had been filed and successfully argued by Sarbananda Sonowal, who became a hero for the Assamese people and was subsequently elected to the Lok Sabha.

The most controversial of Sinha's decisions, which irked many Congress and other political party leaders, was his refusal to sanction prosecution of Prafulla Kumar Mahanta, the then Chief Minister, against whom CBI had submitted definite charges in court in the LOC scam case. Sinha's clarification explaining why he came to his controversial decision could not convince his detractors. Even "the CBI hierarchy was very upset" with his decision. It was pointed that Sinha had erred in drawing the conclusion that "Mahanta's criminal culpability could not be proved" although "he could not escape moral and political responsibility for this scam".

Many people have written about Assam and the North-East in recent years. But Sinha excels in his deep understanding of the sentiments and the aspirations of the people and in his serious concern for their wellbeing. This is one man who really loved Assam.

CHAPTER – 10

Leader with a Vision

Two images of childhood still remain indelibly etched in my mind. These images have not been tarnished or erased by almost seven decades of aging in a milieu of economic development, social transformation and political change. Both these images are of meetings in erstwhile Jubilee Garden of British days in the heart of Panbazar, Guwahati, which was later vandalised by some unimaginative and insensitive engineer planners to build an ugly waterworks. We used to play in Jubilee Garden. We also learnt our political lessons here. Our younger siblings used to enjoy the functions held by "Moina Parijat".

The first meeting was addressed by Muhammad Ali Jinnah. He was dressed in an impeccable English suite with a necktie to match. He travelled in an open car from the residence of Khan Bahadur Muhammad Ida Khan, a rich and prominent PWD contractor, who lived in a brick-walled and colonnaded bungalow in a sprawling compound on the eastern edge of Lakhtokia. There is a multi-storied industrial bank and other establishments in that compound now. A Punjabi by birth Ida Khan was lame. So his friends nicknamed him as Amir Taimur. He was friendly with all sections of society. I do not remember the language in which Jinnah spoke. But his speech was translated into Assamese by Sir Muhammad Saadullah. I did not understand the contents of the speech. But Jinnah seemed to have taken umbrage at what, according to him, was Congress's attitude towards the Muslims. Jinnah compared British India with an orange. While the Muslim League had asked for only one fourth of that orange, the Congress would not agree. The Congress party wanted the whole orange. The crowd, which filled every nook and corner of Jubilee Garden, seemed to have been excited since before the meeting started. They interrupted both Jinnah and Saadullah at regular intervals shouting, *Allah Ho Akbar* and *Larke Lenge Pakistan.* Actually there was a lot of propaganda during the previous few years in favour of Pakistan, especially by the Sayed Abdul Malik edited Assamese periodical *Paigam.* That is why the crowd was so excited.

The second was a public meeting when a huge but quiet crowd awaited at Jubilee Garden for the arrival of Gopinath Bardoloi after his famous meetings in New Delhi, when Bardoloi opposed the "Grouping" proposal of the Cabinet Mission, which would have pushed Assam to East Pakistan. In New Delhi, Bardoloi had obtained the support of Mahatma Gandhi. All the then Congress leaders including Bisnuram Medhi, Muhammad Tayebullah, Siddhinath Sarma, Bijoy Chandra Bhagawati, Fakhruddin Ali Ahmed, Harikrishna Das, Bhubaneswar Barua and others were there in the Jubilee Garden that day. The meeting was organized by Lakshidhar Bora, Radhika Ram Das (my father's brother), Rabin Nabis and Biswa Goswami. Even as a child, I knew all of them by face and by name. I do not remember the date. But the Cabinet Mission's proposal was announced on May 16, 1946 and Bardoloi submitted his Memorandum to the Congress Working Committee in New Delhi on May 19, 1946. The public meeting in Guwahati must have been held in June or July, 1946.

I heard the term *Satyagraha* ('firmly adhering to truth') for the first time in that meeting. This term, coined by Mahatma Gandhi, imbued generations of Indians with an idealism and a fervour to fight for freedom of the country through non-violent methods. The present generation of Indians may not comprehend the strength of idealism and the potency of *Satyagraha* in these days of pragmatism and consumerism. But, they must have read or heard about the movement that was built up and how *Satyagraha* worked against the mightiest universal empire set up through military conquests and trade in all the continents of the world.

All those memories, stored since childhood, zoomed back to me when I saw Dr. Nirode Kumar Barooah's book *Ejon Satyagrahir Rajniti* (Politics of a Satyagrahi) published in January, 2010. The book is sub-titled *Gopinath Bordoloi Aru Assam, Tetia Aru Etiya* (Gopinath Bordoloi and Assam, then and now). Going through the 626 pages of this monumental tome and recollecting the memorable events of small town Gauhati, and not very big Assam of those halcyon days, I really marvelled at the tenacity and perseverance of the author who has brought together so much of data and information within the covers of this remarkable book. Decades of research through innumerable books, newspapers, magazines, correspondence, documents, records of interviews and even personal dairies of a number of important people have made this book readable. But it is the acutely discerning and scientifically analytical mind of Barooah which has brought out the nectar after churning the ocean of research materials.

About Bardoloi's philosophy and his commitment to the cause of Assam, Barooah's book is replete with analytical details and information. Barooah does not mention, but many sensitive members of civil society know how, at Bordoloi's instance, Saadullah joined Congress after partition and became one of the seven member committee which drafted India's Constitution. We also know how Malik changed track and created great literature after partition. Both of them became nationalists after they failed to take Assam to Pakistan.

Today's enlightened, but pragmatic, generation of Assamese youths are not familiar with honesty, sacrifice and ideology of the politicians of Bordoloi's days. They need to be educated about how politicians of those days behaved and performed their duties. Barooah's book will help the present generation to learn about the political leaders who fought for India's freedom.

CHAPTER – 11

Bisnuram Medhi and Bangladeshi Infiltration

During the twentieth century the most acute problem that Assam faced was that of the transformation of its demographic profile due to continuous and relentless immigration of Bengali people from across its borders. One man who sincerely tried to prevent the flow, against all odds, was Bisnuram Medhi both as Revenue Minister (1946-1950) in the Bordoloi cabinet and as Chief Minister (1950-1957). The present generation of Assamese people are not familiar with the events of those times and are unaware of the role that Medhi played during that crucial period of Assam's history. After considerable and painstaking research Pramod Chandra Medhi has now brought into light the different facets of Bisnuram Medhi's life and works in a compact volume entitled *"Louho Manab Bisnuram Medhi"* (Iron Man Bisnuram Medhi). This book in Assamese, with numerous quotations in English, will be an important addition to the literature that is available for a peep into one of the most difficult periods of Assam's history.

This book brings back the memories of what I saw and knew about Bisnuram Medhi during my childhood and youth. I remember visiting Medhi's Latasil, Uzanbazar residence as a child with my mother. In the smalltime Guwahati of the 1940s almost every one knew every one else. Medhi was a successful criminal lawyer and had made plenty of money. The glass windows of his house and the Assamese silk curtains impressed me most. Later, I saw his Hajo residence which is probably one of the finest specimen of Assam-type architecture with timber, mortar and glass. Medhi was a "stylish man".

Once I was summoned to his residence to attend a meeting of important personalities to discuss about arrangements to be made for holding the Hills and Plains Festival in Guwahati. I happened to be the General Secretary of the Cotton College Union Society. In those days students who topped the list in the University examinations used to be normally elected to this position unlike the present day practice of electing politically motivated student leaders. In that meeting I was given the responsibility of providing student-volunteers for the festival which was held on January 26, 1954. When the meeting was over Medhi called me aside and advised me to try for the Civil Services Examinations.

My next meeting with Medhi was in the winter of 1961. In December, Mussoorie becomes very cold with heavy snowfall and all the IAS probationers are taken out on a "*Bharat Darshan*" tour from the Academy of Administration. In Madras we were taken to the Guindy Rajbhawan where Medhi was then residing as Governor. Medhi spoke to us in great detail about our duties and responsibilities and advised us to serve the country sincerely and diligently. Just before we left the Rajbhawan I revealed my identity. Medhi was very pleased to know that I had succeeded in the IAS examination and he told his Personal Assistant - Bhim Sekhar Barua - about my uncle - Radhika Ram Das - who had been Medhi's junior colleague as State Minister of Education and Revenue. My uncle later served in Bimala Prashad Chaliha's Ministry also.

I met Medhi for the last time when he stopped over at Mangaldai Circuit House sometime in 1965 on his way back from Tezpur to Guwahati. Earlier he had demitted office as Governor of Madras. I was about to leave Mangaldai on promotion to the State Secretariat at Shillong. In those days Mangaldai was a sub-division of the erstwhile Darrang district (with headquarters at Tezpur). Mangaldai sub-division consisted of the present day districts of Darrang and Udalguri. I was the Sub-Divisional Officer during 1963-65. Medhi asked me about the progress of work under the Pakistani Infiltration Post (PIP) scheme, which had been started by the Government of India to stop further immigration of Bengali Muslims.

This introduction will show that I had been impressed by Medhi's personality even as a child and as a youth. Reading the book under review I remembered many of the things that I had heard long ago. For example, Medhi had vehemently opposed Assam being used as the dumping ground for East Bengal Hindu refugees. The then Prime Minister Pandit Jawaharlal Nehru and other central ministers and officers were under the wrong impression that Assam had plenty of vacant land. Medhi pointed out that the vacant lands were in the hills where tribal people lived and were unsuitable for refugees and that the plains districts were already over-crowded. But Nehru was angry and he wrote to Bordoloi on May 10, 1949 as follows, "I understand that Medhi your Finance Minister is a strong opponent of any further refugees coming to Assam. I think he is wrong in this. I am sending a copy of the letter to him also so that he may know my views on the subject". In another letter on May 18, 1949 Nehru almost issued a veiled threat. He wrote to Bordoloi that "if Assam adopts an attitude of incapacity to help in solving the refugee problem then the claims of Assam for financial help obviously suffer". Such letters coming from a Prime Minster of Nehru's stature would have created fear in any other state minister's heart, but not Medhi. He stood steadfast in his resolve.

One of Medhi's staunch supporters - Rabin Kakati - has left a note in which he described how Medhi prevented the sinister designs of Muslim League to occupy grazing reserves, forest reserves and other vacant lands by sending hordes of armed Bengali Muslims shouting slogans of "*Larke lenge Pakistan*" in 1946. They even tried to occupy Police Stations, Circle Offices and other Government buildings. Medhi deputed his trusted officers to frustrate such designs.

During the Refinery movement also Medhi played a pro-active role. He pleaded for the Refinery based on Assam oil to be located in Assam. In reply Nehru wrote back to him on June 14, 1957 as follows, "I am sorry we have to disagree with you on this (Oil Refinery) matter. We have every regard for the feelings in Assam. But we cannot obviously decide something against our judgment and we think that it will not be advantageous even to Assam......." In another letter to the then Assam Governor Fazal Ali on June 12, 1957 Nehru stated the following, "The Defence Chiefs having examined these various schemes, said definitely that they would not undertake to protect the refinery if it was situated in Assam or the pipeline of it went to Calcutta along the Pakistan border. The strong and definite statement by those responsible for our defence and security could not be ignored. For all these reasons we could not accept the proposal to have the refinery in Assam". Medhi shot back a reply to the Prime Minister as follows, "We are unable to understand the arguments advanced by the Defence Department against the location of Oil refinery in Assam. If the Defence Department cannot undertake the protection of the Oil refinery located in Assam how will they protect the oil fields and the transport system in the eastern region?" Medhi further argued that "The knowledge of the fact that the refinery is not going to be located in Assam for reasons of defence will scare away all the intending industrialists from coming to Assam and thus prevent the industrial development of the State". Medhi obtained the services of a French expert named Fritz. This expert confirmed that the refinery should be located in Assam (The *Assam Tribune*, August 15, 1957).

The present generation of political leaders are not aware that the Central Government's attitude, particularly its refusal to appreciate the critical problems that Assam faced in the first decade of independence, was responsible for the later disturbances and insurgency in Assam.

CHAPTER – 12

Bomb Blast of October 30, 2008

International attention was drawn by the serial blasts of Thursday, October 30, 2008 at Guwahati, Barpeta Road, Bongaigaon and Kokrajhar. This is for the first time that the Government of India have shown so much concern over an incident in Assam. The Union Home Minister rushed to Assam next day to take stock of the situation. He stayed for two days. The Prime Minister and the United Progressive Alliance (UPA) Chairperson Sonia Gandhi came two days later. The Government of India also deputed teams of experts to assist in police, intelligence and forensic investigations. The international community, including the President of the United States of America, expressed their shock and dismay at the incidents and condemned the perpetrators.

Several aspects of Black Thursday deserve special mention. It is evident that the entire operation must have been planned centrally and meticulously by the terrorists. Therefore, all the blasts could be synchronized to go off within a period of 13 minutes. Remote control and Programmable Time Delay devices (PTD) were used. It was a difficult task and very complicated manoeuvre were involved. Large quantities of explosives were used. In the Guwahati blasts RDX used was estimated to be 80 kgs. Besides, high quantities of ammoniam nitrate was mixed. It is reported that in no other bomb blasts in India such high quantities of explosives were used. Congested locations were chosen in order to maximize the casualties.

According to unofficial estimates about 100 people were killed and 500 were injured. There was heavy loss of property, including destruction of motor-bikes, cars and other vehicles. Shops and trading establishments were badly damaged causing great loss to a large number of marginal businessmen.

Immediately after the bomb blasts one ambulance vehicle was burnt down in Ganeshguri. A couple of fire brigade vehicles were also burnt down. Damage was caused to a number of public and private vehicles. It is not clear whether this was done by the same people who planted the bombs or by the irate crowd who had lost their kith and kin.

The blast affected all communities. An impression is sought to be created that the indigenous people were specially targetted. However, this impression cannot stand scrutiny except in the vicinity of the Baptist church near Kamarpatty, Guwahati, where people from one particular village - Soalkuchi - had their silk shops. No big insurgent or terrorist outfits claimed responsibility immediately after the blasts. Actually, the United Liberation Front of Assam (ULFA) and the National Democratic Front of Bodoland (NDFB) vehemently and repeatedly denied that the respective organizations were involved in the blasts.

There was a feeble attempt to thrust responsibility on an organization called Islamic Security Forces (Indian Mujahidin). An apparently fake SMS message dated 30.10.08 was also flaunted. But it was found that this organization did not exist any more. Therefore, the attempt to project it as responsible for the blast could not be sustained. It was probably a fake claim. Actually, several Muslim organizations had been formed since 1990s to protect the community against attacks by Bodos, specially NDFB and BLT (Bodo Liberation Tigers), whose object was ethnic cleansing. Many of these Muslim organizations combined under the banner of ISF (IM) in about 2000. This arrangement, however, fizzled out within a short time.

Different people, political parties and civil society organizations have tried to blame different terrorist outfits for the bomb blasts. Because of the severity, the spread and the synchronization it was suspected that only a resourceful organization with mass following like the Harkat-ul-Jehadi-e-Islami (HUJI) could have done it. Actually several Muslim suspects were apprehended in different places. On the day of the blast and about the same time that the bombs went off one Azizur Rahman was arrested while carrying a bomb in Tezpur town. One Muhammad Saidul Isra (25), a brick kiln worker from Assam, was arrested in Perambadur area near Calicut in Kerala. He was found to have sent SMS messages to several mobile phones in Assam around the time of the blasts.

The Students Islamic Movement of India (SIMI) had been banned some time ago. It is alleged that SIMI has now reappeared under a new name - Shaheen Force. They are suspected to have played a role in the incidents. One top HUJI leader from Bangladesh - Jehangir - is suspected to have planned the entire operation under the direction of Pakistan's Inter Services Intelligence (ISI). It is reported that immediately after the blasts Jehangir escaped to Bangladesh via Garo Hills in Meghalaya. Another unconfirmed report blamed the blasts on a top official - Ahmad Shah Gilani - who is supposed to be in charge of operations in India's North Eastern Region (NER) and who is supposed to have planned the bomb blasts. Media has reported that according to Rabiram Brahma, President of BPPF, the main culprit is Tahid Molla, who had sold all his wares from his shop in Kokrajhar after the bomb blasts and disappeared. Molla is reported to be in the "most wanted" list of West Bengal police and to have been linked with various organizations.

One Moinul Haque, a professional car lifter, was arrested for supplying the vehicles used in the blasts. Along with him a Guwahati city traffic constable - Anwar Hussain - was also arrested. Car thefts are rampant in Assam. A total of 6,534 cars were lifted in Assam during the past 5 years. Only 852 were recovered. Many of these were used for bomb blasts and decoity. Huge amounts of explosives were recovered from one Moinuddin of Bihubar of Sivasagar district. Earlier, one Niazuddin had been picked up from his residence in Geleki of the same district with 2 kgs of RDX, 26 detonators and 5 meters of cotex cables. But the HUJI leader who is directing the terrorists in Assam - Ikbal - has not yet been identified. Another HUJI - Aziz Raja - stays in Bangladesh but is keeping link with Ikbal. The ISI operations all over India are controlled by Abdur Sovan.

From across the border a HUJI group of 10 are reported to have entered Assam about the time of the blasts. Some names were also mentioned including Md. Mustafa, Alsunal Kabir, Aftab Ahmed, Rizwan Ahmed, Abu Sahib and the only woman - Sahiba. Earlier it was suspected that Sahiba was killed in the Ganeshguri blast. It has been now discovered that Sahiba is alive and she along with her other group members might be planning some more blasts. It has been reported in the local media that some Bangladesh newspapers rejoiced that such great damages have been wrought by the blasts. Local media also stated that an SMS message was received from Bangladesh which expressed satisfaction over the blasts and asked the persons concerned to go to the next destination. It has been also reported that *El Ihsan* of Dacca in its edition dated 04.11.08 had called for a jehad against India because of alleged atrocities on Muslims. It is not certain to what extent these reports can be believed. But in his Press Conference of 11.11.08 the Chief Minister, Tarun Gogoi said that a third force from across the border was the brain behind the blasts. He probably hinted at someone from Bangladesh.

All this must have prompted many people to blame the Islamist terrorists. But Islamic organizations feel that this is unfair because there is no hard evidence to implicate HUJIs or other Muslim outfits with the bomb blasts. That is why many Islamic organizations have protested.

Many arrests were made from among the members of NDFB. Officially, however, NDFB denied any involvement. Its Publicity Secretary, S. Sanjarang, said that NDFB cannot be blamed for the "inhuman acts" simply because the vehicles used in the blasts belonged to some Bodo people. NDFB denied that Bodo people arrested were its cadres. But the most important allegation against NDFB was that its cadres were not observing the terms of the ceasefire agreement. In the Borbari Designated Camp in the Baksha district, for example, the total number of inmates registered were 204. But only 144 were found to be present inside the camp on 21.11.08. The others were absent. Some had gone home on leave but many had just "gone out". In the Udalguri Designated Camp the number registered was 235. The number found on inspection was 209. There are 4 other such camps in Udalguri district. According to Standard Operating Procedure (SOP) there are two commandants - one from NDFB and the other from Police. However, the decision of the Police Commandant prevails. There is no restriction on movement of camp inmates. It has now been decided that entry and exit of camp inmates must be properly recorded and regulated. There are allegations that many inmates go out, make mischief and then come back to the camp. There is a report that the Government of India may review the terms of SOP when the ceasefire agreement comes up for revision.

At least 2 inmates had to be arrested for interrogation in connection with the bomb blasts. They were P. Fawthai alias Pabitra Boro and R. Kherja. Another 4 NDFB cadres had also been arrested. But they had to be released because no evidence could be collected against them. All three Maruti cars used in the bomb blasts in Guwahati - at the district court, Ganeshguri and Kamarpatti - were kept in the house of school teacher named Punkha Brahma at Dantalpara in Ambari-Fatasil area of the city. The day before the blast, i.e., on 29.10.08 these were driven away by Dinesh Boro, Thumpi Narzary and Mridul Basumatari.

One of the most important arrests was that of Chabin Boro alias B. Susungra who was taken into custody on 12.11.08. He was the former self-styled home minister of NDFB. After his arrest his sister and the two wives claimed that he had formally left NDFB 11 months ago. According to them he was in his Zoo Road rented house on the day of the bomb blasts. Along with Chabin a Bhutanese national named Tenzing G. Zangpo was also arrested. Tenzing is wanted in many cases in Bhutan. He claims to have been in the Druk National Congress which opposes the ruling alliance in Bhutan. According to him, India and Bhutan are opposed to the ideology espoused by Druk National Congress. As reported by the BBC Correspondent Subir Bhowmik Tenzing had allied with other insurgent groups (*Dainik Asom,* 15.11.08).

The Bhutan connection is still important. It is reported that after the destruction of ULFA and NDFB camps in 2003 by Indian and Bhutanese forces there have been several attempts to rebuild these again. Presently, there are 30 small camps of ULFA and NDFB. Each of these camps can accommodate about 20 people. If these insurgent outfits are able to start operating again from Bhutan there will be chaos in Northern Assam.

There are many theories about the place or places where the bomb blasts were planned. According to one such theory the entire operation was planned in Khagverbari near Barpeta Road in the house of an NDFB cadre in a series of meetings in July and August, 2008. According to another, the entire operation was planned by Jehadis of Bangladesh under the direction of ISI. The planning was done under the direct supervision of ISI's Ahmed Shah Gilani who is in charge of North-East in that organization (*Pratidin,* 14.11.08). Another theory, citing Army source, says that the planning was done by the HUJI top leader Jehangir in Guwahati itself. That HUJIs and ISI have been active in Assam is known for quite some time. Many arrests had been made in several places in the past. As many as 10 ISI agents arrested in Guwahati were released by the Court of Additional Session Judge because police could not provide enough evidence. It is reported that 8 of these are now missing. They are suspected to have escaped to Bangladesh. Similar cases of police failure to provide evidence and make the charges stick have been quite a few. If the former top insurgent leader and present chief of Bodoland Autonomous Council (BTC), Hagrama Mahilary, is to be believed it is the HUJIs who had planned and implemented the entire operation.

The Government of Assam spokesman had said in the beginning that both ULFA and NDFB were involved in the incidents. Later, the Chief Minister reiterated this when he said in his Press Conference on 11.11.08 that the Government of Assam has got clear indication that beside ULFA and NDFB a third force was also involved. According to him "the brain behind the blasts is in Bangladesh". In fact, the Government of Assam has made a request to INTERPOL for apprehending a few persons allegedly involved in the incidents.

Political parties and others have also expressed their opinions and blamed each other. None of the political parties have any hard evidence. They seem to rely on heresay and impressions based on their ideology. The majority of them see Islamist insurgents as responsible for the blasts. This is because many political parties believe that in terms of manpower, financial resources and mental make-up, the Islamist alone seem to be capable of carrying out such a gigantic task.

But if we go by the number and the nature of arrests it looks almost certain that NDFB had carried out the actual operation. The truth was known publicly only after the Special Investigation Team (SIT) completed its investigations. The impression about NDFB's role was, however, enhanced by a couple of arrests of the key persons. One Bimal Mushahary was arrested from Ambari-Fatasil area of Guwahati. He is supposed to be an arms expert. Although police allege him to be an NDFB cadre, his wife claims that he was a Congress Seva Dal leader. Then there was another Anup Boro, who is reported to have made a confession in which he has implicated quite a few NDFB cadres to have been involved with the blasts.

However, the CBI's charge-sheet submitted to the Special Court shows that it was NDFB and NDFB alone who had planned, executed and completed the entire operations. The arrest of Ranjan Daimari, NDFB chief, and his associates confirm this. Black Thursday (30.10.2010) will be remembered for the worst series of bomb-blasts in Assam's long history of insurgency.

CHAPTER – 13

Lessons of Black Thursday

The serial blasts of Thursday, October 30, 2008 in Guwahati, Kokrajhar, Barpeta Road and Bongaigaon of Assam left about 100 dead and 800 injured beside destruction of public and private property. In Guwahati, blasts took place in 3 locations - Ganeshguri Point, Kamarpati and Panbazar (Chief Judicial Magistrate's Court premises). In Kokrajhar also bombs exploded in 3 places. In Barpeta and Bongaigaon blasts took place in 2 and 1 place respectively. These 9 blasts were orchestrated to take place within minutes of each other. It was found later that all those blasts were master-minded by Ranjan Daimari, chief of National Democratic Front of Bodoland (NDFB), the most dangerous Bodo terrorist outfit.

When this happened there was a genuine public outcry against the terrorists. This is natural because innocent people suffered. The victims and their friends and relatives also gave vent to their ire on the concerned Government departments and officials. The Fire Brigade was attacked for delay in arrival. Two of their vehicles were burnt down. The police and the security forces were criticized for not taking an action in advance and for their inability to identify and apprehend the culprits. The political parties and the Government were criticized for inaction and complacency.

A number of steps were taken by Government in the aftermath of the bomb blasts. Security forces all over the state were altered. Action was taken against known criminals and supporters of terrorists. Police patrolling and searches were intensified. More vulnerable places were identified and brought under security cover.

A Committee was appointed to go into the genesis of the trouble and to suggest ways of avoiding such incidents in the future. The former Director General of Police, DN Dutta was appointed as the Chairman of this Committee. This Committee made several important recommendations. Among these was one for appointing a Police Commissioner for the city. It seems that the State Government accepted this recommendation. But it has not implemented it as yet. Most major cities in India have this system of Police Commissioner. Guwahati has become very big and maintenance of even ordinary law and order has become very difficult. A senior officer fully dedicated to look after law and order has become essential.

Dutta Committee's recommendations regarding increase of police force and vehicles for quick movement have been accepted and partly implemented. Two years after the incidents the State Government have now decided to implement the Committee's recommendations regarding setting up of a Specialized Disaster Response Force. Two companies of this force are being recruited soon. This force will be trained up in the same manner as the National Security Guards (NSG). They will be given the same type of sophisticated weapons and equipments as NSG. This force will work under the State Fire Service.

The State Government have not, however, acted as yet on the Dutta Committee's recommendations regarding placing of close circuit television (CCTV) in vulnerable places. This has become absolutely essential at least in the busy traffic inter-sections of Guwahati such as Ganeshguri Point, Paltanbazar, Chandmari, Athgaon and Jalukbari.

The present condition of Ganeshguri Point will show that the State Governments are smug and rather unconcerned about the future dangers of similar attacks. The Ganeshguri Point has been identified as the most vulnerable spot in Guwahati as far as terrorist activities are concerned. According to media reports the largest number of bomb blasts have taken place in this spot on as many as 28 occasions. A large number of people have been killed and injured in this area. The Government has also taken a number of steps to curb such activities. On both sides of the fly-over iron fence has been fixed so that bombs and grenades cannot be lobbed easily. Below the bridge the parking places have been cleared of vehicles and some of these areas have been fenced off. Proper lanes have been demarcated for cross-traffic to pass below the bridge without hassle. Actually the number of vehicles which have to pass below the Ganeshguri fly-over is huge. Then there are numerous small roads which emanate from the Ganeshguri Point. Traffic is also heavy on these roads. "No Parking zone" sign-boards have been put up in congested areas. Khaki-clad policemen patrol the areas. Traffic policemen direct the traffic in white uniform. Unfortunately, however, all these measures have not been totally effective because lots of vehicles, including Government vehicles, are parked in front of "No Parking" signs at all times of the day. The footpaths have become hazardous to padestrians because of encroachment by hawkers.

The principal accused of the Ganeshguri case, Ranjan Daimari, who is the head of NDFB, along with his 10 other collaborators has been arrested by police in this case. Charge sheets have also been prepared against them. Meanwhile, on the night of December 10, 2010 a key accused in the serial blast case, B. Jwangkhang alias George Boro, deputy commander in-chief of NDFB was arrested from a hotel in Aizawl where he was hiding after return from Bangladesh. His PSO was also arrested.

George has been described as the kingpin of the Guwahati blasts. The trial of all these accused persons should be completed early.

On October 30, 2010, two years after the incidents, people all over Assam organized memorial meetings and remembered the victims. They demonstrated against the terrorists. They demanded immediate and deterrent punishment.

What has irked most people three years after the incidents is the failure of Governments, both Central and State, to pay the compensation packages promised to the victims and their kins. Even the amounts promised by the Prime Minister are yet to be disbursed. Such delays cause hardship and annoy the affected people. Necessary action should be taken by the concerned officials to disburse the compensation immediately.

CHAPTER – 14

The Massacre at the Taj

Mumbai's iconic Taj Mahal Palace and Tower Hotel (Taj, for short) reopened on December 21, 2008 after the carnage of November 26-28, 2008 (26-28/11). On December 22, 2008, I happened to be in the metropolis in some other connection. Immediately after arrival in the city I proceeded to the site.

The magnificent 106-year old edifice of the Taj is the dream child of Jamshedji Nusserwanji Tata who, according to legend, "commissioned the building after being refused entry to the now defunct Apollo Hotel, which had a strict Europeans-only-policy" (*The Hindu*, November 28, 2008). Many people discount this story. But Jamshedji, as RM Lala has recorded, built the Taj as "his gift to the city he loved". He got the architectural design prepared after obtaining two and a half acres of prime land in the reclaimed area of Colaba by signing a 99-year lease agreement on November 1, 1898. Construction started in 1900. There was a simple ceremony in which the traditional coconut was broken and a Parsi *diwa* was lighted. The construction of the solid stone structure was done by Sorabji Contractor. The hotel was formally opened on December 16, 1903 when only one wing had been completed. Since then the Taj has remained the best hotel in Mumbai (*The Hindu*, November 29, 2009).

The 59-hour long siege at the Taj started at 9.25 pm on Wednesday, November 26, 2008 (26/11). After landing at Machimar Nagar (Fishermen's Colony) at 8.45 pm the 10 heavily armed Pakistani terrorists travelled in five batches of two each and attacked different locations. Two of them came to the Taj. Later, they were joined by two others who had attacked the Leopold Café at 9.15 pm, probably as a diversionary tactic, and then ran the few blocks to the Taj. These four terrorists could hold on for so long because the Taj is a warren of rooms: In addition to the 565 guest rooms including 46 suites, there are restaurants, shops, lobbys, dance floors, cafes, beauty saloons, spas, a discotheque, an elite club and a host of other facilities. The terrorists had maps of each floor of the Taj and had studied the important locations thoroughly. Probably they had carried on with simulated exercises during training. There were hundreds of guests - both Indians and Foreigners - who were staying in the rooms and hundreds of others dining or otherwise using the hotel's facilities. The Taj staffers on duty on 26/11 evening numbered 592. Many people ran away, 31 were killed and 345 evacuated. The Maharashtra police were taken by surprise and the Government of India also took quite some time to react. It was almost daybreak on 27/11 when Operation Black Tornado could be commenced by the combined central and state forces. The hotel was ultimately cleared at 8 o'clock on 28/11 morning when the last of the four terrorists jumped out of the Taj window only to be shot dead by NSG commandos. Earlier, two other terrorists had been charred to death and the third one shot dead inside the hotel.

On Monday, December 22, 2008 my first stop in Mumbai was at the famous western-style restaurant called Leopold Café at Colaba. On 26/11 two Pakistani terrorists had reached the Leopold at 9.15 pm and unleashed a mayhem. According to a French eyewitness the terrorists lobbed 3 hand grenades and shot at diners indiscriminately with their Kalashnikovs. Within minutes they killed 8 people. Two Australians who came "face to face" with the terrorists saw them on the rampage. Both the Australians were injured. The Australians were the first to arrive at the Bombay Hospital in a taxi. The two terrorists who had attacked the Leopold then ran to the rear entrance of the Taj.

When I arrived at the Leopold four weeks later the scars on the walls were still there. Foreigners were easily mingling with the locals. All types of drinks and food were flowing from the kitchen through the narrow passage where aging waiters literally rubbed shoulders against each other to rush the filled up plates and glasses to the customers. The discussion on each table seemed to be animated and the drone reverberated throughout the big restaurant.

I took a corner table and sat alone with a plate of warm fish and chips and a mug of black American coffee. I watched the crowd outside in the busy Colaba Causeway through the tall, broad, open windows. Both sides of the road were full of pedestrians: The middle aged Parsi matron with the quaint spectacle tucked to her nose by a gold chain, the itinerant vendor carrying an earthen pot of curd on his head, the tight jean clad young couple probably rushing to a rendezvous, the formally clad executive importantly carrying his briefcase, the intellectual looking researcher with her omnipresent ethnic bag filled with books and notepads and the myriad of other prototypes of their own trades and callings. It was a usual day, a usual crowd and an usual movement on one of Mumbai's most frequented streets. I then reflected on what possibly could be the reason for the two Pakistani terrorists shooting on another such innocent crowd four weeks earlier. According to media speculation the attack on the locations in south Mumbai, including the Leopold, was focused on the foreign tourists and investors. Probably the object of Pakistan's Inter Services Intelligence (ISI), who allegedly inspired the attack by these non-state terrorists, was to scare the foreigners away so that they abandon India as tourist destination and investment hub. This is no conjecture but a distinct possibility because "the terror attack was limited only to the tourist spots in south Mumbai" (*The Hindu*, November 28, 2008). The then External Affairs Minister Pranab Mukherjee rightly said that "the aim of the terrorists was to harm India's economic growth". According to him "this unpardonable criminal attack only underscores the risk all countries face from economic sabotage, irrespective of whether these acts are authored by states or merely carried out by so called non-state actors" (*The Economic Times*, January 13, 2009).

From the Leopold I proceeded to the Taj. The direct route, which also leads to the Gateway of India, was barred. I took the back road and then was driven along the sea to reach the main entrance of the Taj, where a permanent barricade had been established. Each person was frisked. Before 26/11 anyone could pass through these portals freely. Everyone was welcomed by the tall Sikh *darwan* (doorman) with a *Namaste* (greetings). But now the *darwan* is overshadowed by numerous policemen and policewomen, brandishing various latest weapons.

I did not enter. But looked at the magnificent building from the other side of the barricades. There were scaffoldings all along the walls. Workmen were busy cleaning up and repairing the stone walls. Many damaged portions were being replaced with new materials. Some of the scars on the walls were still visible along with the charred remains of the windows and the casements. The crowd of onlookers increased as the afternoon advanced. There was an endless variety of languages in which conversation was going on. But everyone's attention was riveted on the Taj. There was a pervading sadness at the damage caused to this grand edifice. But behind the sadness there was a nationalist feeling of oneness at that sentimental moment. I felt reassured that the Pakistani terrorists could not destroy the unity of India.

When I returned on December 24, 2008 I spent an entire afternoon in the Taj. The sprawling lobby looked spick-and-span. Around the huge carpet the furniture was spread in the same order as in the past. The cut glass chandeliers were lighted up although it was a bright clear day. Various functionaries were in their respective positions including the reception counter assistants, the public relations managers, the announcer with the microphone who calls cars and taxis and the luggage dispatcher who does a hundred odd jobs including dispensing of postage stamps. I had bought some stamps long ago when I came down from the bedroom after writing an important letter, which I posted in the wee hours past midnight. There was, however, an additional piece of furniture, which I spotted in a corner. This had been newly placed after 26/11. It was a tall desk covered by a damask table cloth on which there was a huge register. The parchment paper-leaves of the register were appropriately watermarked and impressed with the Taj insignia.

I turned left and entered the long, wide and tall corridor leading to the offices. Then I saw the real destruction. The Chinese restaurant, the Harbour Bar and the Cake Shop were gone. This area will require major reconstruction. The process has already started and might last the best part of the year. I was told that upstairs also the greater damage was in the section facing the sea. I had a mind to go up the beautiful old staircase but resisted the temptation. The glass doors on the swimming pool side appeared intact. So did the pool itself.

Returning to the lobby I walked towards the bookshop. There I bought the latest publication titled "Change We Can Believe In". Besides the main chapters the book contained a Foreword by Barack Obama and the reprints of 8 of Barrack's key speeches during the 2008 Presidential campaign. This remarkable book by anonymous authors was published only a few days earlier in New York. It claims to "outline his (Barack's) vision for America and its place in the world". It contains "bold and specific ideas about how Barack Obama plans to fix the ailing American economy and strengthen its middle class, make healthcare affordable to all, achieve energy independence and keep America safe in a dangerous world". In the long chapter on "Rebuilding America's Leadership", Barack Obama's plan for fighting in Pakistan and Afghanistan, Iran and the Muslim world are categorically defined.

With this book in hand I recrossed the lobby and entered the Star Board on the other side. There I planted myself in a comfortable sofa in an enclosed space. Only a few people were around - most of them in the Bar inside. For the next couple of hours or so I read through the book while ruminating over the incidents in the hotel during 26-28/11.

Great physical damage has been wrought in several locations in Mumbai by this heinous attack on the country's financial capital, which "targeted to derail a fast growing economy and shatter confidence of global as well as domestic investors". (*The Hindu*, November 28, 2008). It left a total of 173 people dead (including 31 in the Taj) and 288 injured. Among the dead were 14 policemen (including some of Maharashtra's best), 26 foreigners, 1 home guard and 9 terrorists. The security forces actually engaged to fight the terrorists numbered 1,406. Only 1 terrorist could be apprehended.

The terrorist attack on Mumbai revealed many defects in India's national security arrangements. The facts that the terrorists were highly motivated, meticulously trained and perfectly familiarized with Mumbai's landscape, without visiting the city, show how Pakistani state and non-state organizations painstakingly prepare their staffers and agents. Our intelligence agencies did not have a clue about Pakistani intentions, except for general information about possible terrorist attacks. Even after the terrorists had landed in Mumbai's shores, and eyewitnesses informed the nearest police station, the latter's reaction was slow. Media has pointed a number of lacunae including "intelligence failure, ill equipped forces, lack of co-ordination and apathy" and commented that "everything that could go wrong went wrong in Mumbai" (*India Today*, December 15, 2008). Barack Obama has warned that "having seen the mayhem that was created in Mumbai, that there are going to be potential copycats or other terrorist organizations that think that this is something that they can replicate" (*Economic Times*, January 13, 2009).

Before I left the Star Board the waiter brought me an envelope with the bill. Carrying the envelope I first went to the tall desk in the lobby, where I recorded my comments in the register. Besides the usual expression of sorrow I made special mention about Sabina Saikia because she was maritally related to an Assamese family whom I had intimately known for more than half a century.

I then sat down on a sofa in the lobby and opened the envelope. It had an etching of the Taj dome printed in the back flap. When I opened the envelope and looked at the four-page folder I was moved by the way it had been designed and the sentiments expressed in the write-ups. The first page contained a silver impression of the "Tree of Life". The original sculpture on which it is based is in the sixth floor. The sculptor is Jaidev Baghel of Kondon of Bastar district of Chattisgarh state. The material used is a casting alloy of brass and bronze. The beautiful sculpture is 49 inches tall, 35 inches wide and 35 inches deep. "This symbolic tree withstood the attack on the 6th floor and stands immortalized". It is a memorial of the events of 26-28/11. It will be ultimately relocated from its present site to the prime spot below the dome of the Taj.

The second page begins with a quotation from Mahatma Gandhi: "Strength does not come from physical capacity. It comes from an indomitable will". Then there is a statement by the management appreciating the selfless service rendered by those hotel guests, staff members, security forces and firemen who "got us through our darkest hour with true courage and grit; who showed extraordinary strength by selflessly helping others and even laying down their lives". This page ends with a statement that "the Tree of Life is a perfect symbol of our salutation to all of those who lost their lives on the 26th of November".

The third page alphabetically lists the 31 names of those who lost their precious lives in the Taj during 26-28/11. They had gathered in the precinct of one of the most beautiful hotels in the world during the momentous 59 hours. They had come from different corners of the earth and from different regions of India. They belonged to different religions, different ethnic communities and different language groups. Reading the names I was amazed by the variety. Yet they belonged to a distinct group of their own and had an identity separate from all others.

The last page describes the Tree of Life. The write-up harks back to the ancient Egyptian scriptures, the Book of Genesis and the Bhagavad-Gita and refers to various "Trees of Life" which are "recounted in the world theologies, philosophy and mythologies". Looking at the picture of the tree once again before I left the hotel I felt ennobled by the realization that I could also pay my homage to "those who put their commitments before their lives".

CHAPTER – 15

A Post-Mortem of the Mumbai Carnage

The entire world was shocked by the physical damage caused to the metropolis of Mumbai during the massacre unleashed by only ten Pakistani terrorists on November 26-28, 2008. The psychological impact has been devastating. The suddenness of the attack, the unpreparedness to meet the onslaught and the failure to present a co-ordinated defence are some of the responsible factors which will need very careful study and analysis in order to tackle any similar event in the future.

The most important lesson of the Mumbai incident is that our intelligence outfits must be expanded, revamped and made more effective. The newly set up National Investigation Agency has now started work. However, the main objective should be to prevent terrorist attacks by a systematic collection of intelligence and by taking advance action to forestall the nefarious designs of terrorists.

India's most important security concerns are from our immediate neighbours of Pakisatn and Bangladesh. Infiltration from these two countries is easy because of the similarities of language, facial appearance and family affinities. Anyone coming from across the border cannot only get shelter but most often can get absorbed into the local population. This is easier in the case of the Bangladeshis, but not very difficult in the case of the Pakistanis. It is good that the newly elected Sheikh Hasina

Wajed government of Bangladesh is co-operating with India. They have demolished the illegal camps of Indian terrorist outfits inside Bangladesh and have handed over most of the leaders to Indian police. Let us hope that our diplomats and politicians will be able to retain the confidence of their Bangladeshi counterparts in the future also. For that purpose a stable and permanent relationship is being attempted as it will be clear from the discussion of the last chapter of this book.

The relationship between India and Pakistan have to improve in the interest of both the countries. The continuing tension and occasional warfare between the two countries have affected both. Their economic development has been stunted, their social relationship has been strained and their cultural relationship has been distorted. It is apparent that unless the political relationship improves neither country can progress. The large armies each country is maintaining at their common border are costing collosal amounts in terms of money, manpower and materials. Pakistan's Inter Services Intelligence (ISI) is primarily engaged in harrassing India in every way. ISI is eating away resources which could have been deployed for Pakistan's economic development. ISI is training and assisting bigoted jehadi elements who periodically infiltrate into India. They are the ones who perpetrate terrorist acts in different locations in India. It is one such bigoted jehadi named Hedley who planned the Mumbai carnage. It is one such group which came to India by sea and attacked crucial locations in Mumbai. The plethora of information unearthed during investigation into the Mumbai incident indicate very close collaboration of Pakistan's official and non-official agencies in the anti-India campaigns. India has to find a way of improving the relationship so that the two countries can live in peace. That is the only way which can ease the present tension permanently. But how it can be achieved without causing damage to the country's interests is the big question.

While political and diplomatic endeavour must continue to solve the outstanding issues between the two countries and while we must actively endeavour to achieve permanent peace, India has to prepare itself to meet all eventualities. It is true that Pakistan has been receiving support from the USA and China. China is still supporting Pakistan's nefarious activities against India. China does not want India to progress. China has developed so much and at such high speed during the past two decades that India cannot hope to match it even in the next fifty years. In 1990 the per capita incomes of India and China were about the same. The comparative figures for 2007 will show that China has a per capita income (US $5420) which is double than that of India (US $2740). The distance between the two countries is widening further in terms of national income. In terms of Human Development Index (HDI) China is far ahead of India. The respective values of HDI are 0.772 for China against 0.612 for India in 2007. Here also the gap is widening during the past few years. China would like that Pakistan does maximum damage to India so that India can never reach China's level of development. Pakistan is doing the job by keeping India engaged in war like situation along with cross border terrorism. It is also clear that on the international scene China is opposed to India's rise as a great power. That is why it does not support India's bid for permanent membership of the Security Council of the United Nations Organisation.

As far as the US is concerned it has always encouraged Pakistan to keep India down. There are indications that official organizations like Central Intelligence Agency (CIA) had helped anti-India terrorist outfits. However, after the September 9, 2001 incidents in New York, the US has changed its attitude to some extent. Immediately after the Mumbai incident, the State Government appointed a committee headed by RD

Pradhan who had been earlier Chief Secretary of Maharashtra as well as Home Secretary in the Central Government. The other member was the former Intelligence Chief V. Balachandran. They had found a number of lacunae and flaws in dealing with the situation by the security forces. This failure has been described as a "tragic debacle".

In fact, the Committee noted that "no formal de-briefing sessions were held by the Commissioner of Police with all (or) groups of officers to make an assessment of what went why". The Committee found fault with the manner in which the Mumbai Commissioner of Police, Ghafoor, had organized the defence during the incident. It was disjointed and dis-oriented. There was practically no central command from which clear instructions emanated. Even the objectives were clearly spelled out. Ghafoor had complained against almost all his senior officers that they were not at all keen to adequately respond to the situation. But the Pradhan Committee found that Ghafoor himself was not able to provide the leadership. The Committee found that Ghafoor was "guilty of gross violations of standard operating procedures". They also found "certain lack of cohesion and communication in the internal functioning of the Mumbai Police Commissioner's office". It now appears that Ghafoor "who had parked himself just below the NCPA (National Centre for Performing Arts) does not appear to have had any role in the Oberoi-Trident fighting". Ghafoor had also been accused of failing to offer any "back up" to Assistant Commissioner Issaq Ibrahim Bhagwan who successfully organized the action in the Nariman House against the terrorists.

One force which could have been of great assistance - the Quick Response Team stationed at Mumbai - was dispersed over several locations and could not be used properly. The most important failure perhaps was that the Police Commissioner was completely cut off from all "critical intelligence flows". How could he analyse the situation and lay down his priorities to be followed by his juniors?

It is rather unfortunate that even after the incident there have been instances of casualness and apathy on the part of the police. The case of the two bags containing 8 kgs of RDX which were discovered in the busy Chhatrapati Shivaji Terminus, a week after the incident, that is, on December 3, 2008 shows the casualness of search of the spots affected by the Pakistani attack. Many more lapses, issues and problems have been pointed out. Many more lessons have been identified for learning in order to deal with similar future eventualities. But the most important point to remember is that the Government must lead a systematic preparation for defending the country against all eventualities. In this effort it must obtain the co-operation of all concerned primarily including the civil society. Eternal vigilance is the price that we have to pay for having a rogue state like Pakistan on our border, a jealous and strong China as another neighbour and an ambivalent USA with waning strength. The existence of numerous terrorist outfits, encouraged and assisted by our neighbours, with conflicting objectives have complicated the scene. This problem will also have to be addressed properly.

CHAPTER – 16

Insurgency in Tibet

Way back in late 1961, when we were in the Lal Bahadur Shastri National Academy of Administration, Mussoorie, my friend and batchmate Prince Wangchuk Namgyal, uncle of the present King of Bhutan, took me out on a drive one cold afternoon in his powerful Japanese pojero vehicle. We travelled on winding roads drenched by rain and skirted the hills enveloped in a deep cover of snow. It was really cold. I shivered while Wangchuk enjoyed. About 40 kilometres out of Mussoorie and beyond the Kemptee Falls the vehicle stopped in front of a cluster of bungalows. The Dalai Lama had stayed here while Dharamsala was being made ready for him. We entered one of the bungalows. A young lady came out and ushered us into a warm drawing room choicefully decorated with ethnic Tibetan furnishings and a large portrait of the fourteenth Dalai Lama on the mantle. I was told that the lady and her parents belonged to the highest rung of Tibetan aristrocracy and had fled that country in the wake of the Dalai Lama's flight to India for asylum in March, 1959. Her maid served Tibetan tea with plenty of butter mixed in the liquor. The taste was so pungent that I had to ask for tea with milk and sugar. I do not remember the details but the discussion rivetted around Tibet and the Dalai Lama. That was my first introduction to Tibet. Later I found out that the nature of Tibetan insurgency is completely different from insurgency elsewhere. The Tibetans are mild natured. Violence is repugnant to them. They are not capable of killing people at the fall of a hat. Their insurgency does not impel them to cause much damage.

The present Dalai Lama, for example, is a man of peace in words, deeds and appearance. His rebellion against the Chinese is not only non-violent, but also value-based like that of Mahatma Gandhi. Again, the section of Tibetans who turned violent in the face of Chinese aggression are milder than most terrorists. The present Dalai Lama was born on July 6, 1935 in a small village called Tagtser in the Dhome province of Tibet. The name given to him by his parents was Tenzin Gyatso. He was brought to Lhasa in October, 1939 and enthroned as the fourteenth Dalai Lama (meaning "Ocean of Wisdom" in Mongolian language) on February 22, 1940. He assumed full responsibility of his office on November 17, 1950 at the age of 16. I learnt about the Dalai Lama and Tibet only from books and articles as I could never visit that country personally.

A reading of the history of Tibet shows that China had all along had a special relationship with Tibet, which was "nominally subject to the suzerainty of China" but was "for all practical purposes an independent theocracy". After the Communists came to power in China in 1949 their cadres started penetrating into Tibet. In 1951 a seventeen point agreement was signed between Communist China and Tibet under which the suzerainty of China was accepted but it was clearly stated that Tibet would continue to enjoy full autonomy. The control of external affairs and defence would be under China but "there would be no interference by the Chinese Government with the Tibetan religion and customs and her internal administration". The Dalai Lama, however, maintained that "Tibet is a separate country different from China - racially, culturally, linguistically, geographically and historically" (*The Asian Wall Street Journal,* November 8, 1979).

The Chinese did not honour this agreement. They started interfering in Tibet's internal affairs from the very beginning. What the Dalai Lama stated in his press statement of June 20, 1959 is significant: "although they had solemnly undertaken to maintain my status and power as the Dalai Lama, they did not lose any opportunity to undermine my authority and sow dissentions among my people". He also accused the Chinese of letting loose "a reign of terror which finds few parallels in the history of Tibet". According to him, the Chinese have used "forced labour and compulsory exactions, a systematic persecution of the people, plunder and confiscation of property belonging to individuals and monasteries and execution of certain leading men in Tibet". In fact, the Chinese wanted the Hans of that country to completely absorb the Tibetans through marriage and forced procreation. As the Dalai Lama said "the ultimate Chinese aim with regard to Tibet, as far as I can make out, seems to attempt the extermination of religion and culture and even the absorption of the Tibetan race". The Dalai Lama further alleged that "beside the civilian and military personnel already in Tibet 5 million Chinese settlers have arrived in eastern and north-eastern Tso, in addition to which 4 million Chinese settlers are planned to be sent to U and Sung provinces of central Tibet. Many Tibetans have been deported to China, thereby resulting in the complete absorption of these Tibetans as a race, which is being undertaken by the Chinese" (Dalai Lama's Press statement at Mussoorie on June 20, 1959).

The Chinese have destroyed most of the monasteries in Tibet. According to one estimate there were 6,259 monasteries with 5,92,558 inmates, both monks and nuns. They housed innumerable statues and religious artifacts made of gold, silver and other metals. The Chinese have destroyed all but 13 of the monasteries and taken away the artifacts. This has led to the conclusion that "Chinese policy is aimed at bringing about a gradual and natural death of Tibetan culture and religion." (The Eighth Tibetan Non-Governmental Organisation in Exile, 1995).

The Chinese have destroyed the flora and fauna in Tibet. "The rich wildlife, forests, plants, minerals and water resources have all suffered irreparable degradation and Tibet's ecological balance is being seriously disturbed". The situation has been further complicated by militarisation and nuclearisation of Tibet. It is alleged that the Chinese have dumped nuclear waste in Tibet beside positioning ballistic missiles probably for future attack against India. Tibet being the source of all rivers flowing into India the Chinese destruction of Tibet's environment poses grave danger to India.

The Tibetans protested against the Chinese design through uprisings in the end of 1955 and again in 1957 in some of the provinces. These revolts were suppressed mercilessly. More than 65,000 people were killed and others sent away to the Chinese heartland. About 15,000 came to India as refugees. These were in addition to the 100,000 who had come to India along with the Dalai Lama. More people came to Sikkim, Nepal and Bhutan. The rebels organised themselves under the banner of the "*Ten-Soung-Ma-Ghar*" or the National Voluntary Defence Army of Tibet. This army wanted "radical changes in social and political organisation of the country". They pledged themselves to work "for the improvement of the condition of our people and their standard of living. We engage ourselves to introduce all necessary reforms in the country in accordance with the natural conditions, customs and genius of our people. In the field of economic development, we pledge ourselves to improve the life of our nomadic people, of the tillers of the land, of the artisans and the handicrafts men to the best of our ability and to effect changes in all spheres of our national life".

The Army emphasised that "it is our avowed policy to bring about these changes by peaceful means". The Chinese, however, alleged that the uprising was the handiwork of reactionaries and that the poorer people were not involved. The leaders of the upsurge on the other hand claim that their movement is "backed by the masses of the people and they refute the allegation of the Chinese authorities that the rising was the handiwork of a few reactionaries". According to the leaders "the widespread revolt is a national upsurge of people who are fighting for their existence and their identity". The then Prime Minister Pandit Jawaharlal Nehru had clarified in Parliament on April 27, 1959 that "even according to the accounts received through Chinese sources the revolt in Tibet was of considerable magnitude and the basis of it must have been a strong feeling of nationalism which affects not only upper class people but others also". A rather intriguing development was the Chinese leader Mao Zedong's mention about Tibet in his well-known "Hundred Flowers Speech". He is reported to have said that "reforms would not be introduced in Tibet during the period of 1958-62 and that thereafter the introduction of reforms would depend upon the wishes of the Tibetan people." This was never complied with by the Chinese. They forced all types of "changes" without informing or consulting the Dalai Lama or the Tibetan people ("Truth About Tibet").

Earlier the Dalai Lama had come to India once before in 1956 to participate in the 2500th Buddha Jayanti celebrations. He had described the atrocities committed on his people to the Indian and the world media. He did not want to return to his capital Lhasa. The Dalai Lama stated in his press statement of June 20, 1959 as follows: "As I was unable to do anything for the benefit of my people I had practically made up my mind when I came to India not to return to Tibet until there was a menifest change in the attitudes of the Chinese authorities". But the then Prime Minister Nehru persuaded him to go back. Nehru had obtained the assurance of the then Chinese Prime Minister Chou-en Lai about the Dalai Lama's safety and advised the latter on that basis. Chou-en Lai had visited India in December, 1956. This position was confirmed by Nehru in his statement in the Lok Sabha on April 27, 1959. The Dalai Lama also understood that the position was as follows: "According to the Indian Prime Minister, Jawaharlal Nehru, Premier Chou-en Lai told him that the Chinese Government did not consider Tibet as a province of China. The people were different from the people of China proper. Therefore, they (the Chinese) considered Tibet as an autonomy". Prime Minister Nehru told me that he had the assurance from Prime Minister Chou- en Lai that Tibet's autonomy would be respected and, therefore, advised me to make efforts to safeguard it and co-operate with China in bringing about reforms". (Note accompanying Dalai Lama's letter to Deng Xiaoping dated September 11, 1992). It may be mentioned here that the Dalai Lama had met Chou-en Lai at New Delhi in December, 1956. But the Chinese did not honour the trust that Nehru reposed on them.

After the Dalai Lama's return to Lhasa in April, 1957. the situation in Tibet became worse with the Chinese forcing out Tibetan Lamas from many monastries to work as labourers on road projects in China and killing others after destroying the monastaries. Then they started inviting high Tibetan personages to parties given by the Chinese Military Commanders. Four of the topmost personages so invited were Sharkelden Gyalto, Head Lama Amdo, Kunchok Lhunup, Pandit Shi Chen, very famous Lama Kham and Kathok Situ, and famous Lama Kham. The first three were killed and the fourth one was incarcerated. Similarly invited other dignitaries never returned home. They were either killed or imprisoned. The climax came when the Dalai Lama himself was invited to attend a cultural programme on March 10, 1959. He was asked to come unaccompanied by any of his Ministers or his bodyguard. This raised an alarm in the minds of the Tibetans.

A large number of people, estimated to be 10,000, who gathered in front of the Norbulingka palace of Lhasa blocked the gates and stayed on throughout the night of March 10, 1959 in spite of the Dalai Lama's personal assurance to them that he would not go to the function. Next day a meeting of all Government officials was held in the palace at the end of which a proclamation was issued in the name of the Cabinet that Tibet was independent. Earlier a gathering of 5000 women had urged the Dalai Lama to proclaim independence. On March 12, 1959 almost the entire population of Lhasa turned out and held a huge public meeting at Shol below the Potala palace. This meeting was in continuous session till March 17, 1959. The Chinese started firing warning shots to disperse the gathering and probably to force the Dalai Lama to surrender. The firing of shell and machine guns became incessant. But the people also persisted.

On March 17, 1959 at 10.30 pm the Dalai Lama and the members of his entourage left the palace one by one. They were fortunate that the Chinese did not discover their flight almost for two days. When the Dalai Lama and his immediate entourage of 80 people arrived at the Indian border post of Chutangmu on the evening of March 31, 1959, they were properly received by the Assistant Political Officer of Tawang. This could be done because the Government of India had expected some such development and had warned the border check posts accordingly (The Prime Minister's statement in the Lok Sabha, April 3, 1959).

At this point it may be pertinent to mention that India had a special relationship with Tibet. During British times the Viceroy at Calcutta Lord Curzon sent an armed expedition to Tibet in 1903 under Colonel Younghusband which occupied Lhasa and obtained certain concessions including opening three trade marts and the establishment of a British Trade Agent's office at Gyantse. A telegraph line was also laid. In 1910 the then Dalai Lama took refuge in India in the aftermath of the Chinese invasion of his country. In June, 1912 he returned to China and claimed that "the old vassel-suzerain relationship ... had came to an end with the extinction of the Manchu dynasty" during the Chinese Republican Revolution of 1911. After the famous Tripartite Conference at Simla between India, China and Tibet a convention was initialled on April 27, 1914, by which China recognised "the complete autonomy of outer Tibet" skirting the Indian frontier and including Lhasa, Shigatse and Chamdo". It also fixed the frontier between India and China for a distance of 850 miles. This frontier came to be called as the McMahon line after Sir Henry McMahon who, as the Foreign Secretary to the Government of British India, had signed the agreement. Independent India inherited the British legacy (Advanced History of India).

Actually India's relationship with Tibet is much deeper than that. As described by the Dalai Lama himself "India and Tibet have religious, cultural and trade links extending over a thousand years and for Tibetans it has always been the land of enlightenment, having given birth to Lord Buddha" (Statement issued at Tezpur on April 18, 1959).

After the Dalai Lama took political asylum in India in April, 1959 many questions about the Dalai Lama's status in this country had been raised. But the then Prime Minister Nehru, in his statement in the Rajya Sabha on May 4, 1959, clarified the position as follows: "We have received the Dalai Lama and party and, subsequently, some thousands of refugees. We have given them asylum. As a sovereign country we have every right to do so, and nobody else can be a judge of that except ourselves... It would have been utterly wrong for us to do otherwise". That settled matters and during the past half a century the Dalai Lama has been India's "honoured guest". He can visit any part of the country as he wishes. Arunachal Pradesh cannot be an exception as claimed by China. In fact, by October, 2009 the Dalai Lama had already visited Arunachal six times and out of these he had been to Tawang five times. As a "refugee" the Dalai Lama is not allowed to make political statements. He has not infringed this condition. He even clarified that he did not "want to increase tension between India and China".

The Chinese Foreign Ministry spokesman Ma Zhaoxu is reported to have said in October, 2009 that "China's position on so-called Arunachal Pradesh is consistent and clear. We firmly oppose the Dalai Lama's visit to the region. China is greatly concerned over the news. We believe this further exposes the Dalai Lama's nature of anti-China separatism, as is known to all". This, however, is uncalled for because India's boundary with Tibet had been finally settled by the Simla convention of 1914. The McMahon line drawn and agreed to in 1914 must be respected by both countries. Rather than claiming Arunachal Pradesh as the so-called "southern Tibet" China should return to India the large area it has been occupying since long and particularly since the war of 1962.

China has accused the Dalai Lama of having perpetrated serfdom in Tibet when he was in power. The Chinese claim that they have freed the Tibetan serfs and brought economic development to Tibet. China is also firmly opposed to any contact between the Dalai Lama and any foreign powers. It is believed by many that China's opposition persuaded President Barack Obama not to meet the Dalai Lama when the latter visited the United States in October, 2009. Again, before Obama's maiden visit to China in November, 2009, the Chinese Foreign Ministry reiterated that "the abolishment of serf system in Tibet is as significant as the end of the slavery in the United States". China's accusations have been firmly denied by the Tibetan representatives, who on the other hand, say that "Chinese rule has restricted religious freedom and threatened Tibetan culture". (*The Hindu*, November 13, 2009)

Almost 100,000 refugees have came to India in the wake of the Dalai Lama's flight in 1959. Ever since 1963 China has been inviting them to come back to Tibet. But, as the Dalai Lama has averred, "There was no response from our side on this issue because this is not the real issue. The real issues are the feelings and welfare of the six million Tibetans still left in Tibet. Why should an alien rule be forced on them? Why should not they have the choice of holding their own beliefs, traditions, culture and identity?" (*The Asian Wall Street Journal*, August 25, 1977). It is these issues that China should address in consultation with the Tibetans.

While awarding the Nobel Peace Prize in 1989 to the Dalai Lama, in his presentation speech, Egil Aarvik, the then Chairman of the Norwegian Nobel Committee, stated as follows, "We affirm our unstinting support for his work for peace, and for the unarmed masses on the march in many lands for liberty, peace and human dignity". As the leader of the Mahayana Buddhism, the Dalai Lama has always supported movements for peace and non-violence. Once he said that "my religion is simple, my religion is kindness". This one line characterised his entire attitude towards life and human conduct.

My visit to the Taktasang monastery near Thimphu from where Guru Padmasambhava had spread his Tantrik Buddhism to Bhutan, Sikkim and Tibet and my earlier visit to the Tawang monastery made me familiar with the message of peace which the Dalai Lama is preaching.

There is absolutely no doubt that he is committed to the promotion of human values, religious harmony and understanding and also of the Tibetan issues. In November, 2009 the Dalai Lama visited Arunachal Pradesh "to hold religious discourses and bless the people in Tawang and Bomdilla". He also inaugurated the multi-speciality hospital in Tawang which has been built with money donated by his followers in 2003. Why should any one object to such a visit?

The relationship between China and Tibet has been bad ever since the Communist party's taking over of the reigns of power in that country. India's relations with China also became worse after the Dalai Lama's flight from Tibet and asylum in India. China's threats and India's counter statements have created an atmosphere of mistrust and enmity between these two largest countries of Asia. The situation has deteriorated so much during 2009 that there have been troop movements and repositioning of missiles by both the countries. This has created considerable tension.

As already mentioned the Tibetans, being Buddhists, are a very peaceful people. The rebellion that they had mounted faded within a short time in the face of massive Chinese offensive. The Chinese are most unscrupulous. They do not believe in non-violence nor do they respect human rights. That is why, they could kill so many Tibetans. They did not hesitate for a moment before carrying out racial absorption and even racial extermination.

As far as Buddhism is concerned the Tibetans allege that Chinese rule has restricted religious freedom and threatened Tibetan culture. According to one statement the Chinese "have desecrated all the holy places, Buddhist scriptures, images and everything that is sacred to the Tibetans. They humiliated and ridiculed the high Lamas and have demanded them to perform miracles. Lamas, monks and nuns have been tortured and killed in large numbers. People have been imprisoned for reciting Tibetan mantras, turning prayer wheels and having in their possession a photograph of the Dalai Lama. Nevertheless the Tibetan people's faith in Buddhism retains its vital strength, bravely upheld by numerous groups of monks who secretly gather for prayers". (Report of the Second Delegation of the Dalai Lama to Tibet).

A sad Dalai Lama has exclaimed that "the tragedy of Tibet is that a whole race, a people strongly opposed to foreign domination, has been subjugated, oppressed and gobbled up by China". He also felt that it is well nigh impossible to carry on an armed struggle against the Chinese. To do so against the unethical and despotic Chinese hordes would be suicidal. But Tibet and the Dalai Lama have the support of the international community in their struggle. The United Nations have passed three resolutions, one each in 1959, 1961 and 1965, condemning the Chinese invasion of Tibet.

On September 21, 1987 the Dalai Lama presented a Five Point Peace Plan on Tibet. It consisted of the following components:

1. transformation of the whole of Tibet into a zone of peace;
2. abandonment of China's population transfer policy, which threatens the very existence of the Tibetans as a people;
3. respect for the Tibetan people's fundamental human rights and democratic freedom;
4. restoration and protection of Tibet's natural environment and abandonment of China's use of Tibet for the production of nuclear weapons and dumping of nuclear wastes;
5. commencement of earnest negotiations on the future status of Tibet and of relations between the Tibetan and the Chinese peoples;

The Peace Plan has been widely acclaimed all over the world. It has been unanimously supported by the United States Congress, the West German Bundestag, the European Parliament, the Dutch Parliament and the Swedish Parliament. I am sure that a solution to the Tibetan problem will be found with the Peace Plan as the basis and that there will be an end of the state terrorism unleashed by the Chinese in the wake of the mild insurgency of the Tibetans.

CHAPTER – 17

A Framework for Talks with ULFA

The United Liberation Front of Assam (ULFA) received the most severe blow when its chairman Arabinda Rajkhowa was brought back to India after his arrest (or surrender) in Dhaka in December, 2009. Along with Rajkhowa the Deputy commander-in-chief Raju Baruah and a few others were also brought back to India. Only the commander-in-chief Paresh Baruah and the cadres whom he directly controls have remained behind in a badly truncated ULFA. Whether these momentous events will bring back peace to Assam will be known only in the future.

But there was a time in the late 1980s when ULFA used to run almost a parallel government in many areas of the Brahmaputra valley. Selective destructions of property, bomb blasts, killings, large scale extortions, kidnappings and frequent bundhs terrorized the different strata of society. It had adversely affected the economic and social life of the people. ULFA used to recruit its members from amongst the large reservoir of unemployed youths in the villages, train them mainly in the northern parts of Myanmar with the help of the National Socialist Council of Nagaland (NSCN) to whom large sums of money had to be paid as training fees.

ULFA had its support base mainly in the villages where its cadres used to find easy shelter. In the urban areas also many families used to supply money, food and accommodation. Some of them were forced to do so.

While some others did it willingly. There were instances of policemen helping ULFA by passing on advance information about proposed counter insurgency measures and thus enabling them to flee or to avoid arrests. Even otherwise many policemen used to intentionally ignore ULFA's nefarious activities and desist from taking appropriate actions.

ULFA was started with the definite objectives of making Assam independent and making it free from the Bangladeshi infiltrators. It still professes the first objective. But it practically abandoned the second objective when it transferred its base to Bangladesh and got embroiled in the anti-Indian posture of the Pakistani Inter Services Intelligence (ISI) and the Bangladeshi Directorate General of Forces Intelligence (DGFI). ULFA's top leaders took up residences in Bangladesh and reportedly started individual businesses with huge investments with the money that the outfit had earlier extorted.

Things started changing when Operation Bajrang was launched on the night of November 27-28, 1990. The then ruling Assam Gana Parishad (AGP) Government was dismissed and President's rule was imposed on Assam. The Unified Command structure was set up and combined action of Army, paramilitary forces and police started against ULFA. In my capacity as the Chief Secretary I was appointed Chairman of the first Unified Command in Assam which came into existence on the night of November 27-28, 1990. There was co-ordinated effort to strike at ULFA Headquarters in Lakhipathar forest area off Digboi. But the main ULFA leaders had fled away to Myanmar having been tipped off in advance about Operation Bajrang. In a number of strikes in many parts of Assam the security forces inflicted very heavy damages on ULFA in terms of manpower and weapons. Many ULFA leaders and cadres deserted the outfit. They are now known as surrendered ULFA or SULFA. Many attempts were made by pro-talk elements to start a dialogue. But they did not succeed.

The next big offensive was launched on December 15, 2003 to flush out the ULFA cadres from southern Bhutan. ULFA's loss in terms of manpower and weapons was heavy. Since then ULFA has been taking shelter mainly in Bangladesh. But the political situation in Bangladesh has changed recently after the assumption of office by Sheikh Hasina Wajed as the Prime Minister. The new Government has turned on the heat against ULFA. Two of its most important leaders, and Central Committee members, namely, Sasha Choudhury, who was in charge of foreign affairs, and Chitrabon Hazarika, who was in charge of finance, were pushed out of Bangladesh directly into the hands of the Indian police in October, 2009. They are now under custody. The ULFA chairman Arabinda Rajkhowa was arrested in Bangladesh and has been handed over to Indian police on December 2 or 3, 2009. A number of other ULFA leaders were either arrested or handed over to Indian police while quite a few surrendered. Only the ULFA commander-in-chief Paresh Baruah now remains to be arrested. He is reported to be either in China or in Myanmar or in one of the countries of South East Asia. Arabinda Rajkhowa's arrest also has been described officially as surrender. Meanwhile, an extradition treaty has been signed between India and Bangladesh. This will facilitate handing over of the arrested ULFA leaders and cadres to India in future.

The situation at present seems to be that almost all of ULFA's top leaders are in custody except Paresh Baruah. Some of its top leaders, including Mrinal Hazarika, who have surrendered, are now campaigning for formal talks. Large numbers of ULFA's cadres have been decimated by desertions and killed in police and army actions. The small number of its cadres who are still sticking to the outfit are in disarray and scattered.

Media reports suggest that they are trying to regroup in 3 camps in the Mon district of Nagaland under the aegis of NSCN (Khaplang group). About 200 ULFA cadres are reported to be in NSCN(K)'s designated camp at Mynakshubasti. It is also reported that ULFA has opened a transit camp at Chakobasti on the Assam-Nagaland border. Notwithstanding these activities, it is the general belief that ULFA will never regain its earlier strength anytime soon. This belief has been fortified after the arrest of Arabinda Rajkhowa. The situation should not, however, lull the Government into complacence because even if grounded now there is every possibility of ULFA rising again like a sphinx. There is also the distinct possibility of fresh disgruntled elements forming new outfits to replace ULFA.

In order to ensure that the number of disgruntled elements do not increase (and is actually reduced) it will be necessary to generate enough employment for skilled, non-skilled and technical personnel through all round and inclusive development of the state with emphasis on labour intensive industries and self employment opportunities. We are now in the middle of the Eleventh Five-Year Plan. This plan is very well conceived. It will be necessary for Assam to take advantage of the numerous schemes and programmes included in the Plan and to attract the enormous fund allocations made in the different sectors of the Plan. Only such concentrated efforts can wean away the youth from the path of insurgency and reduce the potential manpower reservoir of unemployed from which ULFA has been drawing its cadres so far.

At the moment the problem is that of freeing the state from continuous violence. This can be done by both the Government and ULFA agreeing to talk and sort the differences. Various people and relevant organizations have expressed different views on the subject. After a number of incidents in which ULFA killed innocent people in indiscriminate bomb blasts and pointless violence, majority of people all over the state now want very strict action against ULFA.

The Government of India, and particularly the Union Home Minister P. Chidambaram, seem to be determined to see an end of ULFA. This is evident from Chidambaram's recent statements in which he has asked ULFA to lay down arms and surrender before coming to talk with the Government. ULFA's top brass do not agree to come to talks with such pre-conditions. Even Sasha Choudhury and Chitraban Hazarika claim that they have not surrendered and that a decision about talks can be taken only by Arabinda Rajkhowa and Paresh Barua. It is Mrinal Hazarika who leads the pro-talk faction of ULFA. Hazarika asserts that talks can be held without the presence of either Arabinda Rajkhowa or Paresh Barua. Another leader Mithinga Daimari, who is now in Guwahati jail, has expressed his views in favour of talks but only with both Rajkhowa and Baruah present. Similarly, ULFA leader Bhim Kanta Buragohain (Mama) has stated from Guwahati jail that a final decision about talks can be taken only by Arabinda Rajkhowa. Meanwhile, some of the top leaders have been released from jail on bail. There is now a sizeable number of ULFA leaders who are agreeable to talks with or without Paresh Barua. This atmosphere has been created after PC Haldar started his confabulations as interlocutor.

To my mind talks must be held with a view to a permanent and political solution of the problem. And a permanent solution is essential for peace in the state so that economic development can take place in a proper atmosphere and at the appropriate pace. A military solution can bring only temporary respite.

There can be no question of "Sovereignty" as an issue in the talks. Sovereignty and integrity of India as a nation is sacrosanct and cannot be compromised under any circumstances. ULFA must seek a solution within India (as it is presently constituted), not outside. This should be the first pre-condition for talks.

The second pre-condition is a truce or a ceasefire and, if necessary, setting up of designated camps as in the cases of NSCN and the Bodo outfits. It would be unrealistic to expect that Arabinda Rajkhowa's arrest would persuade all ULFA cadres to surrender because after surrender they will have no locus standi to talk.

The third pre-condition is to have talks at the highest level. The Government of India should be represented by the Union Home Minister P. Chidambaram himself. Lower functionaries may prepare the agenda after sorting the issues. But as in the case of the Assam Accord the actual talks must be held at the highest level. Many organizations including the People's Consultative Group (PCG) and the People's Committee for Peace Initiative in Assam (PCPIA) would like to join the talks. Many other organizations seem to point that ULFA does not represent all the people of Assam. That is true. But it is ULFA which has been fighting against the Government for the past three decades. A solution has to be found with their agreement. It is, therefore, essential that ULFA is represented in the talks at the highest level of Arabinda Rajkhowa and Paresh Barua. No other organization needs be associated at this stage.

I am sure that if talks are held with the three pre-conditions I have advanced, a solution to the vexed problem will be found. As far as the issues are concerned there should be no hesitation in discussing all issues raised by all concerned including those requiring Constitutional and statutory amendments. The talks may require a long time. The sooner the talks are held, the better it is.

CHAPTER – 18

The Bihari-Assamese Riots of 1969

The Bihari-Assamese riots started at Namrup on October 4, 1969. Just a couple of weeks earlier I had joined as Deputy Commissioner of the then undivided Lakhimpur district with headquarters at Dibrugarh after completing my two-year stint as Deputy Commissioner of the erstwhile Goalpara district with headquarters at Dhubri. Two days later I was greeted by riots in Tinsukia over collection of subscriptions. I remember these riots today in the context of the present unrest between both the communities.

Jawaharlal Chaliha, who was organising Durga Puja in the then small fertilizer township of Namrup, was killed after being pulled down from his motorcycle in the main chowk near the police station. The assailants were suspected to be Biharis.

Earlier in Tinsukia also the riots were started by Biharis although the quarrel over collection of subscriptions took place between some Marwari businessmen and some Assamese youths. In Tinsukia the situation could be brought under control immediately mainly because of the excellent co-operation offered by the leaders of the town, prominent among whom was the then Congress stalwart Jadu Bhuyan, who happened to be the chairman of the Tinsukia Municipal Board. Others like late Parama Gogoi, MLA (and later Minister) and late Radha Krishna Khemka, ex-MLA also helped. I was young, but the older people offered me full support.

The maturity, pragmatism and objectivity of the leaders amazed me. What was more surprising was their absolute lack of bias although they belonged to different political parties and came from different communities. In later life I always cited the example of communal harmony of Tinsukia whenever the occasion arose.

At Namrup, however, the disturbances were of a different type altogether. The violence and the animosity unleashed had no parallel or precedent in Assam till then. Chaliha's killing built up such a psychological barrier between the Assamese and the Biharis that all the latent hatred seemed to have erupted in a sudden sprout. It also triggered off a chain reaction. Before the police forces could reach Namrup from Dibrugarh thousands of angry villagers from the surrounding areas started beating up the Bihari labourers and made a violent attack on the hostels where several hundred Bihari engineering students were staying. The hostels were the main targets because these apprentices were suspected to have been brought there to fill up all the posts in the huge fertilizer factory depriving their Assamese compatriots. Police forces had to be brought from Guwahati in order to quell the ensuing riots. Curfew had to be clamped down and continued for several days. In the aftermath of the mass frenzy 6 more people were killed. I was surprised by the ghastly sight of the dead bodies with terrible stabbing wounds. Some of the bodies had to be fished out from Dilli river. Among the dead there were 3 Assamese and 3 Biharis. Many more were seriously injured. More than 700 arrests had to be made. These persons were sent to different jails in Assam. Many Bihari youths left for the Barauni engineering institute to complete their training.

Namrup did not have any credible local leadership. The local MLA did not have any clout. He was so afraid that I had to bring him in my car from his residence for meetings. The nearby Tingkhong MLA and Socialist leader late Bhadreswar Gogoi was, however, very helpful. The Gandhian leaders from Guwahati, Dwarika Baruah and Hemo Kakati (Bajaj Award winner), brought the messages of peace and amity to an embittered neighbourhood and applied the balm of sanity to the angry people and their frayed tempers. Two officers rendered yeoman service. Kamakhya Prasad Chaliha was the Fertilizer Corporation of India's Public Relations Officer. The other one was Bhupendra Kumar Baruah whom Assam Government deputed post haste to Namrup to take up the position of Chief Executive Officer, Fertilizer Corporation India. He saved the MD of FCI Satish Chandran IAS from sure death when the latter was gheraod by 2000 angry workers inside the factory. Both Chaliha and Baruah worked absolutely in tandem with the district administration.

In our days we were fortunate to be free from political interference. The then Chief Minister Bimala Prasad Chaliha had the practice of ringing me up at night, either at Dibrugarh or at Namrup, to enquire about each day's events. But he never gave any directions regarding how to tackle the law and order situation which he left completely to us. The then Chief Secretary Ahmed Nazir Kidwai was a father figure. He was always supportive.

There were three lessons which the Tinsukia and the Namrup riots, along with the later Digboi and North Lakhimpur disturbances, taught me. It is through people to people contact that such riots can be ultimately controlled. Force has to be applied at the first instance. But that cannot be the only method.

Secondly, I found that it would be impossible to retain the north bank areas tagged to Dibrugarh. I wrote a long report to Government for bifurcation of the district which the then Revenue Minister Mahendra Mohan Choudhury supported. There was already a long standing public demand for a separate Lakhimpur district which

Mahananda Bora again started reiterating. He was joined by other public spirited leaders. The Government approved the proposal. This started a process in which most big districts were divided into smaller ones so that it became easier to control the law and order situation and to manage development work.

The Government realised that jobs were at the root of the trouble. They persuaded Oil India and FCI to reserve 100 per cent of the class four jobs for local candidates. The district administration was asked to depute officers to the interview boards to ensure that only local candidates were selected. For the higher posts Government itself appointed an IAS officer to sit in the Selection Board.

The fact that the present Bihari-Assamese fight is entirely irrelevant and harmful to both communities has been recognised by all sensible people. ULFA started these riots in order to chase out the Biharis so that Bangladeshi labour may replace them. The policies pursued and the actions taken by both the Governments of Assam and Bihar this time must also be appreciated. But reservation of jobs in category 'C' and 'D' must be ensured for the local people. Only then will permanent peace be established.

CHAPTER – 19

Why Dima Hasao is Burning ?

Dima Hasao is one of the two hill districts of Assam. This name was adopted in 2010. Earlier the district was known as the North Cachar Hills district. Here the local administration is run by an autonomous district council elected in accordance with the provisions of the Sixth Schedule of the Indian Constitution. During the past few years this district has been affected by one of the worst insurgencies in India's North East Region (NER). Killings, bomb-blasts, extortions, kidnappings, destruction and damages to public and private properties have been quite extensive. In this chapter it is proposed to examine the nature of this insurgency and its background.

Dima Hasao is a small district with a population of only 1,88,079 in 2001. It is projected that in 2011 the population of Dima Hasao will be 2,17,000. The density of population was only 38 per sq.km in 2001. There are 645 villages in the district out of which 605 are inhabited. But only 124 are electrified. The total area is 4,880 sq. kms out of which 21.77 sq. kms are urban and the rest are rural. There are only 4 towns. The gender ratio is adverse against females there being only 884 females against 1000 males. This is the lowest gender ratio of any district in Assam where the state average is 935 females against 1000 males.

Dima Hasao is a very poor district. A few examples will prove this statement. Only 14,133 households have safe drinking water and 12,848 have electricity against a total number of 38,589 households. The rate of literacy is 67.62 percent. As many as 70 percent of the people are Hindus, 26.68 percent are Christians and 2.48 percent are Muslims. Scheduled Tribes form 68.28 percent of the population of the district and Scheduled Castes 1.79 percent.

There is only one hospital in the district along with just 2 dispensaries and 10 primary health centres. The total number of beds in the hospitals and the different types of health centres is 190. There are just 60 doctors. The number of births registered in 2008 was 4408 and the number of deaths 1625. The people living in the district are not properly looked after as far as their health is concerned. They suffer from quite a few endemic and epidemic diseases.

There are only 714 primary schools, 206 middle schools, 86 high schools, 6 higher secondary schools, 6 junior colleges and only 1 degree college. The enrolments are also low. A total of 17,716 are in primary classes, 11,482 in middle classes, 4893 in high schools, 745 in higher secondary schools and 365 in junior colleges.

The indicators of poverty and deprivations outlined in the foregoing paragraphs will show that Dima Hasao district is a fertile ground where the growing disaffection against government is quite natural. What is surprising is that it escalated into insurgency. Moreover, even by engaging a huge troop of 10,000 police and para-military forces it took a long time to control a district with just about 2 lakh people. It was probably because of two reasons. The terrain is difficult and undulating. Moreover, a major portion of the area is covered by dense forests and steep hills. Secondly, the villages are not only sparsely populated but are situated at great distances from each other. Many of these villages are situated at hill tops. The climb is very steep and narrow. These are perfect conditions for guerrillas to operate against organized forces who can normally move only in vehicles. The guerrillas can attack and ambush such forces easily taking cover of the deep jungle. This has happened in a large number of cases.

Several tribes inhabit Dima Hasao district. The largest in number are the Dimasas, a sub-group of the great Kachari tribal group who have lived in the North East since ancient times. There are Dimasas in Karbi Anglong, Cachar and Nagaon districts of Assam and in Dimapur of Nagaland. The word Dimasa means children of a great river. The district is now (2010) named after the Dimasas. That has been one of the demands of the ethnic people. But the other tribes also had their own grievances. The Zemes, for example, would like to be included in Nagalim, or greater Nagaland, along with the territory they now occupy. The Dimasas resent the infiltration and land grabbling by Bangladeshis and Nepalis.

The next tribe in number and importance to the Dimasas are the Zemes who are spread all over the district. The majority of them live in the north-eastern part of Dima Hasao district and the area south of Maibong, which was the old capital of the Kachari kings. Zemes are a sub-tribe of Kacha Nagas. Their compatriots call themselves Zeliangs in Nagaland and Zeliangrongs in Manipur. The Zemes have six different clans. The Hmars migrated to Dima Hasao district from Myanmar and Manipur. The whole tribe has been converted to Christianity. They have built churches in each of their villages. The Kukis are a group of tribes with 37 sub-tribes. They are believed to have migrated to India from Central Asia through Myanmar. They are spread in Dima Hasao district of Assam, in Nagaland and in Myanmar. They are Christians and are very modern in their outlook and appearance. Beside the main tribes described above there are other small tribal groups including the Bietes and the Hronghols who inhabit parts of Dima Hasao district. With very small populations these tribes live apart from each other. They are staunchly individualistic.

The conditions in Dima Hasao district are therefore conducive to insurgency. The rugged hills and the deep jungles provide the shelter. The ethnic aspirations of a variety of tribes inspire the insurgency. The leadership is provided by the elite group of youths with money and social clout. The main insurgent outfit called the Dima Halam Daogah (DHD) was led by Jewel Garlosa, a highly educated youth who enjoyed the very best facilities of life. When he and his main associate were arrested in Bangalore the high life they were living came to light and shocked most people. Jewel was arrested in June, 2009. On October 2, 2009 more than three hundred of DHD(J) leaders and cadres surrendered. The entirely unsavoury operations of this group became known through their statements.

The money for the insurgent groups came from Government coffers. The fact that rampant looting of Government funds had taken place in Dima Hasao district was known for sometime. The cases started by the National Investigation Agency (NIA), as already referred to, showed how funds meant for development were withdrawn by corrupt Government officers and unscrupulous political functionaries. They handed over part of the money to the insurgent outfits for purchase of weapons and to be spent on the upkeep of their cadres. NIA has now submitted chargesheets on October 18, 2010 against 16 people based on NIA's investigations and the concurrent probe conducted by the Central Bureau of Investigation (CBI). Those now in jail on these charges include Mohet Hojai, former Chief Executive Member of the erstwhile NC Hills Autonomous District Council, Jewel Garlosa himself, Niranjan Hojai, Commander of DHD(J) and RH Khan, suspended district social welfare officer, who actually withdrew the money and in whose relative's house at Guwahati almost Rs.14 crores were found in cash stored behind false walls. Khan was instrumental in transferring money to DHD(J) directly and through Hawala transactions in Guwahati and Kolkata.

Meanwhile, the Comptroller and Auditor General of India (CAG) has conducted a special audit into the misutilisation of funds in Dima Hasao Autonomous District Council during the financial years 2007-08, 2008-09 and 2009-10 (upto June 12, 2009). Many irregularities, misappropriations and fraudulent withdrawals were pointed in the chargesheets. Media reports indicate that the scam could involve as high an amount as Rs. 1000 crores and the illegal beneficiaries might involve even the highest political functionaries in the State of Assam. The former Governor Lt. Gen. (Retd.) Ajai Singh is accused by media to have been one of those illegitimate beneficiaries. He is also alleged to have transferred cash by trunk loads from Haflong, the headquarters of the district, to Guwahati, the State capital. All these, however, need to be proved in the court of law.

The CAG has also pointed that an amount of Rs. 272 crores was released by the Government of Assam to the district council in excess of budgetary allocations during 2007-09. How this could happen is really intriguing. The State Government will have to explain such excess payments in the next Assembly session. In any case what has happened in Dima Hasao district is something which has not happened anywhere else in the country. This is a slur on our ethical standards. This is so horrible that it has shocked the entire country. Indian democracy must act and punish the guilty without hesitation.

A Fact Finding Committee of the prestigious organization - Justice on Trial - headed by Justice VM Tamaskar visited Dima Hasao district and after detailed enquiry and consultations made certain important recommendations. These should be implemented early.

CHAPTER – 20

Food Riots of Autumn, 2010

In a number of districts of Assam riots took place in September-October, 2010 when poor people who were denied special ration cards for rice at concessional price virtually revolted and attacked the concerned Government officials and destroyed public property. Valuable lives were lost, large numbers injured and many blocks and other offices were burnt down and damaged.

The villagers were aggrieved because quite a few poor families were left out of the lists of below poverty line (BPL) people. The main reason for such exclusion of poor families was the reduction of BPL percentage by the Government of India in their latest estimate published in March, 2007 based on the 61st round of National Sample Survey operations (NSSO). In case of Assam the BPL estimates were shown as reduced from 40.9 percent in 1999-2000 to 19.7 percent in 2004-05 on the basis of uniform recall period (URP) and from 36.1 percent to 15 percent, during the same period, on the basis of mixed recall period (MRP). There was an incredible fall of Assam's BPL ratio by 21.2 percentile points viewed against only 8.5 percentile points fall for the entire country. This should have aroused the State Government to the dangers ahead. Instead of that the Government started propaganda claiming success for its plans and programmes saying that there was tremendous economic development in Assam. The results are now apparent in the food riots. It is fortunate that a number of State

Governments including Bihar and Kerala started protesting and the Government of India appointed the Suresh Tendulkar Committee to review the situation. This Committee revised Assam's BPL figure to 34.4 percent. Even this is not really reflective of the actual situation at the grassroot level. Assam should conduct an independent survey immediately beside co-operating with the all-India survey to be conducted in accordance with the Supreme Court's dictum published in the media on October 20-21, 2010.

What people objected to are the anomalies in the selection of beneficiaries for distribution of low priced rice and the largesse given under the Anna Surakhsa Yojana. It seems that many families were selected who actually belonged to the high income groups. Families of PWD contractors, commercial vehicle owners, big land lords, government job holders and their cohorts were given BPL cards which meant 10 kgs. of fair price shop rice at Rs. 6 per kg. A few such families got even higher allocations of rice. At the same time in the same villages very poor families were left out and got nothing. It is the members of these deprived families who started the riots.

Many people complained that the members of the ruling party got preference. They alleged that most, if not all, beneficiaries were selected only from among the ruling party supporters by the party apparatchiks, who had been put in charge of preparing the lists of beneficiaries. On the other hand the Government and the ruling party leaders alleged that the opposition parties have fomented trouble unnecessarily in order to make political gains.

After the riots Government became active. According to media reports some amends have been made and enquiries also have been ordered. In order to benefit more people 5000 additional families will be given fair price rice in each of the 126 assembly constituencies. This will mean that in the entire State the number of BPL families getting low priced rice will increase by another 6,30,000. These measures will meet public grievances to some extent.

One Deputy Commissioner told me that since only 10 kgs. of rice is provided to each family at the rate of Rs. 6 per kg and since the market price of that quality of rice is only Rs. 16 per kg. the net gain in cash terms is only Rs. 100 per family per month. This is a small amount. People should not have rioted only for this paltry sum. But he forgot that rights were involved and that people were fighting for their rights. Moreover, people were afraid that when other commodities like sugar, kerosene, edible oils, etc. are also sold in fair price shops at cheap rates they will lose. In fact there is already a proposal to extend the subsidies on other essential commodities also. This proposal was made by the high power co-ordinating body of the United Progressive Alliance Government chaired by Sonia Gandhi herself.

It is not certain whether the State Government and civil society have learnt the lessons of these riots. There seems to be a mood of complacency once again now that the rioting has stopped. But if proper steps are not taken rioting may erupt once again. In this connection the most important step should be to formalize the system of identification of BPL and Antodaya families. For this purpose there is no better agency than the Gaon Sabhas (GSs). It is the local people who will know the pecuniary conditions of each family. It is, therefore, the GSs who will be able to advise Government better on selection of beneficiaries of the schemes. Even otherwise GSs are the constitutional bodies who are empowered to carry the functions of local governments. Therefore, more trust should be placed on them. Government and civil society must realize that in the twenty-first century people will not tolerate distribution of benefits of public schemes in a hush hush manner by a few officials or party members.

The riots show that if the Government is perceived to be unfair, people will take the law into their own hands.

The disaffection will proliferate. Wide spread riots will be difficult to control by the police. It is, therefore, necessary to ensure that Government action is always seen as fair, just and equitable.

It has to be remembered that Maoist ideology has taken roots in many parts of India and nearby countries. In Nepal Maoists have won majority of seats in Parliament. They got the king removed and established a republic. In the northern and central states of India and in West Bengal Maoists have influenced millions of peasants and workers. Many incidents have taken place resulting in death and injury to a large number of people. If the Assam Government allows disaffection to spread through unfair distribution of benefits to the poor, Maoists will take a hold on the State. Meanwhile, Akhil Gogoi and his Krishak Mukti Sangram Samittee (KMSS) have made a deep impression on the poor and even the middle classes in Assam. Gogoi is one leader people seem to trust. He has become well-known in many other States of India. The support he got and the attendance he could gather for his New Delhi Sansad Gherao programme show that his movement is growing among the people at the grassroots level. Gogoi's ideals are similar to those of the Maoists but his methods are non-violent. However, its growing popularity might encourage the insurgent outfits of the State and provide them with a reservoir of disgruntled youths for recruitment to their ranks. Government should keep an eye on these possibilities and see that food riots do not recur due to inequitable selection of beneficiaries.

CHAPTER – 21

The Resurgence of Bodo Society

The fact that the Bodo-Kacharies are one of the original tribes inhabiting the Brahmaputra Valley is well recognised. When the Tai-Ahoms invaded the valley and established their hegemony in the thirteenth century AD the Bodo influence started declining. Meanwhile the Bodos started merging with the main stream of Assamese society. It was at that crucial moment that a great leader appeared on the scene and brought about a resurgence of Bodo society.

I first heard about Gurudev Kalicharan Brahma (April, 1860 - May, 1938) when I was a student of the Cotton College in the 1950s. Quite a few of my Bodo contemporaries including Samar Brahma Choudhury and Prasenjit Brahma (son-in-law and son, respectively, of Rupnath Brahma) were very close to me. They told me about Gurudev. In order to understand the present Bodo insurgency it is essential to know what Gurudev did for the Bodo society in the first half of the twentieth century.

When I joined as Deputy Commissioner of the erstwhile united Goalpara district with headquarters at Dhubri in late 1967 the Plains Tribal Council of Assam (PTCA) movement had just begun. We had frequent problems in the then Kokrajhar sub-division which necessitated my constant attention. I visited almost all the villages connected with Gurudev's activities and only then realised how great an impact Gurudev had on Bodo society and its religious, political and cultural resurgence.

When the then Chief Minister Bimala Prasad Chaliha paid quite an extensive visit to the Kokrajhar sub-division in January, 1968 he attended many meetings and held discussions with a large number of Bodo leaders. I was constantly by his side along with Rupnath Brahma, the then Assam Minister. We had arranged a big public Bihu feast at Kokrajhar which the Chief Minister attended. Chaliha's visit gave me the first occasion when I could have a real feel of the depth of Bodo sentiment. I was convinced that the Bodo problem needed a human touch and a political solution. The PTCA agitation could not be dismissed as a mere law and order situation.

When the Chaliha Cabinet decided to put up to the Assam Assembly the proposal for introduction of Bodo language in the Secondary Schools I drafted the report overnight which the then Minister (and Dhubri MLA) Sayed Ahmed Ali carried personally to Shillong next day. The Assembly took a unanimous decision to adopt the proposal. All this and my academic interest in historical, social and economic affairs of the areas which I had the honour to serve brought me into close proximity with several personalities who had been inspired by the teachings of Gurudev.

One person whom I respected and liked very much was Rupnath Brahma who was a disciple and close associate of Gurudev. I had met him first in 1962 when he visited Silchar and Karimganj to see the pest affected paddy fields as the then Agriculture Minister. I was then the Assistant Commissioner under training at Silchar. I met him several times after that. I met him for the last time only a couple of days before he died. He died on Jaunary 23, 1968. I happened to be in Guwahati on that day. When I was informed about the event I immediately rushed back to Kokrajhar so that I could attend his funeral along with thousands of Bodo and non-Bodo people.

The present Bodo mindset and the process of its formation over the decades of fight against injustice, discrimination and isolation has to be understood and appreciated against the work that Gurudev did during the last decade of the nineteenth and the early decades of the twentieth centuries. It is Gurudev who lifted up Bodo society which hitherto had "remained a stagnant society". Actually the then existing Bodo society's refusal to accept "changes with time" had "contributed to their backwardness, ignorance, neglect and decay".

Gurudev got initiated to the Brahmo religion and started preaching it after his visit to Kolkatta and meeting with Swami Sibnarayan Paramhansa. Gurudev visited Kolkata thrice. During the course of his campaign for that religion Gurudev held many conventions and made many visits all over the Brahmaputra valley. It is not known, however, whether Gurudev had any direct links or connections with the thoughts of the early savants of Brahmo religion such as Raja Rammohan Roy, Dwarkanath Tagore and Keshab Chandra Sen. The ideals which these leaders had propagated brought immense changes in Indian society in the nineteenth century such as the position of women, introduction of widow remarriage, abolition of polygamy and early marriage, provision of higher education and inter-caste marriage. As the *Advanced History of India* records "many far-reaching changes in Hindu social ideals have been and are still being brought about, steadily and silently, by the indirect influence of the Brahmo Samaj".

Gurudev's main concern was to stop proselytising by the Christian and Muslim clerics. Secondly, he did not support of worshipping many gods and goddesses. It is, however, an enigma why he did not support Srimanta Sankardev's Ek Sarania dharma which recognised only one God and eschewed idol worship. Gurudev campaigned to stop absorption of the Bodos in the fold of

Ek Sarania dharma. But Gurudev maintained quite a close link with the Assamese mainstream. At the time of Simon Commission (1929) he opposed the proposed annexation of Goalpara district to Bengal which the Goalpara zamindars had demanded. He also supported restoration of Assamese language in the courts and schools of Goalpara district very strongly.

Gurudev was not only a religious preacher but was also a great social reformer. The organisations he set up did immense good to Bodo society. The various yogyahutis (sacrifical fires) that Gurudev held in different places drew thousands of people. The majority of these people converted themselves to the Brahmo religion. During his three visits to Kolkata Gurudev had obtained permission of Swami Sibnarayan Paramhansa to use "Brahma" as a surname for those Bodos who converted themselves to the new religion. That is why we have so many Brahmas in Assam. Some non-Bodos also became Gurudev's disciples.

The Brahma Boarding which Gurudev had built at Dhubri not only offered shelter to Bodo students and traders but also provided a place where future Bodo leaders could meet. Thus the famous 1925 rally and the protest meetings, against higher caste people's opposition to the adoption of surname Brahma, were held in the Brahma Boarding.

Gurudev organised the first Bodo Mahasanmilany in 1921 at Bhaoragury with Rupnath Brahma as the first Secretary. This was followed by several such Mahasanmilanis in different places in Assam. Many resolutions were adopted in these Mahasanmilanis, which were mostly on matters relating to social reform. In a recent book titled "Journey Towards Enlightenment: Gurudev and the Bodo Society" the joint authors Mitra and Narzary have noted that these resolutions were passed because Gurudev felt that Bodos have to abandon the "habits like excessive liquor consumption, rearing pigs, forced marriages, animal sacrfice, internal feuds, hedonistic religious practices" if they were to "acquire a higher status in the society" and "usher in modernisation and progress". This book is a mine of information about the early Bodo movement. It also records most of the events of those times in Assam.

The third Bodo Mahasanmilani, held at Roumari near Bongaigaon in 1929, was attended by several non-Bodo leaders at Gurudev's invitation. These included Nilmoni Phukan, Ambikagiri Roy Choudhury and Mahadev Sarma. Another distinguished personality - Ananda Chandra Agarwalla - who was then the Superintendent of Police of the united Goalpara district and "a follower of Gurudev" attended the Mahasanmilani.

Again it was Gurudev who inspired setting up the Bodo Students Union. Gurudev had little formal education but as the Chief Guest he made the significant statement that "to live meaningfully education is very necessary" in the first Bodo Students Union meeting held at Kokrajhar in 1919. Later this organisation converted itself into the All Assam Bodo Students Union (AABSU).

Gurudev's encouragement led to the publication of "Bibar" in 1924 which was the first Bodo language magazine. Gurudev was also instrumental in organising a co-operative society, schools, Brahma Company, Ryot sabhas, Mahila samitees, Women's convention at Molandubi and many other organisations.

Gurudev had influenced Bodo society in many different ways. His influence was also felt in Assam's history during the first half of the twentieth century. Gandhiji came to visit the Bodo village of Rupsi in 1934 after he had seen and had been impressed by the beauty of Bodo handicraft and handloom in the 1926 Guwahati Congress session. Gurudev went there to receive Gandhiji.

The large crowd hailed Gurudev as the "Mech Gandhi". Gandhiji was very happy after his visit to Rupsi.

Gurudev played an important role in bringing about the Tribal League after the Roha convention of April, 1933. This Tribal League was the prime mover in the creation of 33 tribal blocks and belts which played an important role in Assam's politics during 1933-1947. When the Simon Commission took interviews in 1929 Gurudev represented the case of the Bodos. He returned a hero after meeting the Simon Commission in Shillong.

Perhaps one of the greatest contributions of Gurudev was the "Boroni Pandulipi" which happens to be "a social law book". This book has "relevance for the entire Bodo community" and is a guide for them "in their day-to-day activities and on social matters". After many rounds of discussions the *Boroni Pandulipi,* along with its 126 by-laws, was adopted in the fourth Bodo Mahasanmilani held in Gurudev's village of Kajigaon in November, 1934. It marked "the beginning of an era of unity, integrity and brotherhood among the Bodo community and was a vital force that would strongly bind them together even in the future".

To sum up, the entire life of Gurudev was dedicated to the upliftment of Bodo Society for whom all the different organisations and institutions were created by him. He was the builder of the new Bodo society.

CHAPTER – 22

Our Bhutanese 'Kurma'

Certain facets of Assam's relations with Bhutan need to be highlighted in order to understand the present political imbroglio in its historical setting. History has recorded the fact that several princes of Kamarupa had founded principalities and ruled over parts of Bhutan. Kumar Bhaskaravarmana (600-650 AD), probably the greatest king of Kamarupa, had established close relations with Bhutan. After his death the political relations weakened. But the social, cultural and religious links survived and flourished. It is this relationship which prevented police action on ULFA insurgents hiding in Bhutan for a long time because the Bhutanese Government did not want to enrage the Assamese.

I had come in contact with the Bhutanese royal family in early 1960s. I had met the late King Jigme Dorji Wangchuk a few times while posted at Mangaldai as SDO (1963-65) and at Dhubri as DC (1967-69). He was the present King Jigme Singye Wangchuk's father. Earlier the present King's uncle, Wangchuk Namgyal, who is now the King's Representative, was my batch-mate in the IAS training College at Mussoorie for a year during 1961-62. Among all the probationers he excelled in horse riding. I was probably one of the worst. He taught me some tricks so that I could pass the final examination by making the mandatory high jump at the back of my horse over the tall barrier at the end of the hurdles. Wangchuk and I had developed a warm friendship. When I went to

Bhutan in April, 1994 he took me and my wife around in his powerful pojero vehicle to some of the remote places.

Guru Padmasambhava, who is also known in Bhutan as Guru Rimpoche or Guru Padmaraja, the Lotus King, came to Taktasang Lahkhang near Paro airport in Bhutan in 746 AD. This monastery clings precariously on the edge of a cliff 2,950 metres above the sea level. Guru Padmasambhava was born in the Swat Valley which is now in Pakistan. Having had his education in the ancient University of Taksashila he came to Dacca Dakshin where Sri Chaitanya Mahaprabhu was born. I had visited Dacca Dakshin near Sylhet city while on an official delegation to erstwhile East Pakistan in early 1963. But no one there knew anything about Guru Padmasambhava who had spent a few years there learning about Hindu religious practices. Then the Guru came to Kamakhya where he had his initiation into Tantrism. After living for a number of years in Kamakhya he went to Bhutan. There he spread Tantric Buddhism which he had evolved out of a blend of Mahayana Buddhism and Tantrism into which Bhutan's earlier Animism or Pon religion of worshipping the Bon deities was also incorporated. The worship of Tara distinguishes Tantric Buddhism from the main religion. Guru Padmasambhava's Kamakhya connection explains the predominance of goddess Tara in the Buddhism of Bhutan, Tibet, Arunachal Pradesh and Sikkim. Ever since then the Bhutanese have been making Tangkha, a colourfully painted religious scroll, usually depicting goddess Tara, Guru Padmasambhava and Lord Buddha. The one with the goddess Tara motif that I was presented on a visit to the Tawang monastery in Arunachal Pradesh is quite beautiful. It is painted with vegetable dyes on the finest silk. Goddess Tara is just another name of mother goddess Kamakhya. Therein lies the significance of Guru Padmasambhava's connection with Kamakhya and his Tantric Buddhism. The Bhutanese have continued that connection by frequent pilgrimages to Kamakhya and Hajo.

Again, to quote Dr. Parmanand, the great scholar on South Asia Affairs, "Buddhism has always played an important role in Bhutan's history and people's life" and it is "the real foundation of the national church of Bhutan today". That is why religion is intertwined with Bhutanese politics. Even their national anthem contains the line "long live the king who directs the affairs of both state and religion". This aspect has been emphasized by the eminent French Anthropologist Francoise Pammaret in her book on Bhutan. Therefore Bhutanese politics and even diplomacy should be examined only against this background.

When I informed the then Chief Minister Hiteswar Saikia that I would be leading a delegation to Thimphu to finalise the agreement between India and Bhutan on the Dhansiri project he immediately recollected our historical ties with that country. Saikia's characteristic attention to details, which his detractors may consider trivial, appeared remarkable to me. Saikia instructed his Principal Private Secretary, Hari Prasad Chaliha, whom he not only trusted but also respected, to send with me Assamese saris and endi chadars not only for the King but also for the Ministers and others. On the road to Thimpu from Jayanagar on the Indian side and Phuntsoling on the Bhutanese side our cavalcade included a landrover loaded with saris, silk gamochas and endi chadars. I felt like Fa Hien or Huen Tsang visiting the courts of Magadha and Kamarupa loaded with Chinese mementoes. Chaliha had selected the biggest saris for the dignitaries. For the King the sari was one and a half meters long. I never believed that such a giant sari existed. This sari is now adorning the palace reception room. All these were entrusted to the charge of the then Flood Control Commissioner Puranjay Sharma who had accompanied me and who had actually signed the formal agreement with the Bhutanese Home Minister. Earlier we had finalized the draft with the help of the Indian Charge de Affaires, one Mathur, a very serious and formal gentleman. He was the antithesis of the Bhutanese Home Secretary, Wangda, who accompanied me throughout our travel.

Wangda was so jovial and suave that we enjoyed every minute of our trip. In a prominent report in the official Bhutanese newspaper - *Kuensel* - it was recorded that "the Chief Secretary conveyed to his Majesty the warm greetings of goodwill and friendship of the Chief Minister of Assam Sri Saikia. He said that it was the desire of the State Government of Assam to further strengthen its close relationship with Bhutan". The present Bhutanese Ambassador to India, Dago Tsering, who was a few years junior to me in the IAS Training College, ruminated over my 1994 visit to Thimphu in a private luncheon at the Bhutanese Embassy in New Delhi recently. Tsering, who was Bhutan's Home Minister during the 1990s, had come to Guwahati twice. We had meals together both the times. On the first occasion I hosted a glittering reception for him below the huge chandellier in the foyer of the Assam Administrative Staff College which Hiteswar Saikia also attended.

My discussion with the King on the insurgency problem was duly reported in personal debriefing in New Delhi and also in Dispur. But the way the King explained the denotation and connotation of the Assamese word "Kurma" in the context of the insurgency problem really left an indelible mark on my mind. His sensitivity to the tender feelings of the Bhutanese, Bodos and Assamese touched me deeply. He said that the Bhutanese considered the Assamese and the Bodo people as "Kurmas". In winter the Bhutanese families follow the practice of coming down to the adjoining northern districts of Assam with their livestock and woollen clothes. They live with families on Assam side. They buy endi and other materials before returning home. In summer the Assamese and the Bodos go up in similar manner to savour the hospitality of their Bhutanese "Kurmas". The *Kuensel* reported that "His Majesty told the Chief Secretary that the Bhutanese people have traditionally enjoyed close and brotherly ties of friendship with the Assamese people and that the existing close relations should be further strengthened through the promotion of closer trade and economic ties between Assam and Bhutan". No wonder that the Bhutanese were reluctant to take violent action against the insurgents and tried to avoid bloodshed till patience was exhausted. I may add that the lower Assam word "Kurma" means "Mitir" in written Assamese and "Sambandhi" in Hindi.

CHAPTER – 23

Geo-Strategic Importance of Look East Policy

Several Indian insurgent outfits have used Myanmar, Thailand and a few south-east Asian countries for their shelter, training and investment of money extorted and taken out of India. Their leaders have directed terrorist activities from these countries. One of the outcomes of the recent agreements between India and these countries is expected to curb insurgent activities. At least the recent agreements with Bangladesh and Myanmar have definitely stipulated this. In this chapter I propose to examine this subject in its entirety and not only in respect of insurgency.

Theoretical economics has long pleaded for removal of all restrictions on trade. The belief is that "in every country it always is and must be the interest of the great body of the people to buy whatever they want of those who sell it cheapest". Stating this in his *Wealth of Nations* Adam Smith also clarified that "the proposition is so very manifest that it seems ridiculous to take any pains to prove it; nor could it ever have been called in question, had not the interested sophistry of merchants and manufacturers confounded the commonsense of mankind".

In the practical field international trade has fostered the wealth of nations all along. In the tremendous economic development which has taken place in the six decades since the end of the Second World War trade probably has played the most important role. When I visited Taiwan in 2003 I went into the genesis of its transformation from a poor fishing island into one of the most prosperous countries in the world. It was in 1950 that Generalissimo Chiang Kei Shek and his wife Sung Li fled to Taiwan (then called Formosa) after Mao Zedong's Red Army swept into power in mainland China. They started the process of Taiwan's economic development through trade. First they harvested and exported fish. Then agricultural and agro-industrial goods. Then the products of village and small industries which included very large consignments of cheap ready-made clothes. This continued for some time when they started manufacturing and exporting computer hardware. Meanwhile the entire young generation went through a sort of knowledge revolution which created a huge human resource base in a small country. Taiwan does not have much natural resources. But it imported raw materials from different countries and transformed these into high quality manufactured goods and exported the same. This value addition became possible through its technically skilled and rich human resources.

A number of countries including South Korea, Thailand, Singapore, Hong Kong, Malaysia and others followed more or less similar growth paths and became prosperous. Even Indonesia and the Philippines are going through the same process. To quote the Nobel Prize winning economist Joseph E. Stiglitz, "the most successful developing countries in the world have achieved their success through trade - through exports". But he has warned that "opening up markets in the developing countries to goods from the advanced industrial countries without full reciprocation" might not work. He quoted the case of Europe when in 2001 it "unilaterally opened up its markets to the poorest countries of the world" and "almost no trade followed". Stiglitz referred to the various trade agreements and opined that "even if trade agreements have been truly free and fair, not all countries would have benefited - or at least benefited much - and not all people, even in the countries that did benefit, would share in the gains. Even if trade barriers are brought down systematically, not everyone is equally in a position to take advantage of the new opportunities".[1]

These are prophetic words with great potency. What I propose to do in this chapter is to examine whether the North Eastern Region (NE) of India is ready to participate fully in the 'Look East Policy' (LEP) of the Government of India and whether NE will actually gain from such a policy. Let me first lay down the expectations of the LEP in its historical perspective.

Ever since liberalization of the Indian economy in 1990 a new orientation is sought to be given to India's foreign policy and trade by a thrust on south Asian and south-east Asian countries. Prime Minister Manmohan Singh described India's LEP as "a strategic shift in our perspective" and further clarified that "the age-old India-Asean linkages have been given a renewed thrust with the impressive growth of connectivity and the ever increasing flows of tourism between India and Asean". In fact, Asean (Association of South East Asian Nations) has reached 40 years of its existence in 2007. Recalling the recent events Singh further said that "in the present phase of our Look East Policy, we in India seek to deepen our economic integration by entering into free trade or comprehensive economic partnership agreements, both with Asean as a whole and with individual countries of the region".[2] Considerable progress has been recorded in trade between India and the Asean countries in the past few years. The volume has risen from US $40 billion in 2007-08 to US $44 billion in 2009-10. A Free Trade Agreement (FTA) was signed between India and the Asean countries in Bangkok on August 13, 2009. It is proposed to increase the trade volume to US $60 in seven years and to reduce the tariff rates drastically. In fact, the growth rate of trade between India and the Asean member countries has been 15.69 percent between 2007-08 and 2009-10. This remarkable growth has been registered with all the Asean member countries: Brunei, Cambodia, Indonesia, Laos, Malaysia, Myanmar, Philippines, Singapore, Thailand and Vietnam.

The very first agreement in this field was the Indo-Myanmar Trade Agreement signed on January 31, 1994. The agreement provided for "establishment of trade on the basis of equality and mutual benefit". The idea was to put in place a "signalling device to monitor the movement of commodities and people". Probably another objective was to provide "an insurance against the perceived threat of Chinese dominance of the region".[3] A memorandum of understanding (MOU) was also signed between the Government of India and Myanmar on the same day. These two agreements were followed by a delegation on June 10, 1994.

Media comments on these events at that time were favourable to the Government of India. For example, Sapra said that "improvement in relations with ASEAN as well as other key East Asian countries like China and Japan would only heighten regional economic bonds. India's increasing integration with this region will only help ensure that these bonds do not snap at any time in the foreseeable future".[4] The MOU is concerned with co-operation between civilian border authorities of the two countries. The minutes of the talk related to banking and trading arrangements, immigration and customs inspection and timing of border trade. Indo-Myanmar trade was formally launched on April 12, 1995 by the Union Commerce Minister P. Chidambaram and his Myanmarese counterpart Lt. Gen. Tun Kyi.

It is appropriate that the LEP first touched Myanmar. Myanmar has a common border of 1643 kms with four of India's states, namely, Arunachal Pradesh, Nagaland, Manipur and Mizoram. For trade with China and the south east Asian countries by the land route all movement has to be through Myanmar. It is true that Myanmar itself is poor. It does not have as much manufactured goods to offer as the other south-east Asian countries. But it has vast natural resources which are yet to be tapped. In recent years the volume of trade between India and Myanmar has gone up to US $1.2 billions. At present India's imports include pulses, wood and wood products, fruits and nuts, natural rubber and paper and paper pulp. India exports drugs and pharmaceutical products, machinery and instruments, steel and transport equipments.

Moreover, Myanmar's geo-strategic location cannot be ignored. That is why India is building the trans-Asian railway network through Myanmar to Singapore. The Asian road highway is also under construction through Myanmar. The ultimate idea is to link up the Indian ocean with south China sea. Besides, India has taken up several infrastructure projects in Myanmar. Tatas are setting up a truck manufacturing plant at Magway, the ESSAR group is joining in the attempt to build the multi-modal Kaladan transport project, the National Hydroelectric Power Corporation will build the Tamanthi power project and the Government of India will help Myanmar to build a new port at Sittwe.

All these efforts to achieve closer Indo-Myanmarese relations reflected India's present pragmatism in matters relating to foreign policy. It may be recalled that writing about India's foreign policy in the Asian context the former Indian Foreign Secretary JN Dixit had suggested that our trade relations with Myanmar should be normalized irrespective of the government that may be in power there because that country is geo-strategically important to India. Such close co-operation with Myanmar is also necessary in order to curb smuggling, border crimes, drug movement and insurgency. Dixit, however, never envisaged LEP although he had devoted three chapters of his book to India's relations with the countries of Asia.[5] In recent years India has changed its policy towards the autocratic junta which controls Myanmar. India is continuing to support the world community's effort towards assisting the Nobel Laureate Aung San Su Ki's fight for democracy in her country. But at the same time it is doing business with the junta government of Myanmar. This is realpolitik. It is in pursuance of this realpolitik that India and Myanmar have exchanged high level visits in recent times. The most important visit perhaps is that of the Myanmarese senior General Than Shwe, who as the "Chairman of the State Peace and Development Council of Myanmar" heads the autocratic government of that country. During his discussion with the Indian Prime Minister on July 27, 2010 India and Myanmar agreed on "close co-operation between the security forces of the two countries in tackling the pernicious problem of terrorism". Arrangements were also finalized for Indian participation in critical areas like medical science, education, telecom services and in major projects and manufacturing industries. Than Shwe was accompanied by a large delegation which included U Soe Tha, Minister for National Planning and Economic Development, U Tin Naing Thein, Minister for Commerce and U Thaung, Minister for Science and Technology. This shows the seriousness with which Myanmar has taken the trade and security relationships with India.

An important and parallel development has been in the spiritual and the cultural fields. The ancient university of Nalanda near Pataliputra (modern Patna) is being revived. The relevant Act has been passed by Parliament in 2010. It was former President APJ Abdul Kalam who made the suggestion in an address to the joint session of the Bihar Assembly and council in March, 2006. Thereafter, the "Nalanda Proposal" of the Singapore Government was received which spelled the details of a great university of the twenty first century. The basic idea of this proposal was to establish a link between south and east Asia through world-class education and tourism. Then the Nalanda Mentor Group, headed by the Nobel Laureate Amartya Sen, made detailed recommendations regarding governance, finance, academic disciplines and other aspects. The leaders who attended the East Asia Summit at Hua Hin in Thailand in October, 2009 endorsed these recommendations and decided to extend their support to the revival of the University. Meanwhile, the celebration of 1000 years of the Vietnamese capital of Ha Noi during 2010 coincided with a similar celebration of the millennia of establishing the Brihadeswara temple at Thanjavur by the Chola dynasty which played the most important role in connecting India with south-east Asia through trade, commerce and maritime activities. These are occasions which will facilitate integration of India and southeast Asia through the spiritual and cultural exchanges under LEP. In this context it is significant that Than Shwe, a powerful Myanmarese visited Bodh Gaya and other pilgrimage sites around it during his official visit to India. Whether the new world-class university to be established at Guwahati can also be assigned a role in this field needs urgent consideration.

The strategic importance of NE in the Asian context was recognized six decades ago by Admiral Lord Louis Mountbatten, the then Supreme Commander of the Allied Armed Forces. He was no development planner nor was he bent on increasing trade. His sole interest in this area was the transport and communication network for supporting China in the war against Japan. It was his South East Asia Command which built the famous Ledo

Road to Kunming in China for supervising the two oil pipe lines, respectively, from Kolkata and Chittagong to Kunming via Tinsukia. This road was also used for movement of troops and military supplies. Its construction was overseen by Mountbatten's quarrelsome Deputy Gen. JW Stilwell. But a magnanimous Mountbatten named the road after Stilwell.[6] According to media report the Stilwell Road has now been rebuilt by China in the Guangzhou Region upto their border with Myanmar. On the Indian side the road is quite good upto a reasonable distance of the India-Myanmar border. The damaged stretch can be repaired within a short time. It is the portion within Myanmar which will need very extensive rebuilding. Myanmar does not seem to have the resources to do this. Whether India and China will carry out the repair is a question which has no answer as yet.

In the second Indo-Asean summit held in 2003 India signed the treaty of Amity and Co-operation in South-East Asia. A separate declaration provided for combating international terrorism as also for comprehensive economic co-operation with a view to step up the current volume of trade. Again, in order to achieve closer trade relations it is expected that India's peak tariff rates would be reviewed to make these at par with the rates in the Asean countries. For this a Free Trade Agreement has been signed already.

During the later half of 2010s there have been many exchanges between India and the south-east Asian countries. As a part of LEP's diplomatic initiative the Indian External Affairs Minister visited Indonesia and Singapore. After that the Prime Ministers of Thailand, Vietnam and Cambodia visited India. A Thai business delegation visited NE. This has not yet borne any positive results in terms of trade and investment. However, the Conference in Bangkok in October, 2007, has promised some investment in NE by Thailand. Earlier India and

Thailand had signed two agreements: one on enhanced co-operation on renewable energy and the other on cultural exchanges.

Regional co-operation has been given a boost ever since the first BIMSTEC summit in July, 2004. The countries included in this summit were Bangladesh, India, Sri Lanka, Thailand and Myanmar. Again, the Thailand Mekong Ganga Co-operation Project aims at revitalizing and developing overland trade, tourism, communications and transport. The countries involved are India, Myanmar, Thailand, Laos, Cambodia and Vietnam. These are developments which will advance LEP and enhance India's economic and diplomatic relations with these countries.

India's most immediate neighbour, Bangladesh, needs special attention. It is believed that close collaboration between these two countries will help achieve growth and prosperity for both. Therefore, the five agreements signed during Bangladesh Prime Minister Sheikh Hasina's visit to India on January 10-13, 2010 have become significant. These five agreements are on mutual legal assistance in criminal matters, on transfer of sentenced persons, on combating international terrorism, organized crimes and illegal drug trafficking, on co-operation in the power sector and a cultural exchange programme. In pursuance of these agreements certain concrete steps were taken including India's promise to export 240 MW of power to Bangladesh and to assist that country to build power plants of 1320 MW each in Khulna and Chittagong. In respect of import trade India will remove 47 (plus the earlier agreed to 56 items) from the negative list. India will give a credit amounting to US $1 billion to Bangladesh for certain infrastructure projects. Bangladesh will facilitate transit of Indian goods and commodities through its territory and will allow the use of Chittagong and Mangla ports to India. India will give access to Bangladesh for trade and travel to Nepal and Bhutan. As far as insurgents are concerned Bangladesh had pushed out some ULFA leaders from its territory and these leaders were taken into custody by Assam police. In September, 2010, a batch of 28 ULFA leaders who had deserted the outfit came back to India from Bangladesh. This method was followed by a large number of others. According to media reports ULFA commander-in-chief Paresh Barua is completely isolated now. He is somewhere in the Yunan province of China.

There are critics in India who do not like that so many of concessions could be given to Bangladesh. Some of them feel that the credit of US $1 billion (about Rs. 5000 crores) is too much. There is a perpetual adverse balance of trade of about US $1 billion annually which Bangladesh has not been able to wipe out. They do not produce the quality goods which India can import. They have plenty of natural gas. But they want to preserve it underground rather than drill out and export to India. Meanwhile, the value of the smuggled goods, on both sides, has been estimated to have increased to US $3 billion per annum. The Bangladeshi smugglers are reported to be making up the adverse balance of illegal trade by illegal export of arms, gold and narcotics according to a National Council of Applied Economic Research (NCAER) study. After the January, 2010 agreements, this type of clandestine trade should end. However, whether that will actually happen is still a moot question.

Bangladesh is expecting to gain considerable improvement of its economy by better connectivity with India. According to the former Bangladesh Foreign Secretary, Farooq Sobhan, the Prime Minister level talks have "opened up a whole new vista, not only simply in terms of Bangladesh's bilateral relations with India, but in terms of Bangladesh becoming a middle income country by 2021". He further stated that "if Bangladesh is to move from an annual growth rate of 6 per cent to 8 or 9 per cent, it must make rapid progress in the integration of its economy with its immediate neighbours, India, Nepal and Bhutan".

According to Sanjib Baruah, foremost scholar on LEP, "Northeast India's isolation from its neighbourhood has much older roots: that which came about as a result of the advent of western dominance over sea routes and over global trade and more particularly the British conquest of the region and the decisions to draw lines between the hills and plains, to put barriers of trade between Bhutan and Assam and to treat Myanmar as a strategic frontier - British India's buffer against French Indochina and China. While the British colonial rulers built a major new transportation infrastructure, aimed primarily at taking tea and other resources out of Assam, the disruption of old trade routes remained colonialism's most enduring negative legacy".[7]

According to Baruah "Northeast India was on the southern trails of the Silk Road". If that was so, this region had connectivity in the ancient times with the world outside. This got snapped during British times. In this connection Baruah alludes to Bhutan. That country realized the importance of connectivity with south-east Asia. The Bhutan King emphasized this when he made the following statement: "No other region in the world needs harmonious and cooperative relations among its states more than South Asia".[8]

The legal and formal arrangements for trade through NE to southeast Asia are now more or less complete. But is NE ready for it ? This region is not yet economically as developed as the rest of India. Moreover, there are no water bodies surrounding it. After partition of India in 1947 NE lost its natural trade routes through what is now Bangladesh. Its land connectivity with the rest of India remained limited to the 26 kms "Chicken's neck" in northern West Bengal.

As far as trade itself is concerned many countries and regions in the world have become prosperous through trade as noted earlier. In fact, countries like Taiwan, South Korea, Hong Kong, Singapore and Malaysia have achieved their present status and level of development through trade. But what has NE to offer to, say, China in exchange for the plethora of goods which that country is already exporting to this region? Industrial products are very limited. Agricultural products will need proper processing and packaging before the same can be exported. The service sector in NE is not doing badly. But the quality is low. Tourism has not been so attractive because facilities are not upto the mark and also because of media's projection of our security environment in very bad light.[9] An extremely concentrated endeavour will be required to achieve economic development of NE and its principal state of Assam before NE can be ready for participation in LEP. When the Thai trade delegation visited Assam in June, 2007 the Union Minister for Development of North Eastern Region (DONER) said that Rs. 15,000 crores would be spent on infrastructure development in NE in the Eleventh Five Year Plan.[10] The Planning Commission Deputy Chairman also announced that substantial funds will be allocated for all round development of NE in a seminar held on October 7-9, 2007. Unfortunately, however, nothing much has happened during the past three years. It will be necessary that the funds are utilized properly for the development of the region.

Let us examine the situation in some detail. Will opening a new trade route or reviving the previous land trade route through NE lead to economic development of this area? There is nothing automatic about it. Before meaningful trade activities can be undertaken our agriculture has to improve both in terms of production and in terms of productivity. Processing industries have to be set up to manufacture quality goods which can be offered in international markets at acceptable prices. The entire infrastructure of roads, railways, communication and air transport will have to be completely revamped. Similarly hotels, restaurants and resorts will have to be built for sophisticated tourists. If that cannot be achieved LEP will not benefit NE. In that case, LEP will only provide a bridge between the rest of India and south east Asia of which NE will forever remain an "underbelly". This type of result probably was not envisaged when the policy was devised. In order that LEP is inclusive it must therefore provide for economic development of NE as a direct objective. In India the indirect effect or "trickling down effect" has not worked so far. Even Stiglitz has opined that "trickle down economics does not work. The fact is that if the economy grows, it is not inclusive and some time the poor can be worse off".[11]

It is not proposed to go into details of the steps needed to achieve this objective. But an attempt is made to identify, to the extent possible, the exports which are within the range of possibility. Agriculture is the mainstay of majority of people in all the states of NE. However, no scientific study of the varieties of plants available in this area has been made. Such a study is already overdue. According to experts there are more than 200,000 "domesticable" plants available in nature.[12] Again, except for Tripura and Manipur agriculture is not doing well in the other states. In Assam there is a process of declaration during the past few years when production, productivity and land use have all declined. During 2009-10 there is a slight improvement in the situation according to latest reports. However, the potentialities are great in agriculture because of good climate, plenty of water except in certain patches, reasonable cost of land and availability of cheap labour. It is the state government which must stir itself and make concentrated effort for agricultural development taking advantage of the Government of India's present initiative for a second green revolution. In the allied sector insufficient development can be taken up on a large scale. There is a huge market for chickens, ducks, pork and meat on hoof in the Indo-Chinese countries as well as in China. I may mention that I have visited most of these countries during the past one decade. Except for China, Thailand, Malayasia and the city states of Hong Kong and Singapore all the other countries are under-developed. However, the big markets in these countries gave me the impression that they can import many commodities from India.

Export possibilities are quite high in plantation crops. Tea, for example, has been exported ever since the first batch of Assam tea was auctioned at London in 1834. Even now Assam produces more than half of India's and 15 percent of world's tea. Its export has declined somewhat due to increasing cost and lack of demand for high quality tea which Assam produces. Kenya and Sri Lanka produce tea all around the year against Assam's nine month season. Hence the high cost and limited per hectare production. But proper branding and educating the Asian middle class about the value of high liquoring, properly blended and carefully produced Assam tea should be able to increase tea export to these presently non-traditional markets.[13] There was an Assam tea logo launched in March, 1990. It has been reported that the Indian Tea Board is launching another in the near future. This will promote export. Again, the green tea market is quite extensive in Asia. Assam can put some of its area under green tea.

Fresh fruits and vegetables of NE are very tasty. Assam alone produces 1.56 million tones of fruits, 3.88

mt. of vegetables and 0.219 mt. of spices. Spices of Assam include turmeric, black pepper and black-cummins. Once cold storage and cold chain are provided these can be exported in plenty. Cold chain involves pre-cooling at farm yard, deep freezing in heavy vehicles during transportation and retail sale from refrigerators. Preservation and packaging are also important. NE's major fruit products include pineapples, pears, bananas, plantains, oranges and now even apples. Vegetables include chillies, ginger, pumpkins, gourds, lemons, jack fruits, orange, cucumber, tomatoes, egg plants and onions.[14] The surplus of bananas from Assam has been estimated at 3.06 mt.

According to the Export Import Bank of India's assessment "Asia region accounted for nearly 15 percent of share in the global fruits and vegetable imports. Major importers include Japan, Hong Kong, Singapore, India, Saudi Arabia and China. In terms of exports, major Asian players include China, Turkey, India and Thailand".[15]

NE is till now outside the traditional rubber-growing area. However, its climate is very favourable for rubber. A good beginning has been made in Assam with 10,500 hectares under 400 varieties of rubber and in Tripura with 23,500 hectares under high yielding varieties. In fact, Tripura has been declared as the "second rubber capital of India" (next to Kerala) by the Indian Rubber Board. Again, Assam produces 40 percent of India's rubber honey. It appears that 500 tonnes of honey can be produced from an average rubber plantation. Its export possibilities need to be explored.[16] India is the third highest rubber producing country in the world and has the highest rate of rubber productivity.[17]

NE is believed to be very rich in medicinal plants. Arunachal, NE's largest state in area, is reported to have more than 500 species of medicinal plants. In Manipur the investment requirement on medicinal plants has been estimated at Rs. 100 to Rs. 132 crores. In Nagaland ginseng is available among medicinal plants. Here the investment requirement is estimated at Rs. 80 to 104 crores. The plants include agar, tejpatta, dalchini, mint etc. Similarly, in Mizoram the investment requirement on medicinal plants will be Rs. 100 to 132 crores. In Tripura it will be Rs. 55 to 71 crores. Assam's depleting expanse of dense forest reserves even now have "medicinal herbs with an investment potential of Rs. 173 crores to Rs. 195 crores which include cultivation, drying and storage, herbal formulation, homeopathy, plants and spices processing etc".[18] Identifications and preliminary estimations have already been done. There are 3000 species of medicinal and aromatics plants. What is needed is to bring up the units in co-ordination and collaboration with India's export oriented pharmaceutical industry which has registered high growth during the past few decades.

Assam has plenty of tuber crops, the annual production being 0.219 mt. Similarly, coconuts and arecanuts are produced in plenty. The annual production of arecanut in Assam is estimated at 72 million tonnes of nuts and that of coconut at 165 mt. of nuts. Some of these are exported outside NE.

The Asian market has already shown its appreciation for some of the industrial products of NE. Products manufactured from plantation crops such as jute, mesta and ramie have proved their popularity in the Asian market. Assam is one of the leading producers of good quality jute in the world and it "enjoys a competitive advantage in the availability of superior fibre and inexpensive, semi skilled labour. There is tremendous scope for production and export of jute commodities and value added items and the industry has been identified as a thrust area".[19] Assam produces 4 to 6 lakh bales of jute annually. The items which can be produced from jute include bags, sofa covers, curtains, wall hangings, flooring material, shoes and even clothes.

In the case of cane and bamboo products also, NE has vast potential. Considerable work has been done in this industry and the demand has been seen in various national and international exhibitions and expositions. Another area with great possibilities is handloom and handicraft. Assam's silk, and particularly muga, can earn megabucks abroad.[20]

To sum up NE has to be an integral part of LEP. In order to achieve that the states of the region must develop their agriculture and industry to such a status that their agricultural and industrial products can compete in the international market. The funds are available under various schemes of the Government of India and in the banks and financial institutions. The natural resources are all there. Some of these have already been identified. NE does not have the required number of entrepreneurs and technical manpower. It cannot transform its natural resources into finished products without the human resources. It must have skilled technical manpower as in Taiwan. For that NE has to become a "knowledge society" or a "knowledge economy" as the management guru Peter Drucker has defined.[21] In this age of information technology, biotechnology and nanotechnology, knowledge has become the most important input into economic development.[22]

The planners and builders of NE have to realize this cardinal fact. What is necessary is the vision and concentrated efforts in various thrust areas after micro studies and appropriate project formulation which can bring NE to a standard in which it will be able to stand the challenge of LEP and will also be able to fully participate in the new milieu. The macro studies have already been done. Considerable work of identification of agricultural, horticultural, floricultural and industrial products have also been carried out. But the real work has to start in the field. Only then NE can hope to be a part of the bridge connecting India and south and south-east Asia.

Endnotes

1. Joseph E. Stiglitz, *Making Globalisation Work*, W.W. Norton & Company, New York and London, 2006.
2. *The Economic Times*, Issue dated February 12, 2007.
3. Amar Yumnam, "Indo-Myanmar trade through Moreh: Status and Assessment". Seminar paper in the National Seminar on Promotion of Border Trade between India's North East and Myanmar: Problems and Prospects. Imphal, November 8 and 9, 2004. The present writer attended this seminar and chaired a session in which trade through Stilwell Road was discussed.
4. "India: Looking East", Editorial in *Sapra India Bulletin*, November, 2006 issue, New Delhi. This magazine on security, insurgency, etc., is one of the most important in this line under the overall guidance of Gen. (Retd.) Shankar Roy Choudhury, former Chief of Army Staff.
5. JN Dixit, *My South Block Years: Memoirs of a Foreign Secretary*, UBS Publishers, New Delhi, 1997.
6. The Earl Mountbatten of Burma, *Report to the Combined Chiefs of Staff by the Supreme Allied Commander, South East Asia*, 1943-45. The English Book Store, New Delhi, 1960. Also see HN Das, *India-China Trade through the Stilwell Road: Dialogue*. Vol.6 No.1. July-September, 2004. Astha Bharati, Delhi, 2004. I have described about my travel on the Stilwell Road upto the Myanmarese Army Camp in the hill overlooking the Lake of No Return and my overnight stay there.
7. Sanjib Baruah, *Between South and South East Asia: North East India and the Look East Policy*. Omeo Kumar Das Institute of Social Change and Development, Guwahati, 2004.
8. Parmanand, *The Politics of Bhutan: Retrospect and Prospect*. Pragati Publications, Delhi, 1992. The Bhutan King expressed similar sentiments when the present writer had an audience with the King while leading an official delegation to Thimphu in April, 1993. Baruah refers to a paper by Francoise Pammaret (maiden name) on Bhutan, Cooch Bihar and Assam. But Francoise Pammaret - Imaeda has described Bhutan in glowing terms in her jointly authored (with Yoshiro Imaeda) coffee table book. *Bhutan: A Kingdom of the Eastern Himalayas,*. Times Books International, New Delhi, 1989.

9. HN Das, Economic Consequences of Insurgency in Assam, *The Indian Police Journal*. Vol. L. No.1. January-March, 2003, New Delhi.

10. *The Assam Tribune,* "NE to reap maximum benefit from Look East policy", issue dated June 27, 2007.

11. Joseph E Stiglitz, "Go Micro for Macro Speed". *The Economic Times,* issue dated March 23, 2007.

12. Jared Diamond, *Guns, Germs and Steel. A Short History of Everybody for the Last 13,000 Years,* Vintage Books, London. 1997.

13. As a member of the Indian Tea Board delegation the present writer witnessed the launching of Assam logo in the UK in March, 1990 when Satchi and Satchi, then the world's biggest advertisement firm, targeted the sophisticated south of London Thames Valley housewives with the message of higher price for better quality Assam tea. The German and the Iranian markets prefer Assam's highest priced second flush tea produced in June-July and they often airlift their consignments to retain the freshness. The present writer witnessed this during his 11-year (1986-1996) term as Chairman, Guwahati Tea Auction Centre, which he had then made the largest CTC Tea Auction Centre in the world.

14. Ginger is grown in plenty in Mizoram and Assam. In Assam an agricultural export zone has been set up consisting of the districts of Kamrup, Nalbari, Barpeta, Nagaon, Morigaon, Karbi Anglong and N.C. Hills. In this zone ginger is raised in 13,908 hectares and production is 61,259 metric tonnes. The total area under ginger in the state is 18,748 hectares and production is 1,35,000 metric tonnes. Special attention is now being paid to its marketing by government. Assam's chillies have received high accolades in the international market. See (i) *National Geographic,* May, 2007. "Bih/Bhut Jalokia". (ii) *Time,* Special Summer Issue. June 25-July 2, 2007. "Global warming. How the chili spread from its South American home and spiced up world cuisine".

15. Export-Import Bank of India, *Fresh Fruits, Vegetables and Dairy Products: India's Potential to Export to other Asian Countries,* Quest Publications, Mumbai, 2005.

16. North Eastern Development Finance Corporation Limited (NEDFI) "Resources and Investment Potential in North Eastern Region", Guwahati.
17. Export–Import Bank of India. *Export Potential of Indian Plantation Sectors: Prospect and Challenge.* Sita Publications, Mumbai, 2004.
18. NEDFI. Op cit.
19. NEDFI. Op cit.
20. Indian Institute of Entrepreneurship, Guwahati. "Prospectus of Border Trade with Myanmar and Bangladesh". Pre-investment Feasibility Study done for NEDFI. Similar studies are required for the other countries of south and southeast Asia.
21. Peter Drucker. All his books have some reference to "Knowledge". But he speaks of a "knowledge society" in *Managing for the Future,* Tata McGraw Hill Publishing Company Ltd., New Delhi, 1992.
22. David Warsh, *Knowledge and the Wealth of Nations,* WW Norton & Co., New York and London, 2006.

CHAPTER – 24

A Paradigm Shift in Bangladesh

Indian ultras were sheltered by Bangladesh Government and specially by DGFI for a long time. Both ULFA and NDFB terrorists have caused considerable damage to the NE region from their safe haven in Bangladesh. The present Government of that country has, however, shown enough goodwill by apprehending and handling over to India the main leaders of ULFA and NDFB and dismantling their camps in early 2010. These leaders have been living in Bangladesh for a long time. They were directing their cadres in India from their hide-outs in Bangladesh. They stashed away their money, extorted from India, in Bangladesh banks. After their apprehension the level of terrorist activities in NE India has come down considerably.

The fact that there has been a paradigm shift (*Din Bodol*) in Bangladesh politics after the December, 2008 General Election has been recognized the world over. Sheikh Hasina Wajed's return to power as Prime Minister has been hailed as the beginning of an age of secular politics, uninterrupted growth and better Indo-Bangla relations. Better Indo-Bangla relations and connectivity have been stressed for Bangladesh's integrated development. Whether the present euphoria can be sustained will depend upon the goodwill and sincerity of both the countries and the proper implementation of the decisions taken in the Prime Minister level talks held recently.

Hasina has promised to take Bangladesh back to the 1972 Constitution which had enshrined, in its Article 12, the values of democracy, secularism, linguistic and cultural nationalism and economic and social justice. The Constitution had been amended several times since then. The most notable among these are the following : The 1977 deletion of Article 12. The replacement of the word "secularism" by "absolute trust and faith in the *Almighty Allah*". The addition, in the Preamble, of the words "*Bismillàh-ar-Rahman-ar-Rahim*" (In the name of *Allah*, the Beneficent, the Merciful). The 1977 inclusion of a separate clause stating that "the state shall endeavour to consolidate, preserve and strengthen fraternal relations among Muslim countries based on Islamic solidarity" and declaration of Islam as the state religion. It would be really interesting to see how Sheikh Hasina reverts to the secularism of the 1972 Constitution.

Meanwhile, Bangladesh has made some progress in the economic front. In the latest edition of the United Nations Development Programme (UNDP)'s Human Development Report, Bangladesh is shown to have advanced two places during 2006-07 to the 146th position among 182 nations in 2007. India's position is 134th. It is also reported that the Bangladesh economy has been growing at the rate of more than 6 per cent in the past few years. The per capita income has gone up to US $ 600 which, however, is still very low. The poverty ratio has come down from 70% in the 1970s to around 40% in 2005. Rural poverty is higher at 44%. After Hasina's coming to power the people of Bangladesh are expecting that the government would "take up strategic plans to implement its commitments made in the "charter for change" before it finishes its second year". This is because "Hasina ran on the promises of change, hope and progress". After one year of her rule "around 72%

approved her role as Prime Minister while the rest were either indifferent or disappointed". Even the ruling party - Awami League - was "rated positively within the range of 50-60%". ("*Forum*", February, 2010, Dhaka).

Bangladeshi intellectuals seem to feel that "the resilient Bangladeshi people are still with Hasina's government". But they would like to see that it does much more in areas such as food security, effective steps against corruption and establishment of good government. Such steps have to be in addition to the overall thrust on growth and poverty alleviation. It is in this context that they plead for and endorse the attempts at better connectivity with India in respect of trade and mutual co-operation. The intellectuals have come to believe that "there is now at long last, the political will and determination on both sides (India and Bangladesh), to see the relationship move forward. The benefits for Bangladesh through increased trade and investment, through improved connectivity not only with India, but with Nepal, Bhutan, China and the Asean countries, will be immense" ("*Forum*", February, 2010, Dhaka).

Therefore, the five agreements signed during Sheikh Hasina's visit to India on January 10-13, 2010 have become significant. These five agreements are on mutual legal assistance in criminal matters, on transfer of sentenced persons, on combating international terrorism, organized crimes and illegal drug trafficking, on co-operation in the power sector and a cultural exchange programme. In pursuance of these agreements certain concrete steps were taken including India's promise to export 240 MW of power to Bangladesh and to assist that country to build power plants of 1320 MW each in Khulna and Chittagong. In respect of import trade India will remove 47 (plus the earlier agreed to 56 items) from the negative list. India will give a credit amounting to US $ 1 billion to Bangladesh for certain infrastructure projects. Bangladesh will facilitate transit of Indian goods and commodities through its territory and will allow the use of Chittagong and Mangla ports to India. India will give access to Bangladesh for trade and travel to Nepal and Bhutan.

In regard to sanctuary to the terrorist outfits of North East (NE) India in Bangladesh it is suspected that the most powerful and the most important leader, Paresh Barua, ULFA commander-in-chief, was tipped off by Pakistani Inter Services Intelligence (ISI) and Bangladeshi Directorate General of Forces Intelligence (DGFI) so that he could flee Bangladesh and find a safe haven in China before the Hasina Government's crack down. It is believed that the ULFA leaders who were pushed out had become inconsequential and ineffective over time. There is a strong suspicion that the elements inimical to India in DGFI and Bangladesh's security forces are awaiting a chance to re-start their anti-India activities.

The fundamentalist elements in Bangladesh have a stranglehold on the poor and illiterate masses of that country and also on quite a large section of the politicians. Many people, therefore, doubt whether Hasina will succeed in her attempt to amend the Constitution and re-introduce secularism.

It is good that Bangladesh will provide transit facilities for Indian goods by train and through the ports at Chittagong and Mangla. In the past, however, Bangladeshi dacoits used to loot Indian trains and harrass passengers. How far the new government will be able to control such nefarious activities is a million dollar question. India should, therefore, expedite development of the Shittwe port in Myanmar and use it as an alternative to the maximum.

The India-Bangladesh agreements of January, 2010 seem to have deliberately avoided any discussion about the illegal Bangladeshi immigration to India and particularly to NE and Assam. The Assam Chief Minister was invited to join the two Prime Ministers on the sidelines of the summit. But illegal immigration issue was not even mentioned. I believe that the talks provided one opportunity when some assurance could have been obtained from Sheikh Hasina for co-operation in stopping such illegal immigration which has now assumed such proportions that India's security and integrity have been threatened by 5 million Bangladeshis in Assam. More than one third of Assam's population now comprise of Muslims against 22.60% in 1951 and 16.23% in 1911. It is also believed that Bangladeshis dominate 45 out of 126 Assembly constituencies in Assam. They are already in a majority in 7 Assam districts. There are several more millions of Bangladeshis in other states of NE.

Bangladesh is expecting to gain considerable improvement of its economy by better connectivity with India. According to the former Bangladesh Foreign Secretary, Farooq Sobhan, the Prime Minister level talks have "opened up a whole new vista, not only simply in terms of Bangladesh's bilateral relations with India, but in terms of Bangladesh becoming a middle income country by 2021". He further stated that "if Bangladesh is to move from an annual growth rate of 6 per cent to 8 or 9 per cent, it must make rapid progress in the integration of its economy with its immediate neighbours, India, Nepal and Bhutan". I personally feel that in return for so much favour shown by India, Bangladesh should at least agree to discuss the problem of illegal immigrants.

CHAPTER – 25

The Story Behind Liberation of Bangladesh

The War of Liberation in Bangladesh was based on the realization of a unique Bengali identity surpassing the Muslin identity of a vast majority of people of erstwhile East Pakistan. To quote Nobel Laureate Amartya Sen, "The identity division that fed the 'struggle for liberation' was firmly linked to language and culture (and, of course, to politics), rather than to any religious difference." ("Identify and Violence, The Illusion of Destiny")

In further elaboration of the genesis of Bangladesh Sen opined that "a Bangladeshi Muslim is not only a Muslim but also a Bengali and a Bangladeshi, typically quite proud of the Bengali language, literature and music, not to mention the other identities he or she may have connected with class, gender, occupation, politics, aesthetic taste, and so on. Bangladesh's separation from Pakistan was not based on religion at all, since a Muslim identity was shared by the bulk of the population in the two wings of undivided Pakistan. The separatist issues related to language, literature, and politics".

The Bihari Muslims, who lived in East Pakistan, and the members of a few extremist Muslim organizations such as Al-badr and Al-shams, tried to win over the Bengali Muslims to the cause of a united and Muslim Pakistan. But they failed in their attempt because Bengalis realized that West Pakistan had looted their resources and had humiliated them in several ways. The Bengalis were "seething with discontent due to West Pakistan's undue domination over them in all respects - administrative, economic and cultural. The key administrative positions were held by West Pakistanis; in economic and industrial matters the people of East Pakistan were exploited and discriminated against; and attempts were made by the West Pakistan ruling authorities to impose on the people of the eastern part a culture alien to them and to make Urdu the sole official language ignoring the claims of the people whose mother tongue and vehicle of culture had been Bengali all along". (Advanced History of India). In fact, the West Pakistanis treated East Pakistan as their colonial possession. After the December, 1970 election, Sheikh Mujibur Rahman's Awami League achieved a clear majority in the National Assembly. Even then he was not allowed to become the Prime Minister because he was a Bengali. This infuriated the Bengalis.

A civil disobedience movement was launched on March 8, 1971. Not only the students, the youths and the intellectuals but even the judges joined the movement. The judges refused to swear in Lt. Gen. Tikka Khan as the Governor of East Pakistan on March 9, 1971. On March 25, the Pakistani Dictator Gen. Yahya Khan started a "military campaign" against the people of East Pakistan. "A reign of terror was unleashed. Men, women and children were indiscriminately slaughtered while the women were dishonoured. In what became a cold blooded campaign of genocide - the intellectuals, academics and professionals - and the flower of youth, the students, were massacred".

The Mukti Bahini, which was essentially a student organization, started fighting against the Pakistani forces. On March 28, 1971 the Liberation Army Chief, Major Ziauddin Khan, announced the formation of an independent Bangladesh Government with Sheikh Mujibur Rahman as its Premier. The struggle continued. On

December 4, 1971 Pakistan declared war on India. On December 6, 1971 India formally recognized Bangladesh as an independent democratic state. A joint military command of India and Bangladesh was constituted and Lt. Gen. Jagjit Singh Aurora became its Chief Commander. On December 16, 1971 at 4.21 p.m. the entire Pakistani Army in the eastern sector, totalling 92,000, under Lt. Gen. Niazi surrendered to Gen. Aurora at Dacca Race Course grounds. This ended one of the most infamous wars in the Indian sub-continent.

This is history. But behind the history there is a human face. The human face is of poverty, squalor, insult, annihilation, destruction and mutilation. That human face is of injury, murder and rape. Literal description of the events and of the perpetrators, however, do not bring out the quintessential Bangladeshi of 1971. His sufferings and humiliations do not get reflected in plebeian essays about how Bangladesh won freedom.

This is where Dr. Bharat Chandra Kalita, an eminent historian and a former Reader of History of the National Defence Academy, Pune, has stepped in. Instead of writing another book of history he has fictionalized the events of those turbulent times in his eminently readable book "A Mole in the Breast". Through the pen of an astute storyteller, Kalita has brought out what actually happened in those days. How the important personalities of India, Pakistan and Bangladesh behaved in that intimate human drama can be perceived only through Kalita's sensitive rendering in his remarkable book. For example, Kalita has highlighted the machinations of the crafty Zulfiqar Ali Bhutto and his role in the conference which the then Pakistani dictator Gen. Yahya had called in an attempt to resolve the crisis over formation of a Government after the December, 1970 election. Bhutto stalled a democratic decision, that is, to appoint the leader of the majority party, Sheikh Mujibur Rahman of the Awami League, as Prime Minister of Pakistan.

In another chapter Kalita has graphically described the shock and trauma of two innocent college girls thrown into the bed room of two important Pakistani army officers at dead of night. The idea was that they should be raped and impregnated. But the officers refused. One of the officers was a Punjabi with a rare spirituality. The other was Major Zia, who was destined to become the first Commander of the Bangladeshi army and then ultimately to become the President of the country. In fact, it was that night's experience which led Zia to leave the Pakistani army and to form the Bangladesh army along with a few other Bengali officers. The armed struggle for liberation of Bangladesh began that night.

Through a multitude of fictional characters, Nazma and Fatema being the chief ones, Kalita has built up a web which encompassed the trials and tribulations of those times. The strength of characters that Kalita has portrayed, the picture of dogged determination of Bengali youths that he has drawn and the indomitable charge forward of the Mukti Bahini that he chronicled are factors which make "this little novella compelling reading".

Whose was this mole in the breast? Kalita was successful in keeping it a secret, like most writers of thrillers, till Nazma revealed it in a fit of remorse when she heard about her fellow girl students' sufferings at the hands of the Pakistani army personnel. Nazma's anguish knew no bounds when she realized that the mole in her breast was the cause of so much physical and mental pain to so many girls.

During the past four decades Bangladesh has lost its secular identity. The fundamentalist Muslim organizations such as Jamat-e-Islami have been able to convince the people and the Government of Bangladesh that it was India's interest that the liberation of Bangladesh served. As a result Hindus are being systematically pushed out so that their percentage in Bangladesh has come down from 28.3 percent in 1941 to only 9 percent in 2001. The figure is still going down. Meanwhile, the Constitution has been amended and Islam has been adopted as the State Religion of Bangladesh. Bangladesh has become a haven for Indian terrorist organizations who are completely under the control of Inter Services Intelligence (ISI) of Pakistan and Directorate General of Forces Intelligence (DGFI) of Bangladesh. India's contribution to Bangladesh's independence is forgotten. It has been now discovered that even in the early days (December 15, 1972) Sheikh Mujibur Rahman had asserted that "keeping away from India guides the basic of Bangladesh's foreign policy" (Jaideep Saikia : "Bangladesh : Treading the Taliban Trail").

Kalita's book, however, is based on Bangladesh's secular democratic identity of 1970s. It is nice to contemplate that once upon a time Bangladeshis were enthused by their Bengali identity to revolt against Islamic fundamentalists. They had tried to negate the two nation theory of 1940s. But after 1970s they themselves have become Islamists.

Index

Notes

Notes